Arkansas Valley Mountain Biking

Leadville to Salida and Everywhere in Between

Mark Wolff

Barking Dog Guides

Published by: Barking Dog Guides Press
P.O. Box 1486, Lyons, CO 80540
mwolff@arkvalleymtb.com

ISBN: 978-0-615-19413-4

PRINTED IN THE UNITED STATES OF AMERICA

Arkansas Valley Mountain Biking

Area map

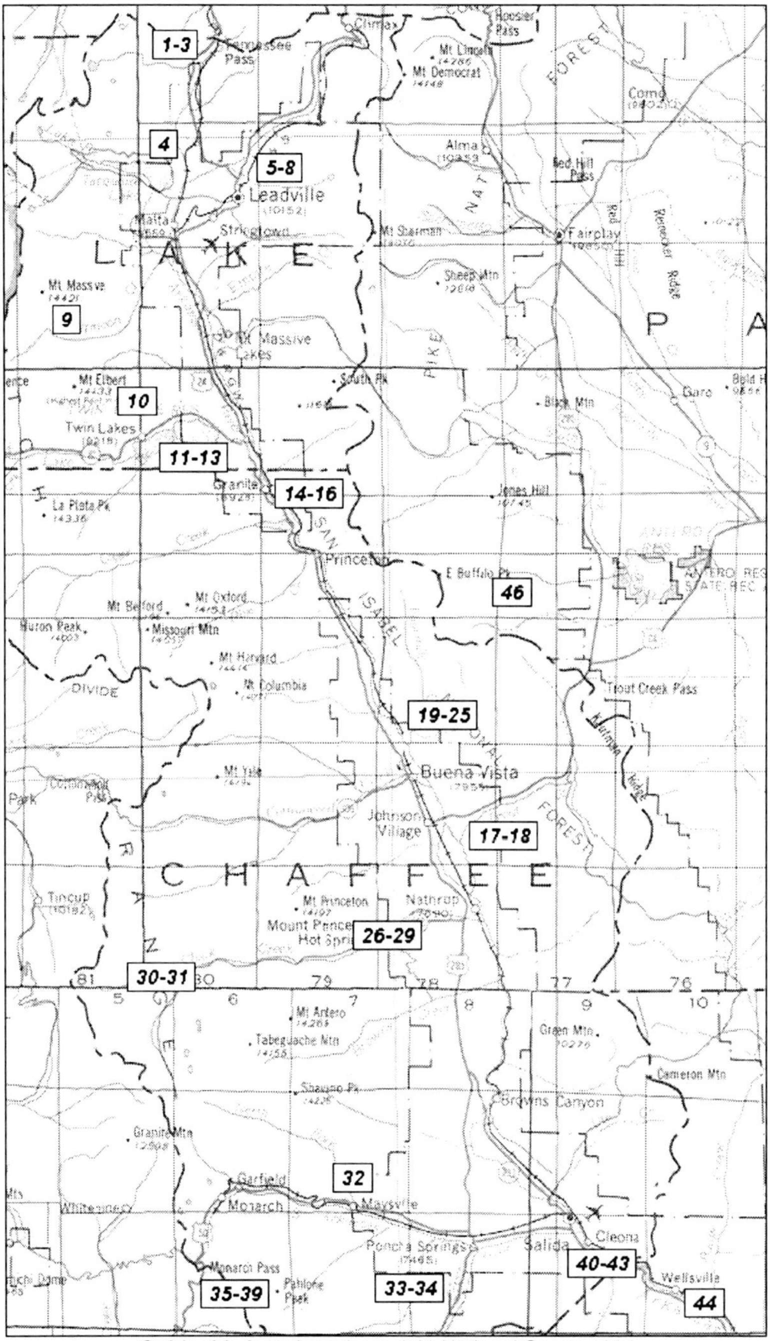

Guide ride locations *(copyright National Geographic)*

Disclaimer

Warning! Ride at your own risk!

Mountain biking is inherently dangerous and there is no way to eliminate all risks. This book tells you where to do it, not how. Therefore, any information provided by this guide is strictly informational and not instructional. You should not attempt these routes unless you have sufficient experience to manage the potential hazards of backcountry travel. Every rider is solely accountable for his or her own abilities to ride in a safe and responsible manner.

Documenting current trail conditions is beyond the scope of this book. Changes in routes, whether attributed to human efforts, natural events, or property closures, are possible. Such changes may impact the technical and aerobic difficulty of a route.

The technical and aerobic ratings for each ride reflect the experiences of the author and may not be agreed upon by others. In addition, all mileage and elevation data included with the route descriptions are estimates.

Getting lost is possible whenever you venture into wilderness. Be prepared and always carry extra maps and a compass, and know how to use them. You should also consider carrying GPS devices and cellular telephones, but be aware of the risks involved with using electronic gear in the backcountry.

All mountain bikers must take responsibility for their actions. The author, publisher, or any other persons or organizations mentioned in this book are not responsible or liable in any way for incidents, property damage, accidents, injuries, or deaths that may result from attempting the routes described in this guide.

The information in this book is based upon the experiences of the author and may not be perceived as accurate by others. There are no warranties, either perceived or actual, that the information contained in this book is accurate.

Using this book indicates a user's acceptance of all potential risks.

No book serves as a substitute for sound judgment. Know your limits and be safe. You alone are responsible for your fate.

Acknowledgements

Many people helped make this book possible, but I'd especially like to thank the following:

Keith and Evelyn Baker of *The Trailhead* in Buena Vista for giving me a place to plant my feet as I explore the Valley.

Andy Applegate of *VeloSports Performance Center* and *Cannondale/Land Rover* for helping me keep my old butt moving.

And I especially want to thank my wife for her great patience, enduring faith, and steadfast support. Without her, none of this would have been possible.

NATIONAL GEOGRAPHIC

All Maps and elevation profiles created with TOPO!
© National Geographic Maps.
http://www.nationalgeographic.org/maps

In addition, thanks to the **International Mountain Biking Association** for their great advocacy work with the Continental Divide Trail and for permission to reprint their "Rules of the Trail." (http://www.imba.com)

About the author

Mark has been mountain biking for nearly twenty years and currently splits his time between Buena Vista and Lyons, Colorado. Over the years he has aggressively explored numerous trails in Washington, Utah, Pennsylvania, Kansas, California, Oregon, and Hawaii. In addition to mountain biking, he is an avid snowboarder and enjoys alpine climbing.

The author at work

Categorized ride index

This list breaks the rides into categories for quick reference

Single-track
1: Camp Hale to Tennessee Pass
2: Mitchell Creek Loop
4: St. Kevin's-Turquoise Lake Loop
10: Twin Lakes to Mount Massive
11: Interlaken Loop
12: Twin Lakes to Clear Creek
13: Cache Creek Loop
14: Lost Canyon to Twin Lakes Loop
16: Spring Creek Short Loop
19: Davis Meadow Loop
21-23: Midland Bike Trail routes
26: Frontier Ranch to South Cottonwood Creek
28: Raspberry Gulch Loop
31: Alpine Tunnel to Tin Cup Pass Road Loop
32: US 50 to Chalk Creek
33: Marshall Pass to Silver Creek Loop
34: Silver Creek Loop
35-39: Monarch Crest routes
40: Bear Creek to Methodist Mountain Loop
41: Methodist Mountain to US 285 Loop
46: Salt Creek-McQuaid Loop

Monster climbs
7: Mosquito Pass
15: Lost Canyon Road
27: Mt. Princeton Road
33: Marshall Pass to Silver Creek Loop
40: Bear Creek to Methodist Mountain Loop
41: Methodist Mountain to US 285 Loop
45: River Park to River Park

Experts only
7: Mosquito Pass
19: Davis Meadow Loop
31: Alpine Tunnel to Tin Cup Pass Road Loop
32: US 50 to Chalk Creek
33: Marshall Pass to Silver Creek Loop
38: Monarch Crest descending Silver Creek
41: Methodist Mountain to US 285 Loop

Beginners' delight
2: Mitchell Creek Loop
20 Lenhardy Cutoff
24: Trout Creek Pass to Buena Vista
28: Raspberry Gulch Loop

Family-friendly
17: Castle Rock Gulch Loop
25: Buena Vista River Road
29: Cascade Railroad Grade
42: Spiral Drive / Tenderfoot Mountain
44: Upper Bighorn Sheep Canyon

Historically significant (ghost towns, mine sites, etc.)
3: Jenny June Mine Loop
6: Ball Mountain Pass
8: Mineral Belt Trail
9: Halfmoon Road
11: Interlaken Loop

Welcome to the Upper Arkansas Valley

Imagine a region central to the some of the best sections of the Colorado Trail, the Rainbow Trail, and the Continental Divide Trail. Next, surround that area with the greatest concentration of mountains exceeding fourteen thousand feet in the contiguous United States. Finish that dreamscape with an ideal climate of moderate summer temperatures and brilliant sunny skies.

That's what you will find in Colorado's Upper Arkansas Valley.

Running more than sixty miles from Leadville to Salida, the region is as of yet a little-known fat tire Nirvana. An advanced cyclist can literally spend an entire summer riding and exploring the region without repeating a single route. With routes ranging in difficulty from beginner to expert, however, there is enough varied terrain to cater to every skill level.

While the Monarch Crest Trail is the best-known ride in the region, the other major trail systems that thread the Valley offer miles of superb riding. In addition, there are countless miles of old mining routes and rugged jeep trails, all prime for fat tire exploration. Whether you seek the sublime single-track of Salida, the screaming jeep trails of Buena Vista, or the celestial lung-busters of Leadville, this guide will lead you to the best rides in Colorado's Upper Arkansas Valley.

Stomp on those pedals and let it rip!

History lesson

Long before the discovery of gold near Leadville sparked widespread settlement of the area, Native Americans of the Ute Nation sought winter refuge in the mild climate of southern Valley. In addition to the Ute, other native nations, such as the Comanche, Kiowa, Sioux, and Cheyenne, utilized the Upper Arkansas River Valley as a gateway to the buffalo hunting grounds of South Park.

The first recorded visit of U.S. citizens to the area did not occur until the Pike expedition of 1806. Sent to find the headwaters of the Arkansas River, Zebulon Pike's group entered the region in mid-December of that same year. By December 22, Pike and some of his men almost reached the river's headwaters near Leadville, but snow forced them to retreat south where they spent Christmas Day camped on the river near Poncha Springs. There's a plaque posted along US Highway 285 (near CR 165) to memorialize this event.

In 1860, the discovery of gold in California Gulch, a small valley just outside of Leadville, changed everything. Within months, a rough and tumble settlement of tents and cabins, dubbed Oro City, housed thousands of miners and prospectors, all drawn to the area with hopes of striking it rich.

Just as the gold yields ebbed, bountiful silver strikes in the same vicinity created a second boom. By 1880, Leadville blossomed into a city of more than 30,000, becoming one of Colorado's largest cities of the time. The city was so vibrant that some people talked of making Leadville the capitol of the newly formed state of Colorado.

The repeal of the Sherman Silver Act in 1893 brought and end to the boom. Many of the region's aristocrats lost their fortunes and abandoned the mines. The most famous tragedy to emerge from the sudden economic downturn is the legend of Baby Doe Tabor. The once young and beautiful widow of Horace Tabor froze to death in her one-room shack on the grounds of the Matchless Silver Mine as she waited for the next silver rush.

To support the mining enterprises of the northern Valley, the southern towns became important rail centers. Buena Vista, established in 1879, started as a railroad town with three lines: the Denver & Rio Grande, South Park & Pacific, and Colorado Midland. Founded in 1880, Salida was a significant link in the Denver & Rio Grande railroads.

The legacy of this rich heritage becomes apparent as you explore the area by mountain bike. Many of the routes in this guide either exploit old railroad grades, access abandoned mine sites, or pass through ghost towns and vacant homesteads. Even though the once bountiful mines are now depleted, the mountains surrounding the Upper Arkansas Valley still hold many treasures awaiting your discovery.

How to use this guide

Understanding a few conventions will help you get the most from using this guide. Included for each ride are:

- *maps*
- *brief route descriptions*
- *mileage information*
- *riding time estimates*
- *ride surface descriptions*
- *elevation data and profiles*
- *aerobic and technical ratings*
- *recommended riding season*
- *trailhead GPS coordinates*
- *directions for access to the trailhead*
- *alternate route options*

Maps

The maps provided in this guide serve to give you a general perspective of and orient you to the nature of a route. The latitude/longitude coordinates provided at the top of each map represent the geographic center of that map. These data are provided to assist you with finding the area on larger scale maps. Additionally, this guide provides a list of the relative USGS 7.5-minute maps for each route.

Unless you are already familiar with the area, you should also carry additional maps. Good quality, highly detailed topographic maps provide a better interpretation of terrain than any guidebook can. While many maps do not include some of the trails included in this guide, you stand a much better chance of staying oriented if you have a map.

In addition to USGS maps, National Geographic's *Trails Illustrated* regional maps and Delorme's *Colorado Atlas and Gazetteer* are also excellent resources.

Mileage information

It's probably worth taking a few words to discuss mileage. While great pains were taken to record accurate mileage readings, the final work can only serve as an estimate. As anyone who has spent a fair amount of time in the backcountry already knows, all cycling computers, global positioning systems, computer software, and maps contain a certain margin of error. Compiling data using all of these tools combined results in compounded, albeit small, errors. It's an unavoidable fact of life.

I used to scoff when I encountered discrepancies of 0.1 miles (or greater) between my cycling computer readings and those recorded in a guide. After gaining a great deal of experience working with GPS units and multiple mapping tools, however, I found that if I repeated a route ten times, the result would yield ten unique mileage readings. While the differences were often miniscule, they were there nonetheless. Go figure.

Forewarned with this information, be aware that all mileage data are estimates and serve only to give you a frame of reference for where you are in relation to other relative data points.

Riding time estimates

The riding time estimates provided give a general idea of the time needed to complete the ride. Obviously, more experienced riders may find these times very generous while others may find them too tight. In general, the estimates are based on what most recreational bikers will find to be a relaxed, steady pace. Since these estimates do not include breaks taken along the trail, you may want to budget a little extra time.

Surface

The surface describes the riding surface of the route: paved road, dirt road, jeep track, double-track, single-track, etc.

Elevation data and profiles

The elevation data and profiles provide elevation statistics and a visual depiction of the climbing and descending nature of the route. Once again, all data are estimates based on GPS and USGS 7.5-minute map values.

Ride ratings

Two criteria determine a route's rating: the *aerobic level* of the route and the *technical difficulty* of the terrain.

Aerobic level

The aerobic rating describes the physical fitness demand of a route. There are three primary levels: easy, moderate, and strenuous. Altitude plays a significant role; if you aren't acclimatized, expect the rides to feel a little tougher than the rating.

Easy rides generally involve little climbing or brief climbs on well-graded terrain.

Moderate rides typically involve some climbing. The climbs may be steep but relatively short, or sustained at a gradual grade. The technical difficulty also pays a factor. For example, a gentle grade may be physically moderate due to loose rocks or sand. Most recreational cyclists will be able to complete moderate rides with minimal walking.

Strenuous rides demand a high level of physical fitness. Steep climbs can be sustained and littered with technical obstacles. Riders without significant endurance and the power gained through many hours of training are likely to find these routes exceedingly difficult. Less fit riders may encounter long stretches where they must either take breaks or walk the bike.

Technical difficulty

The quantity and nature of the obstacles encountered along a route determine the technical difficulty of a ride. Technical ratings are divided into five levels from 1 to 5, with 1 being the easiest.

Level 1 rides have few obstacles and do not require any special bicycle handling skills. The riding surface is generally smooth and descents are gentle.

Level 2 rides may have some rocks or patches of loose gravel or sand, but novice mountain bikers should have little problem riding through these obstacles.

Level 3 rides are technically moderate and typically on single-track or jeep trails. Riders may encounter rocks, roots, erosion damage, or other obstacles that require specific cycling techniques. Line selection, or the ability to direct a bicycle along a specific, narrow path, becomes important at this level. Some intermediate and most novice riders will encounter short sections of hike-a-bike.

Level 4 rides have combined obstacles and fewer line choices than Level 3 rides. Riders may encounter sections of trail that are both loose and rocky. Laterally eroded single-tracks may be steep. Some intermediate riders may have to push their bikes through stretches of these routes, increasing the time it takes to complete the ride.

Level 5 rides typically feature very steep sections that are frequently littered with many obstacles. Intermediate riders will struggle and find themselves at an increased risk for sustaining serious injury on these routes. As such, only expert riders should attempt these rides.

Season

Each route has an optimal riding season listed. Late or early snowfall will affect this range. Don't ride on snowy or wet trails as doing so damages the trail surface. Call a local bike shop or Forest Service office for current conditions.

Trailhead GPS coordinates

Provided with each route are the GPS coordinates for the trailhead. These will assist GPS-equipped riders with finding a route's starting point. In addition, GPS route files (.gpx format) for all the rides in this guide are available free on the Internet at: *www.arkvalleymtb.com*.

Getting there

Directions to the trailhead originate from a distinct location in the closest town and follow major thoroughfares. If you are already familiar with the area, you may know shortcuts or alternate ways of getting to a trailhead. If a route has alternate riding options or multiple access points, directions to those locations may also be included.

Alternate route options

Most routes have interesting, alternate ways of riding them. The options provided are suggestions for approaches that some riders may wish to explore. There are many ways to do these routes and as you become more familiar with the area, you are bound to find variations better suited to your style.

What to expect

The Upper Arkansas Valley is predominantly high desert where one can expect dry weather and sunny skies throughout the year. The Sawatch Mountain Range bounds the Valley to the west, the Sangre de Cristo Mountains to the south, and the Mosquito Range to the east. The northern end of the Valley is bounded by the Continental Divide, which runs east to west above Leadville.

Coursing the entire length of the Valley is its namesake river, the Arkansas. Well-known to whitewater enthusiasts, the river crashes down nearly one vertical mile from its headwaters just below the Continental Divide at Fremont Pass north of Leadville to the Royal Gorge east of Salida.

When surveying the area, one cannot ignore the fact that in some places the valley floor is more than seven thousand feet below the highest peaks surrounding it. The net result is three distinct climate zones, each with unique characteristics.

Routes at elevations of less than nine thousand feet typically run through sage and stands of scraggly pinon. The single-track and jeep/ATV trails in this zone are typically comprised of crushed granite and may be sandy in summer. Many of these trails are dry and snow-free for much of the winter, and some routes can be ridden year-round. Since this zone can get uncomfortably hot in summer, it's best to ride in the early morning or late afternoon. The Arkansas Hills north of Salida and the Fourmile Recreation area east of Buena Vista are good examples of this zone.

Higher up, the landscape slowly changes to classic Colorado sub-alpine forests of pine and aspen. It's in this zone where trails are frequently loamy and fat tire knobs are at their best. You'll sail over trail-beds that are at once soft and fast. Furthermore, the forests offer relief from the summer sun and higher temperatures of the lower valley. Trails through here are typically dry and snow-free from mid-May through October. Much of the Colorado Trail and Rainbow Trail run through this zone.

Routes accessing terrain above the trees, at elevations of twelve thousand feet or more, slice through alpine meadows of brightly blooming wildflowers and fragile grasses. Without the shelter of trees, you are likely to encounter higher winds, cooler temperatures, and intensely strong ultraviolet rays. This is also the last place you want to be in the event of a storm. Trails here have the shortest season: July through October. Much of the Monarch Crest Trail, some sections of the Continental Divide Trail, and many of the rides in the Leadville area access this zone.

There are a few things to keep in mind when visiting the area. Summer daytime temperatures in Salida average in the mid-eighties, but can reach into the nineties on some days. Leadville, due to its high altitude, is typically ten or fifteen degrees cooler than Salida. Nighttime temperatures may be up to forty degrees cooler than day, so if you plan to camp, pack accordingly.

Hunting season begins in fall (check with the Colorado Division of Wildlife for more information). This is also an ideal time to ride because the aspens are at peak color and the weather is great. If you plan to ride after the start of hunting season, be sure to wear bright clothing and avoid popular hunting areas.

Try to avoid riding when trails are muddy or remain covered with large areas of snow. Riding in mud damages trails and may affect the quality of the riding surface for a long time. If you encounter a small mud patch, ride or, better yet, push your bike directly through the center of the trail. Bypassing mud damages a trail by making it wider.

In addition, resist the temptation to ride on trails closed to mountain bikes and don't ride illegal (rogue) trails. This is a serious problem in some places and jeopardizes bike access to the region. If in doubt, don't do it. If you find a trail that interests you, but are uncertain of its status, contact a local bike shop or the proper land management agency to learn more before riding it.

Weather

In general, the weather in the Upper Arkansas River Valley is exceptional. Mountain weather, however, is notoriously fickle and requires some preparation. Summer storms are usually fast moving and can be fierce. With little warning, perfect crystal-blue skies turn gray, the temperatures plunge, and thunder shakes the Valley as lightening dances across the sky. If caught by surprise, cherry-sized raindrops, hail, or even snow could fall on you.

Fortunately, these storms often pass as quickly as they arrive.

If you see a storm forming, it's best to turn back and head for the car. If caught in a storm, here are a few things you can do to reduce your risk of injury. First, be prepared. Always carry rain gear. If you get wet, your chance of developing hypothermia (the cooling of your body's core to dangerously low levels) increases exponentially. This potentially life-threatening condition is possible even when temperatures are in the low 50's. Altitude, dehydration, and fatigue all contribute to your susceptibility. A light, waterproof/breathable shell tucked into your pack can literally be a lifesaver. If you are going high, you should also bring extra insulating layers.

If you hear thunder, you are within the striking range of lightening. If caught in an exposed area, ditch the bike and look for a gully or low spot where you can crouch or sit on your pack. Do not lie down and avoid all puddles and running water. Do not take shelter under lone trees or close to isolated rock outcroppings. If you are in a forested area, descend as much as possible and take shelter in a dense stand of uniformly tall trees. If you are part of a group, spread out so that a single strike doesn't disable everyone.

Though the day may be warm and balmy, be prepared for as much as a forty-degree drop in temperature when the sun goes down. This may be fine as you slip into your sleeping bag at camp, but if you underestimate the time it takes to complete a ride it could mean trouble. Imagine shivering in your shorts and short-sleeve jersey as you walk your bike through the dark. No fun. So, if you are attempting an epic be sure to pack extra clothes, food and consider taking a headlamp as well.

Sun

Don't underestimate the sun. Most of the rides in this guide are in excess of eight thousand feet, where there is little atmosphere to protect your eyes and skin from powerful ultraviolet rays. Even though the air may feel cool, the sun quickly burns unprotected, exposed skin. Always wear sun block with a minimum of SPF 30 and wear protective sunglasses. If you are riding with small children in tow, be sure to take measures to protect their eyes and skin as well.

Equipment

How much stuff to bring? It depends on you. Your standard gear should include a helmet, gloves, sport sunglasses, and a cycling computer. A helmet is a no-brainer, or at least it will help prevent you from becoming a no-brainer in the event of a crash. Gloves add comfort to your ride and help protect your hands if you fall. Sunglasses shade your eyes from ultraviolet rays and protect them from bugs and trail debris kicked-up by your tires. A cycling computer/odometer is essential because you won't know where you are if you don't know how far you've gone.

One of the most versatile yet least expensive pieces of gear I own is a urethane-coated nylon rain poncho. Costing less than thirty dollars, I have used it for everything from an emergency camping shelter to a highly effective rain garment. It packs small, weighs about twenty ounces, and fits easily into my hydration pack. While it isn't practical to wear it while riding, when caught in a shower I simply throw it over my head and find a comfy place to sit until the storm passes. I stay dry. My pack stays dry. Perfect!

At a minimum, you should also carry:
-this trail guide
-bicycle multi-tool
-spare tube(s)
-patch kit
-pump
-small first aid kit
-sun block of SPF 30 or more
-rain gear
-extra layers if accessing higher altitudes
-cigarette lighter

Other wise things to include:
-chain tool
-tire levers
-area map and compass
-spoke tool
-wrist watch
-headlamp

If you attempt a longer ride, consider taking:
-sports drink with electrolytes
-spare cables
-2 extra spokes and nipples
-water treatment tablets

Super gear-heads may also want:
-global positioning system (GPS)
-CO2 inflation tool with extra cartridges
-heart rate monitor

Always give your bike a quick checkup before you ride. Visually inspect your wheel skewers, rims, brakes, cables, headset, and cranks to be sure everything is in good condition. Check your tire pressure and your tires (healthy tread, no sidewall cracks, etc.). Take a quick spin around the parking area to check seat height, pedal cleats, and brakes.

One mistake many riders make is that they never check or change their chains. A dirty or dry chain quickly wears out, and a worn chain has a greater chance of breaking on the trail. Additionally, a stretched chain will silently ruin the components of your drive train, a very costly repair. Do yourself a favor and check, clean, and lube your chain frequently, or take it to a shop to have it done professionally.

Safety

Both Chaffee and Lake Counties are predominantly rural and sparsely populated. Many of these routes, therefore, go deep into remote wilderness. Help may not be expedient or readily available in the event of an emergency. Use common sense and always ride well within your ability.

At best, cellular telephone reception is spotty in the backcountry. In addition, some providers either do not offer service or have limited coverage in some parts of the Valley. If possible, however, always carry a cell phone. Signals frequently improve as you gain altitude, especially when riding in areas adjacent to the larger towns. The number of places you have service may astonish you.

In addition, consider purchasing a Colorado Search and Rescue (CORSAR) card. For a nominal cost, this card will cover any search and rescue fees you incur should you get in a jam. You can find them at many outfitters and retailers throughout the Valley.

Water

You'd be surprised how quickly you can dehydrate while riding. The dry climate and high altitude conspire to desiccate you even on easy rides. While a single bottle may be more than adequate for your single-track outings at home, you will need to carry more when you venture into the high country of the Arkansas Valley.

Hydration packs work well and are available in sizes of 80 -100 ounces. On longer rides, you should *also* carry a bike bottle or two of electrolyte-replenishing sports drinks. One trick is to mix the sports drink in your bottles a little "thick" so that it is slightly more concentrated than the recommended serving. This gives you a few extra calories with each gulp and works to prevent hyponatremia, a dangerous depletion of your body's electrolytes. If you super-concentrate your sports drink, however, be sure to also drink plenty of water to offset the potential dehydrating effect of the concentrate.

If you run dry on the trail, your best bet is to bum water from your friends or others on the trail. If that doesn't work, filter or treat water from streams following the directions of your water treatment tablets. Unless it is an extreme emergency, ***DO NOT DRINK UNTREATED WATER FROM STREAMS***. Giardia cysts are common in the Arkansas Valley and ensure that you, or at least your bottom, will never forget the time you sipped from that sparkling Rocky Mountain stream.

Altitude

Locals are acclimatized to the high elevation and won't have any problems with altitude. If you are visiting from a lower elevation, however, there are a few precautions to take to reduce your risk of developing Acute Mountain Sickness (AMS). First, give your body a day or two to rest and acclimatize. Take it easy and don't hammer on your first few rides. Drink plenty of fluids, but try to avoid heavy consumption of caffeine and alcohol.

You might experience mild symptoms of AMS, such as faint headaches, light-headedness, and slight fatigue during your first couple days. If symptoms intensify or don't subside within a few days, however, consider moving to a lower altitude. Descending as little as one thousand feet may be enough to make you feel much better.

If you experience two or more severe symptoms, such as aspirin resistant headaches, irregular breathing, a rapid resting pulse rate, nausea, dizziness, or difficulty sleeping, descend immediately. Though uncommon in Colorado, it is possible for these symptoms to develop into a life threatening build-up of fluids in the lungs and brain.

IMBA Rules of the Trail

The way we ride today shapes mountain bike trail access tomorrow. Do your part to preserve and enhance our sport's access and image by observing the following rules of the trail, formulated by IMBA, the International Mountain Bicycling Association. These rules are recognized around the world as the standard code of conduct for mountain bikers. IMBA's mission is to promote mountain bicycling that is environmentally sound and socially responsible.

1. Ride On Open Trails Only
Respect trail and road closures (ask if uncertain); avoid trespassing on private land; obtain permits or other authorization as may be required. Federal and state Wilderness areas are closed to cycling. The way you ride will influence trail management decisions and policies.

2. Leave No Trace
Be sensitive to the dirt beneath you. Recognize different types of soils and trail construction; practice low-impact cycling. Wet and muddy trails are more vulnerable to damage. When the trailbed is soft, consider other riding options. This also means staying on existing trails and not creating new ones. Don't cut switchbacks. Be sure to pack out at least as much as you pack in.

3. Control Your Bicycle!
Inattention for even a second can cause problems. Obey all bicycle speed regulations and recommendations.

4. Always Yield Trail
Let your fellow trail users know you're coming. A friendly greeting or bell is considerate and works well; don't startle others. Show your respect when passing by slowing to a walking pace or even stopping. Anticipate other trail users around corners or in blind spots. Yielding means slow down, establish communication, be prepared to stop if necessary and pass safely.

5. Never Scare Animals
All animals are startled by an unannounced approach, a sudden movement, or a loud noise. This can be dangerous for you, others, and the animals. Give animals extra room and time to adjust to you. When passing horses use special care and follow directions from the horseback riders (ask if uncertain). Running cattle and disturbing wildlife is a serious offense. Leave gates as you found them, or as marked.

6. Plan Ahead
Know your equipment, your ability, and the area in which you are riding -- and prepare accordingly. Be self-sufficient at all times, keep your equipment in good repair, and carry necessary supplies for changes in weather or other conditions. A well-executed trip is a satisfaction to you and not a burden to others. Always wear a helmet and appropriate safety gear.

Keep trails open by setting a good example of environmentally sound and socially responsible off-road cycling.

Leadville

One of the most interesting facets of exploring Colorado's backcountry is encountering the legacy of its mining heritage. Few places reveal the extent of that past as much as Leadville. As you ride through the area, you'll see more prospect and mine sites than you can count. The backcountry is literally filled with old structures, piles of tailings, and many open mine shafts. Feel free to explore, but heed all private property postings, do not climb on any structures, and stay away from open shafts.

While the infamous Leadville 100 running and mountain biking races give the town its well-deserved hardcore reputation, the area has some easy and fun rides for novice cyclists and families. The Mineral Belt Trail, for instance, may be the best municipal, multi-use trail in the in the country: it's scenic, easy, and they groom it for skiing in winter! This, however, does not imply they are all easy. The Mosquito Pass route, for example, may be the most difficult ride in this guide.

No other city in the United States provides as much easy access to high altitude terrain. Before setting out, please bear in mind the unique demands of this environment. First, you will want to get early starts to avoid potentially dangerous afternoon storms. Many of the local routes access terrain above tree line, the last place you want to experience a storm. Next, visitors to Colorado from lower altitudes may want to take a few days to acclimatize before going nuts in the saddle.

Since a number of these rides start at the center of town, they offer easy access to post ride comforts such as food, showers, and lodging. If you need any gear or have any questions, there is also a great, full service bike shop right in the center of town.

While visiting, take a tour of the Matchless Mine or ride the Leadville, Colorado and Southern Railroad. The National Mining Hall of Fame and Museum, and the Tabor Opera House provide fascinating diversions if you need time to rest your weary legs. Discover why Leadville is one of the state's most fascinating, and perhaps greatest towns.

That says it all!

Ride 1: Camp Hale to Tennessee Pass

39°23.614' N, 106°18.725' W WGS84

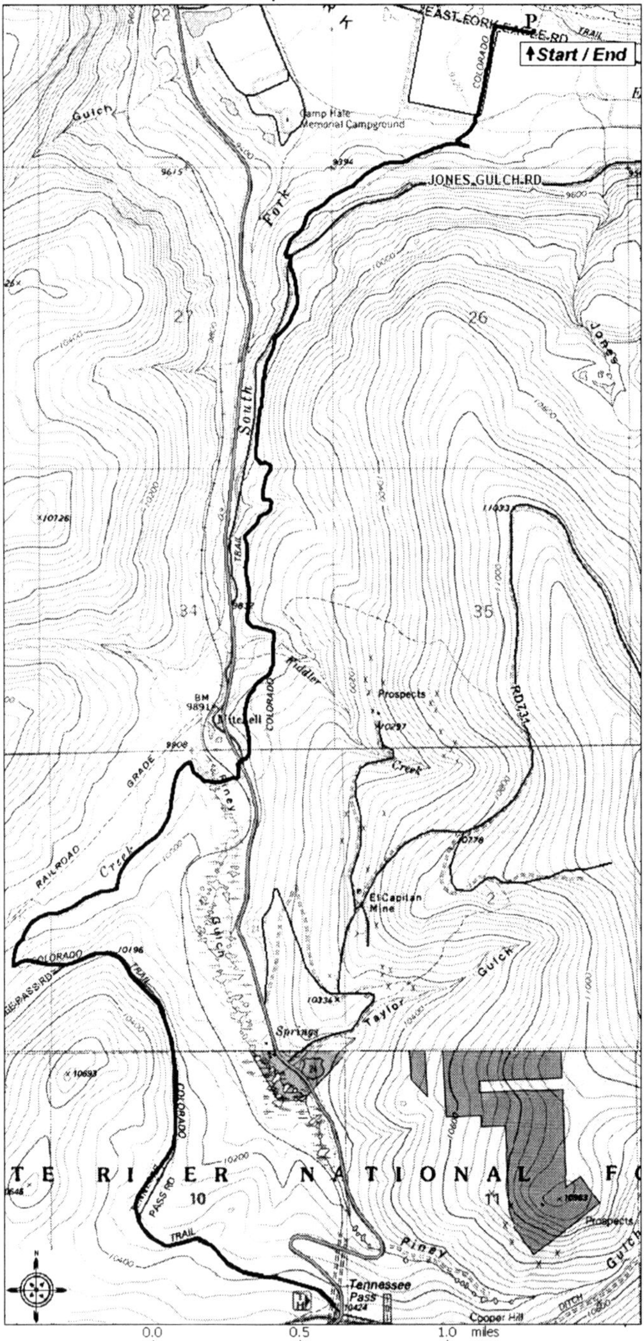

0.0 0.5 1.0 miles

0.0 0.5 1.0 1.5 km

Map 1: Camp Hale to Tennessee Pass (copyright National Geographic)

In 1941, the U.S. Army realized the need for a specialized division trained in skiing and winter survival. In addition to building Camp Hale to serve as the base for this unit, the Army built the country's longest T-bar lift at the present site of Ski Cooper for the troops to practice downhill skiing. After two years of rigorous training, the Tenth Mountain Division deployed to Europe where they played a key role in the liberation of northern Italy.

If there is such a thing as the perfect cross-country single-track ride, this may be it. Most of the grade is mild enough to crank in your middle ring and the technical obstacles are just challenging enough to test your skills without slowing you down. The icing on the cake, however, is the return trip from the pass. It's so much fun that you will not be able to stop smiling and you may have to scrape bugs from your teeth when you finish.

Do this ride. It will make you happy.

Elevation profile:

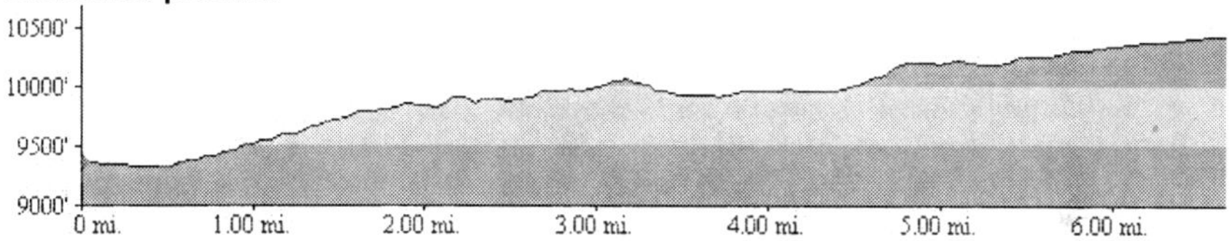

Ride length: 12.9 miles
Ride type: out-and-back
Riding time: 2 hours
Surface: dirt road/jeep track (5.0 miles); single-track (7.9 miles)
Elevations: start/end 9,360'; max 10,440'; min 9,330'
Total climbing: gain/loss 1,410'

Aerobic level: moderate (on the easy side of moderate; some climbing on single-track)
Technical level: 3 (a few tricky spots, but mostly smooth trail)
Season: June through October
USGS Quadrangles: Leadville North, Pando

Trailhead GPS coordinates: 39° 25.446' N; 106° 17.919' W

Getting there: from the stoplight at 6th St. and Harrison Ave. (US 24) in downtown Leadville, drive north on US 24 for 15.8 miles to the Camp Hale Forest Service Campground exit. Turn right and drive 0.1 miles to the intersection with Road #7161D. Turn right and continue east for 0.5 miles, crossing the bridge over the Eagle River East Fork. At the "T" intersection with Road #714, turn right and drive approximately 1.5 miles to the trailhead and parking lot on the left.

The ride:

- **0.0** Start at the parking lot of the Camp Hale trailhead of the Colorado Trail. Turn right (west) on Road #714.
- **0.1** Turn left (south) on Road #7141C, following the Colorado/Continental Divide Trails markers.
- **0.5** Turn left and cross the bridge. Look for trail markers to help you find the route. The ride is now on really nice single-track.
- **1.2** Pop-out on a dirt road. Head left, pass through a gate, then immediately turn right and continue on the single-track. Trail markers lead the way.
- **1.5** Pass an overlook with a bench. Stop to wave hello to the cars speeding by on the highway below you.

2.2 Cross a gnarled jeep track and continue riding the sweet line on the other side.
2.6 Cross a stream on a plank bridge.
3.0 Cross the highway. Watch for traffic! Head left, dropping down and around the gate. At the bottom, bunny-hop the train tracks (or walk your bike across as I do) and continue riding the fine line ahead.
3.1 Cross the water on tricky bridges. Ride them if you don't mind swimming if you don't clean them.
4.5 Pop-out on a well-graded dirt road and continue riding left (east) toward the pass.
5.3 Continue straight on the double-track after crossing a bridge.
5.4 Enter a clearing. Look left to see the slopes of Ski Cooper.
6.5 Arrive at the Tennessee Pass trailhead. Turn around and return the way you came. What a blast!

Options: You can extend this ride by riding south on the Colorado Trail and incorporating the Mitchell Creek Loop, turning the ride into a lollipop-loop (clockwise) of approximately 18 miles.

Or, you may want to shuttle it from Tennessee Pass for a fun, short downhill blast into Camp Hale.

Ride 2: Mitchell Creek Loop

This is a nice ride to start any sunny day. The single-track is manageable for beginners yet interesting enough to satisfy more experienced riders. Strong riders can probably blast through two laps in less than two hours.

The route starts with a pleasant roll through a pine forest where a few rocks keep things interesting without getting too technically demanding. After a short stretch on a dirt road, the single-track descent into Mitchell Creek basin is smooth and effortless. The ride ends along easy-graded double-track and the route's only sustained climb.

Elevation profile:

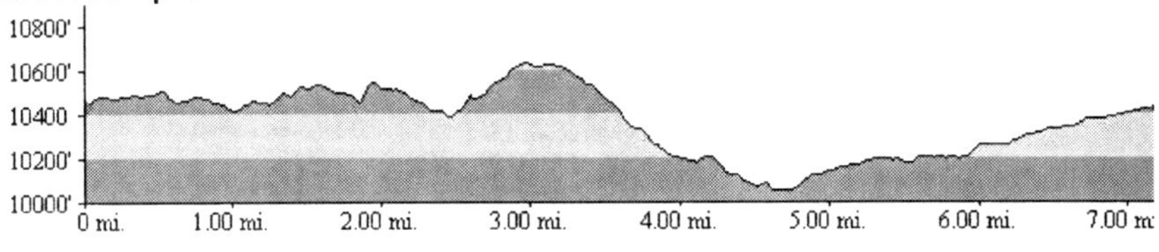

Ride length: 7.1 miles
Ride type: loop (clockwise)
Riding time: 1 hour
Surface: single-track (4.1 miles); double-track (2.6 miles); dirt road (0.4 miles)
Elevations: start/end 10,440'; max 10,630'; min 10,060'

Total climbing: gain/loss 900'
Aerobic level: easy (but the entire ride is over 10,000')
Technical level: 2+ (easy overall with a couple short rocky sections)
Season: June through October
USGS Quadrangles: Leadville North, Pando

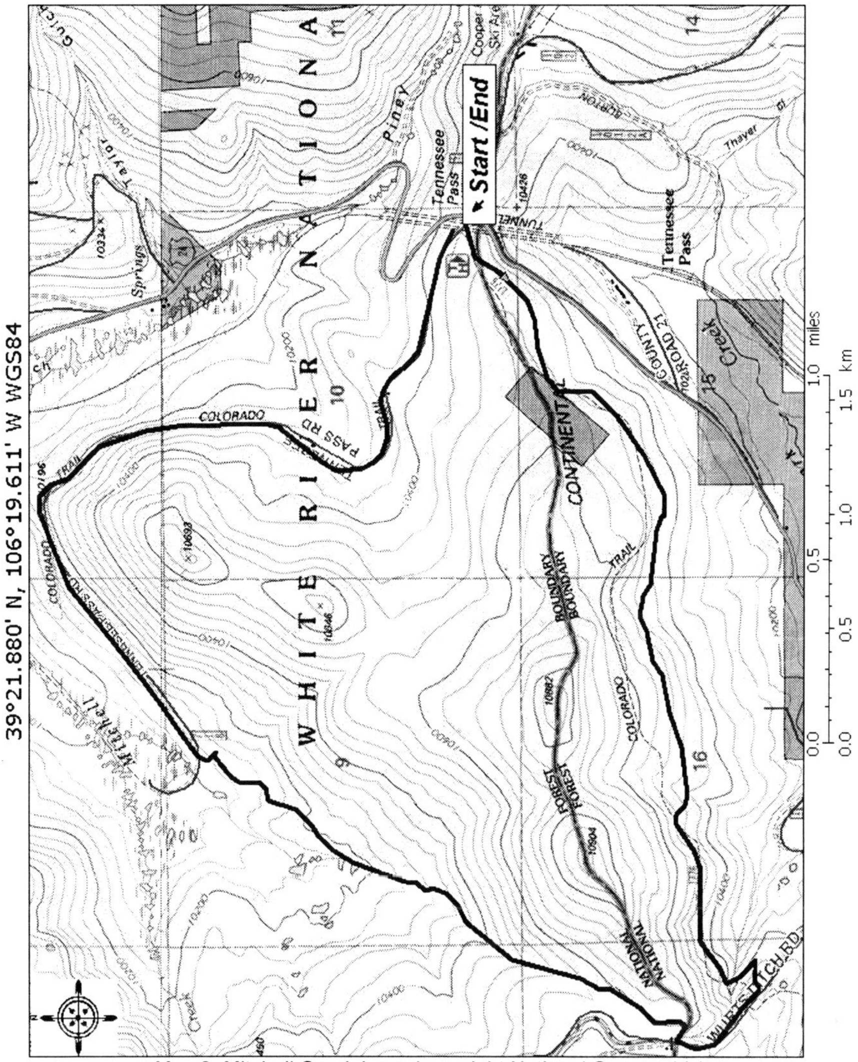

Map 2: Mitchell Creek Loop (copyright National Geographic)

Trailhead GPS coordinates: 39˚ 21.761' N; 106˚ 18.675' W

Getting there: from the stoplight at 6th St. and Harrison Ave. (US 24) in downtown Leadville, drive10.0 miles north on US 24 to Tennessee Pass. Park in the large parking area on the west side of the highway. The ride begins at the trailhead entrance adjacent to the highway on the southeast corner of the parking lot. *This parking area has pit toilets.*

The ride:

0.0 Start at the Colorado Trail trailhead adjacent to the highway at the southeast corner of the parking lot. Get ready to roll on some nice single-track.

0.9 Pass a trail sign for the Colorado Trail and "Tree line" (huh?). Continue straight on the Colorado Trail.

2.3 Start a downhill with a bridge at the bottom.

2.4 Cross the bridge and continue straight on the single-track. Cross another bridge in 50 yards. Follow the sign directing you to the "10th Mountain Division Hut." (*Pass the spur on the left that leads to Crane Park.*)

2.5 Turn right at the intersection with Wurt's Ditch Road and ride uphill. ***Note-*** *the Colorado Trail continues for approximately 3.5 miles before entering a wilderness area where mountain bikes are prohibited. Add miles to this ride by riding this section of the Colorado trail as an out-and-back.*

2.9 Turn right onto FSR 705. Ride about 10 yards then turn right again at the trailhead sign. Continue riding past the sign, bearing right onto the obvious trail. (*The faint left spur leads to a campsite.*)

4.5 After a very fun and easy downhill, the trail enters an open meadow in a boggy area. The trail gets a little hard to follow, but stay left and ride along the southern edge of the meadow. As you ride through the Mitchell Creek basin, be sure to either ride or walk your bike through the center of any muddy spots; riding around the mud damages the trail.

4.7 The trail widens to a double-track and starts to climb.

5.3 Continue straight on the road as the Colorado Trail intersects on the left.

7.1 Arrive back at the parking lot. Do it again?

Options: ride to the end of Wurt's Ditch Road for a pleasant out-and-back spur. Return to the trailhead by resuming the Mitchell Creek Loop.

Ride 3: Jenny June Mine Loop

This route begins atop Tennessee Pass at the Tenth Mountain Division memorial that pays tribute to the 992 troops who gave their lives in the brave service to our country and to our allies during World War II.

The ride is a moderate spin to the Jenny June Mine site along somewhat rough jeep trails. Start by making your way into Ski Cooper then head south to the mine site. The crux of the ride is the three-mile climb following a steep and loose descent near the midpoint.

Elevation profile:

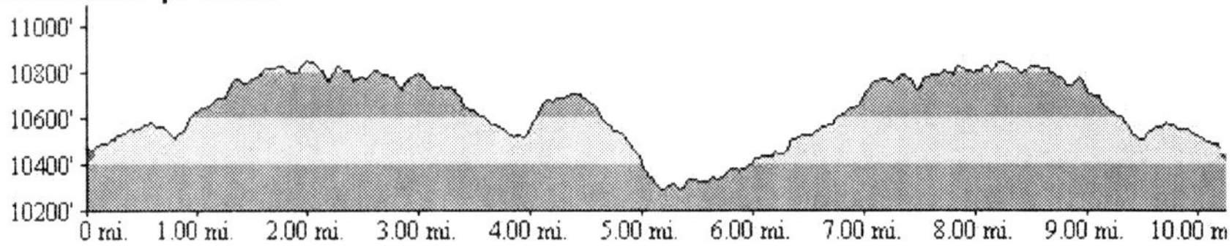

Ride length: 10.1 miles
Ride type: lollipop-loop (clockwise)
Riding time: 1.5 hours
Surface: jeep road
Elevations: start/end 10,440'; max 10,850'; min 10,290'
Total climbing: gain/loss 1,500'

Aerobic level: easy/moderate (some climbing)
Technical level: 3 (some rocky sections)
Season: June through October
USGS Quadrangle: Leadville North

39°20.732' N, 106°17.966' W WGS84

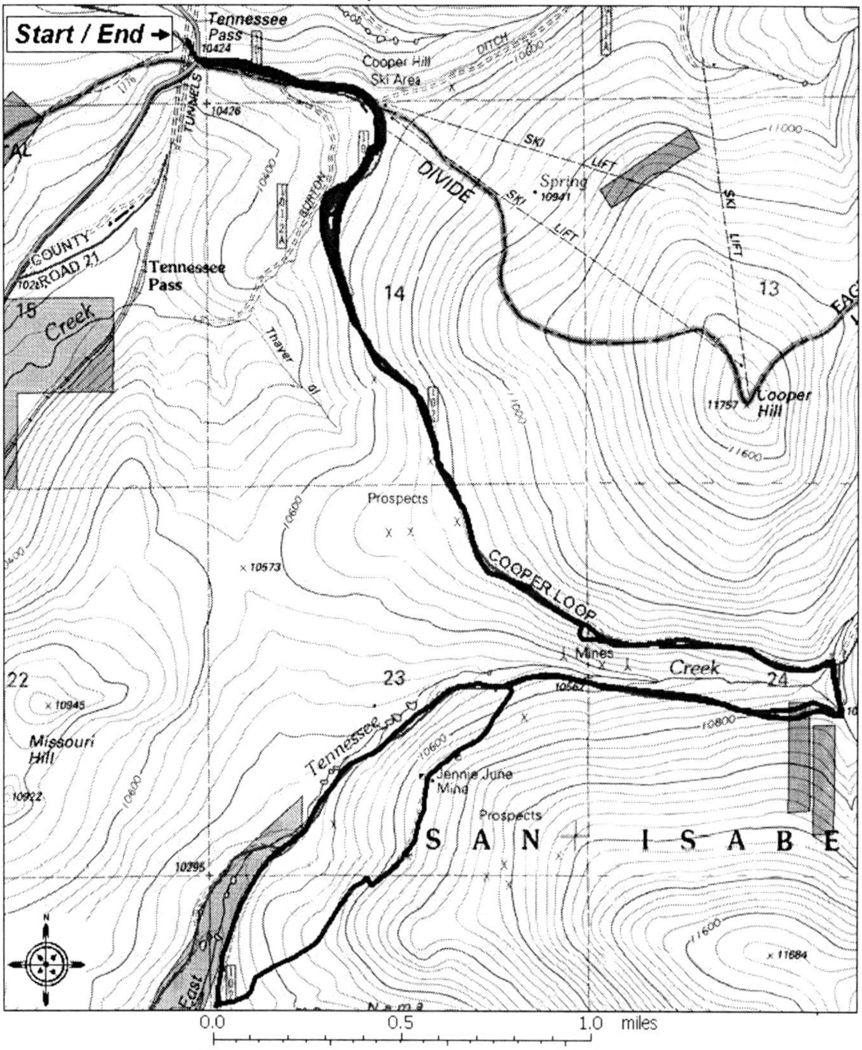

Map 3: Jenny June Mine Loop (copyright National Geographic)

Trailhead GPS coordinates: 39° 2.729' N; 106° 18.645' W

Getting there: from the stoplight at 6th St. and Harrison Ave. (US 24) in downtown Leadville, drive 10.0 miles north on US 24 to Tennessee Pass. Park in the large parking area on the west side of the highway. The ride begins at the Tenth Mountain Division Memorial on the east side of US 24. *Use caution when crossing the highway! This parking area has pit toilets.*

The ride:

0.0 Starting at the Tenth Mountain Division Memorial, ride east on the road leading into the ski area.

0.3 Enter the ski area gate. Continue riding toward the lifts and base area.

0.5 Turn right at the base area and follow the road south to the maintenance building. If it's in bloom, take note of the wonderfully fragrant clover growing along the road.

0.6 Turn right onto TR 102.

1.6 Pass the "Tennessee Pass Cook House" sign.

1.7 Bear left at the unmarked fork and continue along on a short section of double-track.

1.9 Stay on the main road, passing a faint jeep spur.

2.8 Cross through a green gate at the bottom of a relatively short descent. Continue over Tennessee Creek, then turn right at the intersection with TR 102A. Continue on west on TR 102 (*East Tennessee Creek Road*).

3.0 Turn right and cross a small stream at an unmarked intersection.

3.9 Make a hard left and look for a sign directing you to the Jenny June Mine. This intersection marks the start of the loop and it begins with a climb to the mine site.

4.2 Arrive at the Jenny June Mine. Heed all warnings and if you explore the area use common sense. Also take note of the sign that reads, "You are here:" (wherever that may be). Get ready to rip a rocky downhill.

5.0 Turn right at the junction with TR 102. Brace yourself for a bit of climbing.

6.2 Close the loop by staying left at the fork. Start the return trip back to the Pass.

7.2 Cross the creek and turn left.

7.4 Bear left at the fork, continuing over the creek and through the green gate on TR 102.

8.4 Pass into the open meadow littered with tree stumps. Continue straight, passing a spur.

9.6 You are back at the ski area. Stop, smell the clover, then continue.

10.1 Arrive back at the memorial. Carefully cross the highway and find your car. Head off to your next adventure.

Options: throw in an out-and-back spur along TR 102A en route, but be prepared for some burly climbing. Whenever you feel like quitting the climb, think of the soldiers of the Tenth Mountain Division for inspiration.

Camp Hale cantonments

Ride 4: St. Kevin's-Turquoise Lake Loop

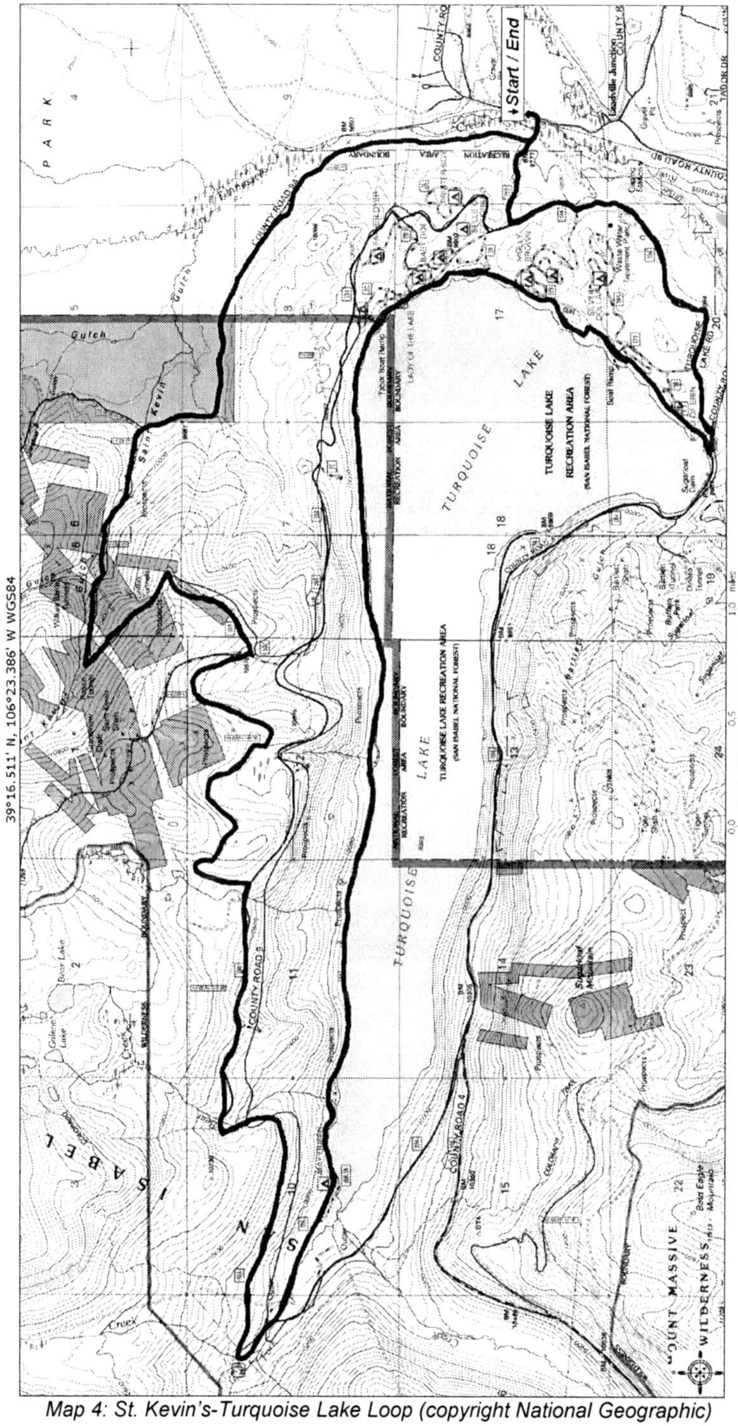

Map 4: St. Kevin's-Turquoise Lake Loop (copyright National Geographic)

The single-track of the Turquoise Lake Trail is one of the most popular rides in the Leadville area. The grade is easy and the majority of the single-track is a smooth spin on the north shore of the lake. Visitors to the area will be tempted to take it easy, stopping to behold the outstanding views of Mount Elbert (14,433') and Mount Massive (14,421'), Colorado's two highest peaks. Locals, on the other hand, will hammer their way through the rock gardens with an amazing display of grace.

This route incorporates the climb through St. Kevin's Gulch, the first major climb of the Leadville 100 mountain bike racecourse. As you sweat and grind up this grade, bear in mind that this is the easiest of the three major climbs of the course. Whew!

Elevation profile:

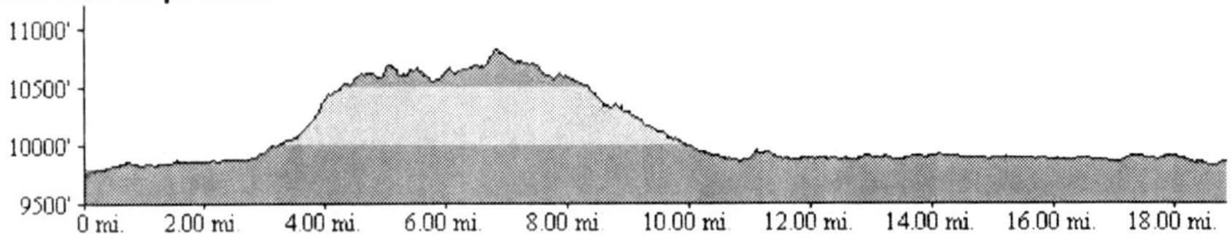

Ride length: 18.6 miles
Ride type: loop (counter-clockwise)
Riding time: 2-3 hours
Surface: jeep road (7.0 miles); paved road (6.1 miles); single-track (5.5 miles)
Elevations: start/end 9,790'; max 10,820'; min 9,770'

Total climbing: gain/loss 1,590'
Aerobic level: moderate (climbing)
Technical level: 3 (some of the rock gardens on level terrain are more difficult, but the escape is easy)
Season: June through September
USGS Quadrangle: Leadville North, Homestake Reservoir

Trailhead GPS coordinates: 39° 15.882' N; 106° 20.365' W

Getting there: from the stoplight at 6th St. and Harrison Ave. (US 24) in downtown Leadville, drive 0.8 miles north on US 24 to the traffic light at Mountainview Drive (at the Safeway). Turn left and drive 2.7 miles west on Mountainview Drive. Turn right at the intersection with CR 9 and continue for roughly 0.5 miles to the large parking area on your right. The ride starts at the southern edge of the parking lot.

The ride:

0.0 Ride out of the south entrance of the parking area, past the pit toilets. Cross the road and train tracks as you head west on CR 9.
0.2 Turn right on CR 9A.
1.0 Stay on the main road, passing intersections with a few jeep spurs.
1.3 The road bends left (northwest).
1.9 Pass through a gate and over a cattle guard. Be sure to stay on the road, as it now passes through private property.
2.8 Cross another cattle guard and start the climb.
3.0 Bear left at the fork to climb on FSR 103.
3.1 Pass an old mine site on the right.
3.5 Bear left at the fork and continue climbing.
4.1 Take a hard left at the switchback.
4.6 Stay left at the fork. Orange blazes on the trees will help guide you through this section.
4.9 Continue on the main road as you pass several campsites.
5.2 Approach a "T" intersection where FSR 103 meets FSR 107. (*FSR 107*

climbs to your right.) Look 45 degrees right for the gate just past FSR 107. Ride around the gate and continue on a slightly faded double-track.

7.0 Pass through a gate as the road widens. Continue to the intersection with paved CR 9 then turn right on the paved road.

7.7 Pass the Shimmering Point Overlook on your left. Keep rocketing downhill.

9.9 Turn left into the May Queen Campground.

10.4 Bear left at the pay station fork. Pit toilets are on the left if you need them. It's also possible to refill water bottles here, but be discrete if you are not a paying visitor.

10.5 Pass another water spigot on the left.

10.6 Last call for pit toilets. Enter the small loop and proceed to the Turquoise Lake Trail entrance. The single-track starts here. Finally!

10.9 Cross a bridge over a stream then contend with the rocks on the other side.

11.3 Pass a mine site and enjoy its sulfurous scent.

12.5 More mine tailings.

14.2 Cross the paved boat ramp and continue riding the trail. Stay on the Turquoise Lake Trail as it skirts the lake. You will soon pass the Baby Doe and Father Dyer Campgrounds, and many access points to the lake.

15.4 Stay right at the fork then pop into a large, paved parking area. Cross the parking area and boat launch then continue skirting the lake on the right fork of the single-track.

15.6 Continue past the Molly Brown Campground on your left. Stay on the trail.

16.0 Bear right at the fork and continue on the single-track as you approach the dam.

16.1 Arrive at the dam and CR 4. Turn left on CR 4.

16.2 Turn left on CR 9C. Climb.

16.5 Continuc straight past the entrance to the Silver Dollar Campground and Matchless Boat Launch.

17.7 Bear right past the access road to the Molly Brown Campground and the Turquoise Lake Nature Trail.

18.1 Turn right at the intersection with CR 9. (*CR 9C continues straight to the Baby Doe Campground.*)

18.5 Pass CR 9A on your left. Cross the tracks and the road. Find your car and get a gut-bomb cheeseburger in Leadville.

Options: want a shorter, less taxing ride that skips all the roads? Park at the dam and ride the single-track as an out-and-back. If you want to skip the bulk of the rocky terrain, turn around whenever the mood strikes.

Dread the climb through St. Kevin's Gulch? Park at the damn on CR 4 and ride the pavement around the lake. You can ride to the trailhead on either the north or south sides of the lake. This option cuts the total climbing by about half.

Ride 5: Ball Mountain Loop

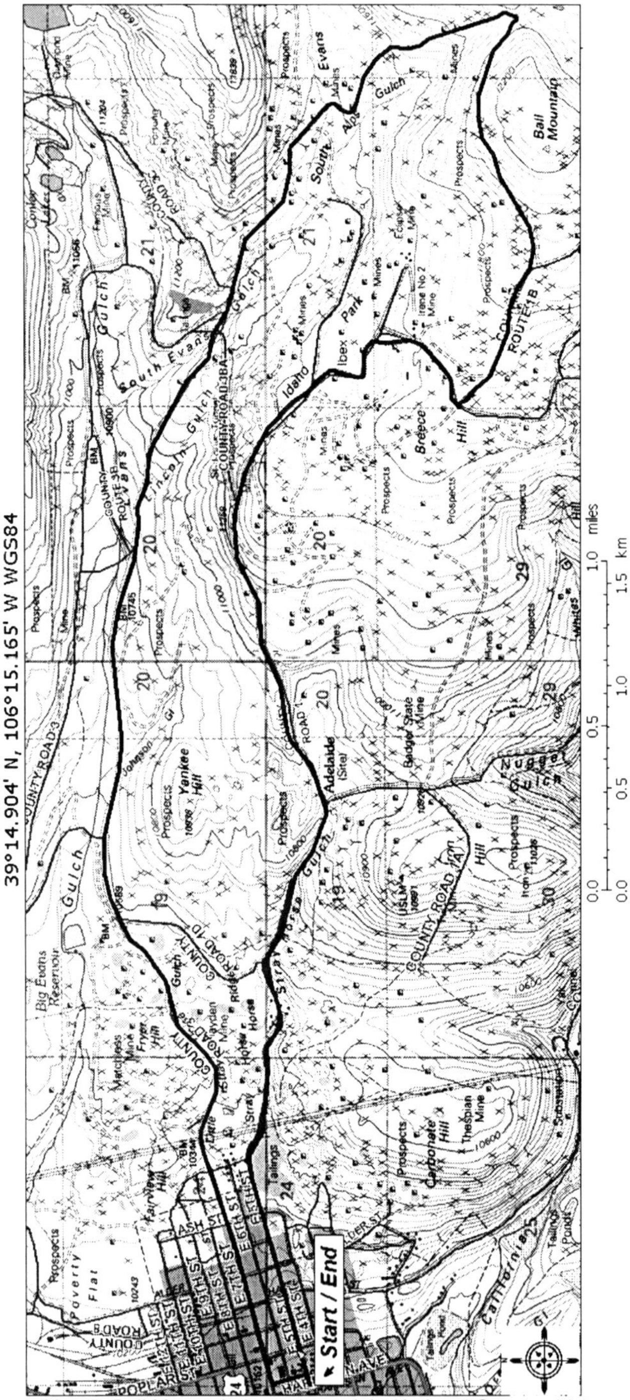

Map 5: Ball Mountain Loop (copyright National Geographic)

So, you're looking for a great workout with a killer descent that starts from the center of Leadville. Try this one. It starts with a pulse-pounding climb to an amazing, but very short (only 0.6 miles!) stretch of alpine single-track. Next, the white-knuckled descent into Alps Gulch is breathlessly steep, technical, and fast. The remainder is an easy glide back to town.

Do this in morning, before the afternoon storms blow in. Because mining was so active in this area, finding your way might be challenging. So many unmapped and unmarked roads zigzag across the route that a wrong turn or two may prove inevitable. If you don't have a GPS, be sure to carry quality maps and a compass as a supplement to this guide.

Elevation profile:

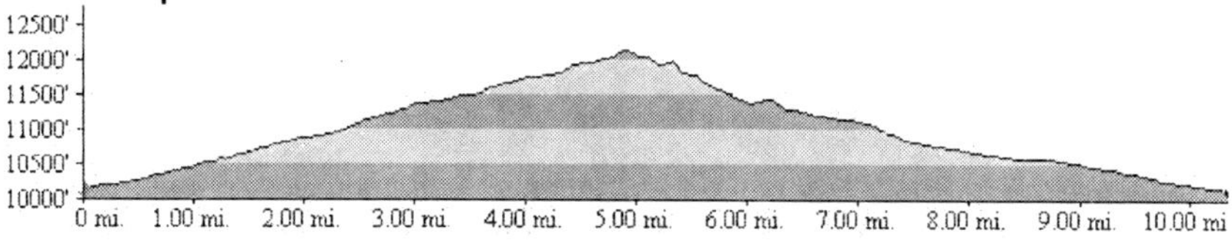

Ride length: 10.4 miles
Ride type: loop (counter-clockwise)
Riding time: 1.5-2 hours
Surface: paved road (2.1 miles); dirt road/jeep trails (7.7 miles); single-track (0.6 miles)
Elevations: start/end 10,150'; max 12,140'; min 10,150'
Total climbing: gain/loss 2,000'

Aerobic level: strenuous (sustained climbs at high altitude)
Technical level: 4 (the descent from the pass is rutted, loose, steep, and fast)
Season: July through October
USGS Quadrangles: Leadville South, Leadville North, Climax, Mount Sherman

Trailhead GPS coordinates: 39° 14.886' N; 106° 17.49' W

Getting there: park anywhere in downtown Leadville. From the stoplight at 6th St. and Harrison Ave. (US 24) in downtown Leadville, ride one block south to E. 5th St. The ride starts at the intersection of Harrison Ave. and E. 5th St.

The ride:

0.0 From the intersection of E. 5th St. and Harrison Ave. (US 24), ride northeast (uphill) on E. 5th St. ***Note-*** *in about 70 yards, you'll pass the historic home of Horace and Augusta Tabor on your left.*

0.7 The road bends east and becomes CR 1 as the pavement ends.

0.9 Enter the mining district and continue climbing on CR 1.

1.2 Pass an entrance to the Mineral Belt Trail on your left. Continue riding uphill, passing beneath the bridge.

1.4 Continue climbing on the main road, passing a spur on your left.

1.9 Stay left on CR 1 as CR 2A intersects from the right. Keep climbing.

2.5 Continue climbing on CR 1 as it bends left. A mining spur will be on your right.

2.9 Continue climbing straight on CR 1. An unmarked road descends on your left and an unmarked jeep road climbs to your right.

3.3 The road levels as you pass another mine access road on your right. Continue straight for another 50 yards and bear right as CR 38 descends to your left.

3.6 After passing a large mining area, bear right at the fork and resume climbing on CR 1A.

4.0 Top-out and look left for a jeep trail that heads southeast toward the rounded summit of Ball Mountain. Turn left at this unmarked junction and cross the rocky runoff channel. Continue ascending on the double-track/jeep trail.

4.5 Bear left at the fork and continue riding the steep jeep trail toward the now visible line of single-track to the east.

4.6 Bear left at the fork and continue riding toward the single-track. The double-track here is very faint.

4.7 Continue climbing as the skinny, single-track begins. What a fine line.

5.1 ***USE EXTREME CAUTION*** as the trail skims the edge of an open mineshaft! It doesn't look deep, but don't tempt fate; it may not be done collapsing.

5.2 Break out your machete and cut a path through the brush. No machete? Narrow your grip and plow through. You will be out in less than 100 feet.

5.3 Arrive at Ball Mountain Pass. Descend left along the obvious, rough jeep track into Alps Gulch. Brace for a fast, technical descent.

6.1 Finish the intense descent and cross a stream on a plank bridge.

6.3 After a quick climb, turn left at an unmarked intersection and descend along a rough jeep track.

6.7 Pass CR 3C on your right as you continue descending.

6.9 Pass the intersection with CR 3B on your right as you continue zipping down hill.

7.1 Continue your descent straight on the main road (CR 38) as you pass a couple roads on your left.

7.7 Continue descending as CR 38 merges into CR 3.

8.6 Continue straight on CR 3, passing CR 3A on your right.

8.9 Pavement! Continue descending. You'll soon pass under the Mineral Belt Trail and zoom past Tabor's Matchless Silver Mine on your right.

10.3 Arrive at the intersection Harrison Ave. and E. 7th St. Ride two blocks south to close the loop. Very nice.

Options: have fun exploring the numerous spurs in the area, but stay away from all structures and open mine shafts.

Leadville, Colorado and Southern Railroad

Ride 6: Ball Mountain Pass

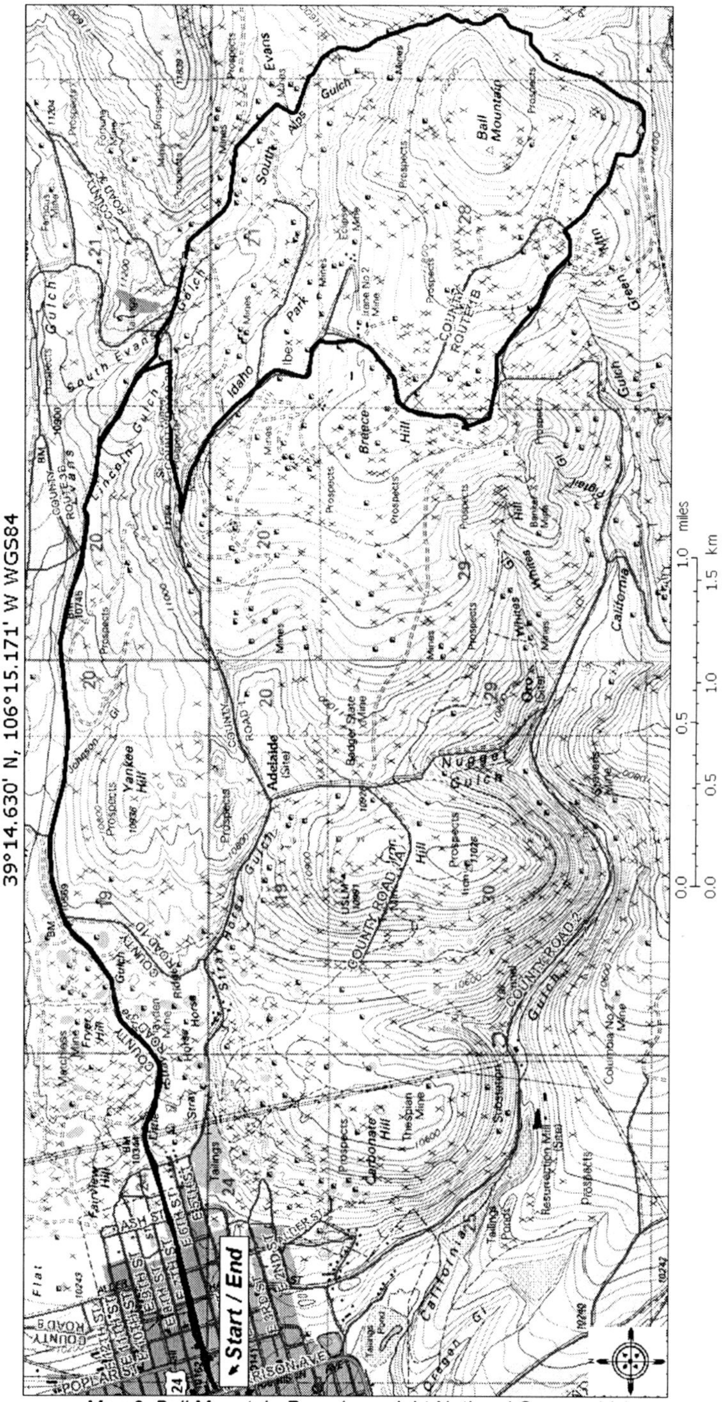

Map 6: Ball Mountain Pass (copyright National Geographic)

Along this route, you'll pass more abandoned mines and prospect sites than you can count, including the famous Matchless Mine just outside of town. You'll see numerous collapsed structures and ride right next to sulfurous tailings that emit the faint scent of rotten eggs. It's the kind of place you dreamed about if you played with Tonka Trucks as a kid. The ride itself is a lot of fun. Sure, you'll work a little for that fun, but it only makes the reward so much sweeter.

Ride this one in morning, before the afternoon storms roll in. Because mining was so active in this area, finding your way might be challenging. So many unmapped and unmarked roads zigzag across the route that a wrong turn or two may prove inevitable. If you don't have a GPS, be sure to carry quality maps and a compass as a supplement to this guide.

Elevation profile:

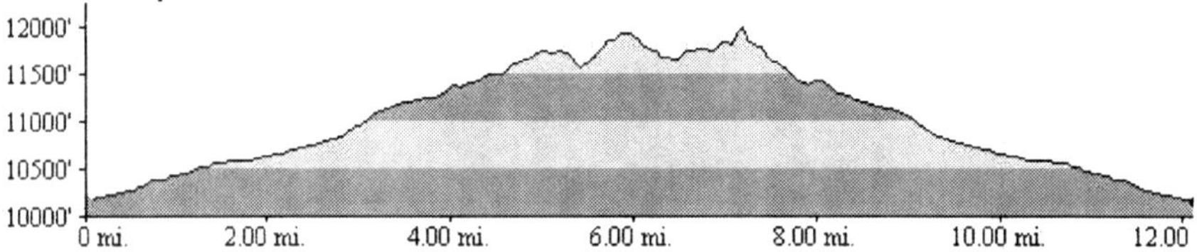

Ride length: 12.2 miles
Ride type: lollipop-loop (counter-clockwise)
Riding time: 2 hours
Surface: paved road (3.0 miles); dirt road/jeep trails (9.2 miles)
Elevations: start/end 10,160'; max 11,990'; min 10,160'

Total climbing: gain/loss 2,325'
Aerobic level: strenuous (sustained climbs at high altitude)
Technical level: 4 (the descent from the pass is loose, steep and fast)
Season: July through October
USGS Quadrangles: Leadville North, Climax, Mount Sherman

Trailhead GPS coordinates: 39° 14.976' N; 106° 17.52' W

Getting there: park anywhere in downtown Leadville. From the stoplight at 6th St. and Harrison Ave. (US 24) in downtown Leadville, ride one block north to E. 7th St. The ride starts at the intersection of Harrison and E. 7th.

The ride:

0.0 From the intersection of E. 7th St. and Harrison Ave., ride east (uphill) on E. 7th.

0.7 7th St. becomes CR 3. Continue climbing on CR 3 toward the Matchless Silver Mine.

1.2 Pass the entrance to the Matchless Mine. ***Note-*** *the bridge you are about to pass under is the Mineral Belt Trail; an entrance to it is just past the bridge.*

1.5 Stay right on the main road as it changes to dirt.

1.6 Continue on the main road, passing a road on your right.

1.8 Continue straight on CR 3, past the intersection with CR 3A on the left.

2.7 Bear right at the fork and continue riding uphill on CR 38. (*CR 3 heads left.*)

2.9 Continue climbing on the main road, passing a road on your right.

3.3 Approach a confusing intersection at the top of a climb. Take the middle fork that climbs right toward the mine site.

3.9 At the top of another climb, take the hard left and continue climbing on the well-graded road. This road is CR 1 (5th St.).

4.4 Continue straight on the main road as it levels. (*Don't take the right that heads up to a mine site.*) Ride for another 50 yards to the fork and bear right (uphill), away from CR 38.

4.6 Turn right on CR 1A and continue climbing.

4.9 Pass some yellow-tinted (sulfurous) tailings and note the scent. ***Note-*** *when rain hits the tailings, the sulfur reacts with the water to create sulfuric acid. This acidic runoff has the potential to contaminate ground water and streams, adversely affecting plant and animal life in the area.*

5.0 Top out and continue straight on the main road through an unmarked intersection.

5.2 Take the left-most fork at the 3-way split. You'll soon approach a mine site with a tremendous overlook of Leadville and Turquoise Lake. Take only pictures; leave only tread marks.

5.5 After a quick dip, go left at the fork and resume with a climb on a rough section of road.

6.0 After topping out on a literally breathtaking climb, turn right at the 4-way intersection. You will now descend toward the power lines.

7.0 Turn left at the fork and start the final climb to the pass.

7.3 You made it! (*Is that single-track you smell on the left?*) Take the obvious descent into Alps Gulch. Get ready for some speed.

8.0 After the hairy descent, cross a stream on a plank bridge.

8.2 Fork left on the double-track after a small climb; ride downhill toward some mine sites.

8.6 Pass CR 3C on the right and continue straight downhill.

8.8 Continue straight and downhill, passing CR 3B on the right as you go.

9.2 Close the loop by staying right at the intersection while descending on CR 38.

9.6 Rejoin CR 3. Keep flying downhill on CR 3/E. 7th St. all the way back to town.

12.2 The end. Grab a tasty beverage at one of the town's fine watering holes. Life can be good.

Options: explore the many spurs in the area, but stay away from all structures and open mine shafts.

Imagine... riding here

Ride 7: Mosquito Pass

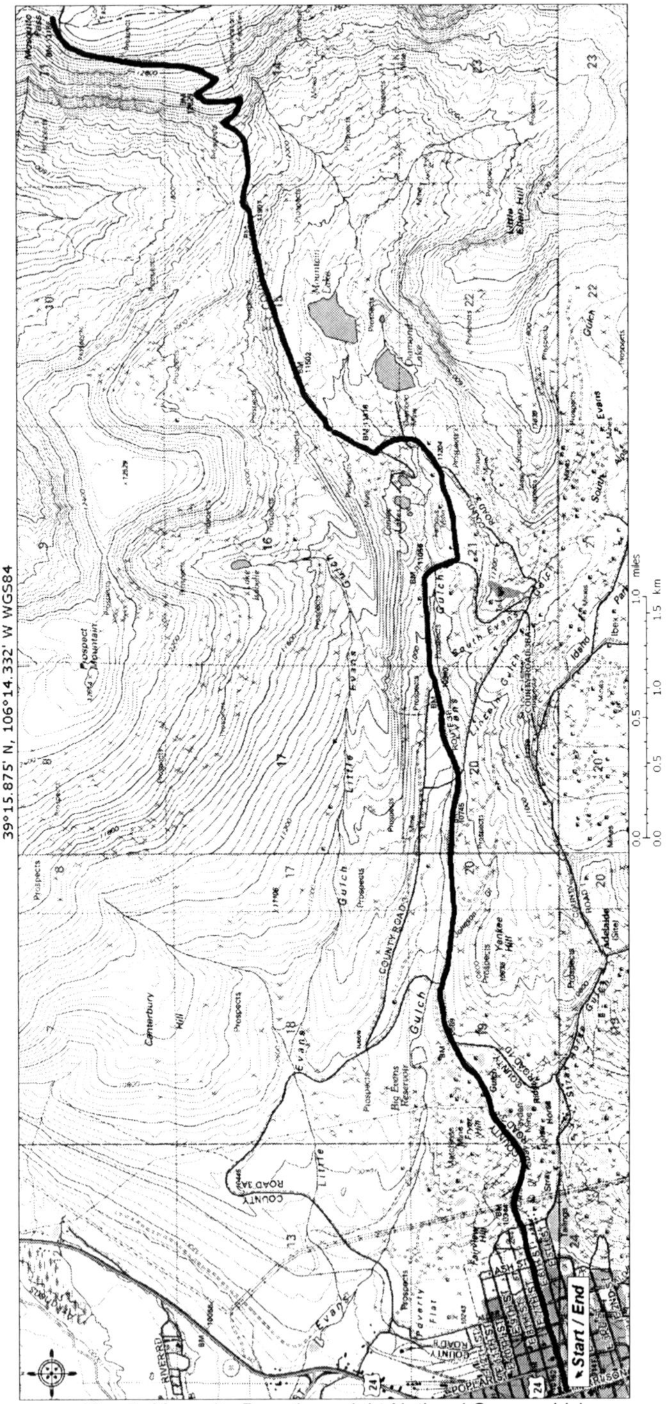

Map 7: Mosquito Pass (copyright National Geographic)

An old sage once told me there are many paths to enlightenment. When I first spied this line from a distance, I wondered if this was one. As I finally reached the summit, however, I wasn't sure if it was Nirvana or simply hypoxia.

Overall, this is probably the most difficult ride in this guide. The steeps are steep and the road surface above 12,000' feels like you are pedaling up a streambed of coconuts. Putting that aside, the route tops out at 13,185', and how many other rides claim that? At times, it almost feels like you are attempting a 14er on a bike, especially when looking way down at tree line.

The upper stretches of the descent will certainly put both your bike's suspension and your technical riding skills to the test.

If you relish a stiff challenge, this is for you. Do it!

Elevation profile:

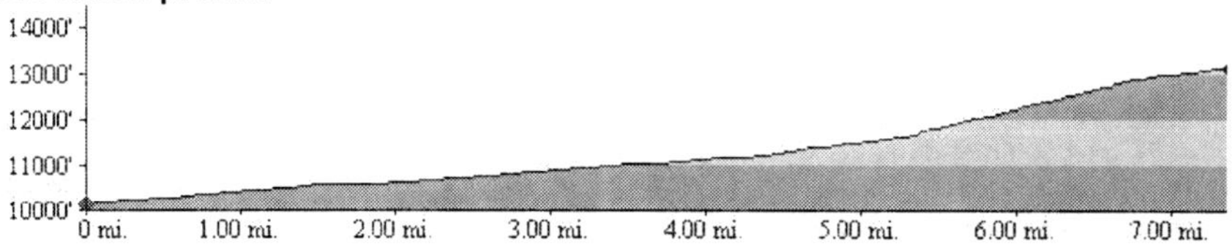

Ride length: 15.0 miles
Ride type: out-and-back
Riding time: 2.5 hours
Surface: paved road (3.0 miles); dirt road/jeep trail (12.0 miles)
Elevations: start/end 10,160'; max 13,185'; min 10,160'
Total climbing: gain/loss 2,990'

Aerobic level: beyond strenuous (altitude + steep grade + loose rocks = a fair amount of suffering)
Technical level: 5 (the descent from the pass is loose, steep and insanely fast)
Season: July through September
USGS Quadrangles: Leadville North, Climax

Trailhead GPS coordinates: 39° 14.983' N; 106° 17.524' W

Getting there: park anywhere in downtown Leadville. From the stoplight at 6th St. and Harrison Ave. (US 24) in downtown Leadville, ride one block north to E. 7th St. The ride starts at the intersection of Harrison and E. 7th.

The ride:

- **0.0** From the intersection of E. 7th and Harrison in downtown Leadville, ride east (uphill) on E. 7th St.
- **0.7** E. 7th St. becomes CR 3. Continue climbing on CR 3 toward the Matchless Silver Mine.
- **1.2** Pass the entrance to the Matchless Mine.
- **1.5** Stay right on the main road as it changes to dirt.
- **1.6** Continue on the main road, passing a road on your right.
- **1.8** Continue straight on CR 3, past the intersection with CR 3A on the left.
- **2.7** Bear left at the fork and continue riding on CR 3. The sign says, "NARROW ROUGH ROAD." Take it as a friendly warning of things to come. (*CR 38 heads right.*)
- **3.0** Pass a driveway on the left.
- **3.1** Pass another driveway on the right.

3.8 Stay left on CR 3 as CR 3B heads right.

4.1 Take the left-most fork, CR 3 (unmarked), at this 3-way intersection. (*CR 3C peels off hard to the right and the middle fork is a mining access way.*)

4.4 Bear left on CR 3, passing the Diamond Mine entrance on the right.

4.5 Stay right at the fork and climb through the rocks.

4.9 Continue straight on the "narrow, rough road" as you pass a couple jeep tracks on the left.

5.4 Look right for dazzling views of Mountain Lake (left) and Diamond Lake (right).

5.8 Stay on the main road, passing more jeep tracks on the left.

6.0 Pass the jeep spurs on your left. Continue climbing on the main road. ***Note-*** *Bird's Eye Gulch, another popular Leadville ride, departs left from CR 3 at this point.*

6.4 Pass a spur on the switchback, heeding the "Do Not Enter" sign. Continue on the main road.

7.0 Continue straight, passing an unmarked spur on the right.

7.1 Continue climbing, passing the rugged spur on the left.

7.5 Raise your arms in victory! You made it! Have a goo shot and some water, then brace for the intense return trip along the same route.

Options: try descending via Bird's Eye Gulch. It'll drop you on CO 91 a few miles north of town.

Or, in the spirit of Father Dyer, ride down the eastern side of the pass. Either ride it as an out-and-back or have someone meet you in Alma or Fairplay.

Along the Mineral Belt Trail

Ride 8: Mineral Belt Trail

39°14.678' N, 106°16.988' W WGS84

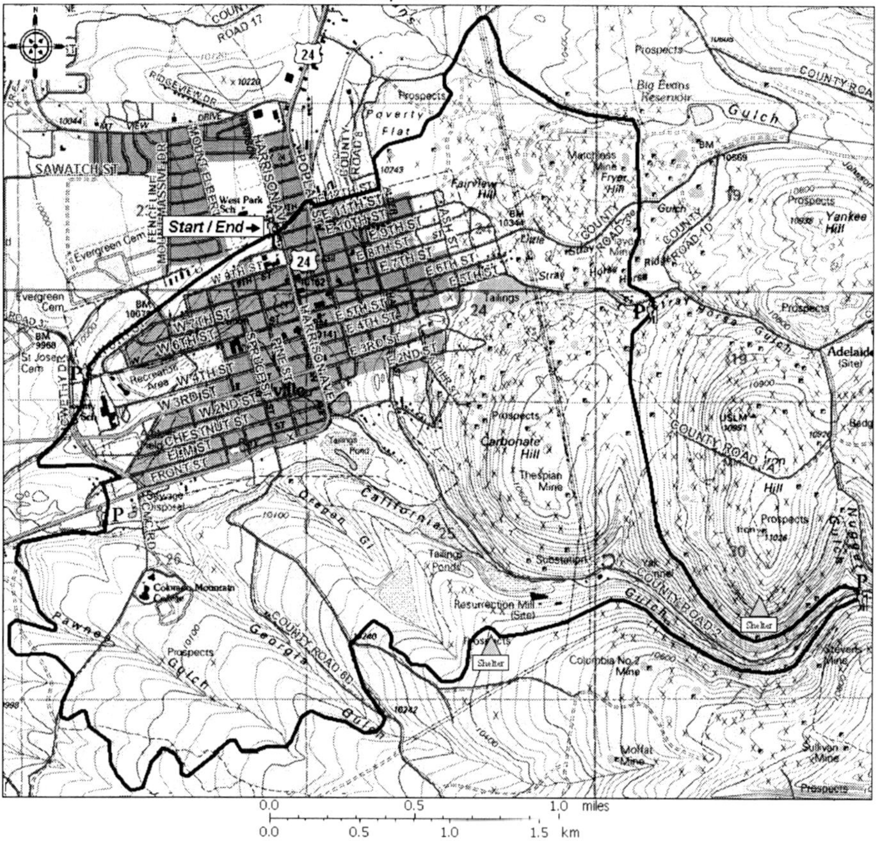

Map 8: Mineral Belt Trail (copyright National Geographic)

Take a journey through the pages of history as you explore this absorbing and exquisite trail. Appropriate for everyone, this trail is both well planned and well built. Interpretive signs and plaques scattered throughout give one an unparalleled appreciation for the town's rich and diverse heritage.

As the plaque says, "Built in the Leadville spirit through the cooperation of many for the enjoyment of all."

Elevation profile:

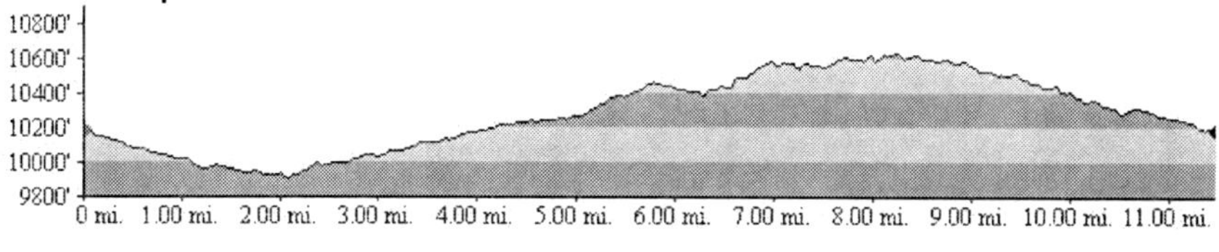

Ride length: 11.6 miles
Ride type: loop (counter-clockwise)
Riding time: 1-2 hours
Surface: paved multi-use path
Elevations: start/end 10,200'; max 10,630'; min 9,910'

Total climbing: gain/loss 800'
Aerobic level: easy
Technical level: 1
Season: May through October
USGS Quadrangles: Leadville South, Leadville North

Trailhead GPS coordinates: 39° 15.173' N; 106° 17.614' W

Getting there: park anywhere in downtown Leadville. From the stoplight at the intersection of Harrison Ave. (US 24) and 6th St. in downtown Leadville, ride about 0.20 miles north on Harrison Ave. to Ice Palace Park (behind the National Mining Hall of Fame and Museum). The ride starts at the intersection of the trail and Harrison Ave.

The ride:
For the sake of convenience, this route description and elevation profile start in the center of town and proceeds counter-clockwise. There are, however, several other trailheads and parking areas; choose the one that suits you best.

The trail itself is extremely well marked and a mileage log isn't necessary. Having said that, it is highly suggested that you stop at the visitor center between E. 8th and E. 9th Sts. on Harrison Ave. to pick up an official map and guide to the trail before setting out on your ride.

While slightly more difficult than riding the loop clockwise, starting at the Ice Palace Park and riding counter-clockwise gives the route a nice flow. You'll begin with a swift descent through modern Leadville. After crossing US 24 at the southwest edge of town (approx. 1.6 miles), you'll pass a parking area and trailhead, and then pass some historical buildings. Next, you'll ascend into a peaceful, forested stretch that gives you a sense of what the area may have been like prior to development.

After passing the first shelter at the Leadville Overlook (approx. 5.6 miles), you'll enter California Gulch (approx. 6.2 miles), the site of the area's first major mining development. It was here that they first discovered placer gold in 1860. The adjoining camp, dubbed "Oro City," drew more than 8,000 hopeful prospectors to a rough-and-tumble assortment of tents and shacks.

At approximately 7.2 miles, you'll pass another trailhead and parking area at CR 2.

Pedaling the leg between California Gulch to the Matchless Mine is like riding through a museum exhibit. The path weaves between interpretive signs, old mining carts, and heaps of mining waste tailings.

At the Matchless Mine site (approx. 9.3 miles) just past E. 7th St./CR 3, Baby Doe Tabor's last home, nothing more than a weather-beaten, one-room shack, still stands less than 100 feet from the trail. Nearly forty years after the repeal of the Sherman Silver Act in 1893, she froze to death in that hovel as she waited for the return of silver's boom days.

The rest of the route is almost a coast all the way back to town. At the intersection of E. 12th and Alder Sts., the route runs down E. 12th St. for about 265 yards. You are less than 0.25 miles from the Ice Palace Park after crossing US 24 at the north end of town.

Options: if you are riding with small children, people not acclimatized to the altitude, or if bad weather rolls in, there are several shortcuts back to town: descend CR 2/Hazel St. through California Gulch (at approx. 7.2 miles); descend CR 1/E. 5th St. (at approx 9.0 miles) at the bridge just north of the infamous red pond (no swimming!); or descend CR 3/E. 7th St. (at approx 9.3 miles) at the bridge just south of Tabor's Matchless Mine site.

Ride 9: Halfmoon Road

This short, surprisingly difficult route leads you from the Mt. Elbert trailhead to the old Champion Mine site. There isn't much in the way of climbing, but the road is steep and littered with rocks. Because there are three deep stream crossings, you may want to save this one for late summer, when water levels are down and water temperatures up.

The ride is an interesting diversion if you are camped in the area for summit attempts on Massive and/or Elbert. The Champion Mine Site is one of the best-preserved mining structures in the region. Be aware that this is a popular weekend area for ATVs, motorcycles, jeeps, and trucks. Keep your ears and eyes open.

Elevation profile:

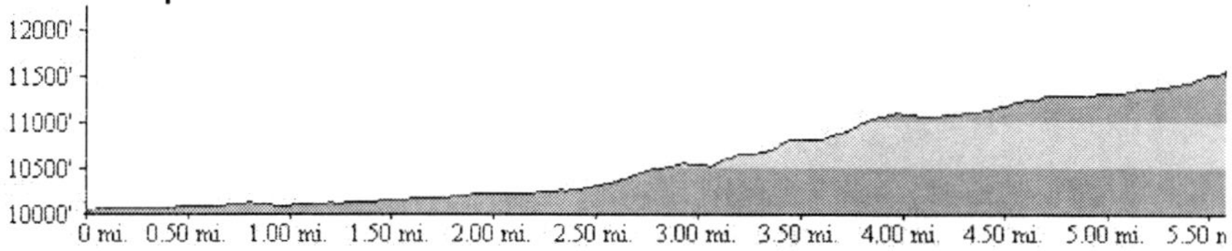

Ride length: 11.2 miles
Ride type: out-and-back
Riding time: 2 hours
Surface: jeep road
Elevations: start/end 10,060'; max 11,560'; min 10,060'
Total climbing: gain/loss 1,500'

Aerobic level: strenuous (steep, loose climbing)
Technical level: 4 (riding this line cleanly demands mad skills)
Season: August through September
USGS Quadrangle: Mt. Massive

Trailhead GPS coordinates: 39° 9.135' N; 106° 24.72' W

Getting there: from the stoplight at 6th St. and Harrison Ave. (US 24) in downtown Leadville, drive 3.6 miles south on US 24 to the intersection with CO 300. Turn right on CO 300 and drive 0.8 miles to the intersection with CR 11. Turn left on CR 11 and drive 1.3 miles. Turn right, following the signs for Halfmoon Creek and continuing on CR 11 for the next 5.1 miles. Turn left into the Mt. Elbert trailhead parking area. If this lot is full, continue west on CR 11 to find a space in either the Mt. Elbert overflow parking area or the Mt. Massive trailhead parking area.

Note- *do not park in one of the formal Forest Service Campgrounds or Picnic Areas unless you are prepared to shell out the appropriate fee.*

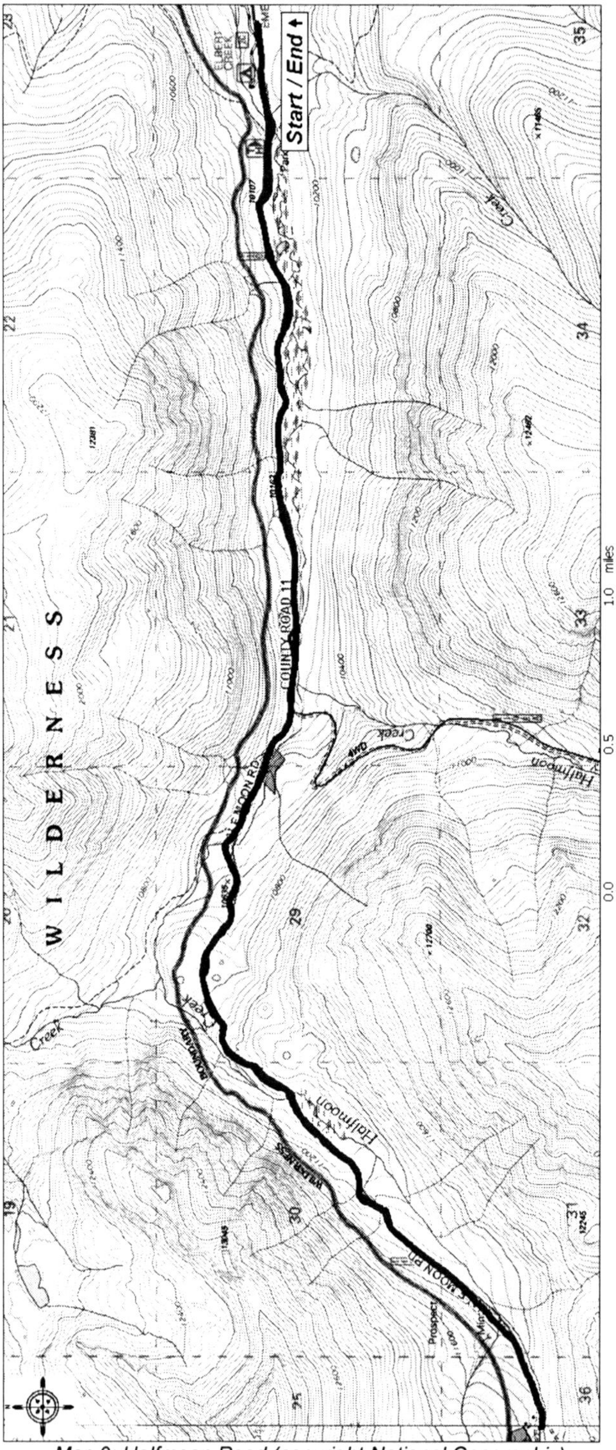

Map 9: Halfmoon Road (copyright National Geographic)

The ride:

- **0.0** Start from the Mt. Elbert trailhead parking area. Turn left (west) onto FSR 11 and start pedaling. In about 100 yards from the start, pass the Elbert Creek Campground on the right.
- **0.4** Pass the Mt. Massive trailhead on the right. The road gets a little steeper and a little rougher just ahead. ***Note***- *this is also the intersection with the Colorado Trail. Bikes are permitted south to Twin Lakes along the COT, but not permitted on the northern leg leading into the Mt. Massive Wilderness Area.*
- **1.3** Stay right as FSR 110J peels off to your left. The route now gets down to some serious climbing.
- **2.7** Pass the Mt. Massive Halfmoon trailhead on the right. Get ready to wade across a wide and somewhat deep section of Halfmoon Creek.
- **3.8** Another deep and wide stream crossing. Some beaver dams slightly down stream make this one very deep. Best to shoulder the bike and, as much as possible, follow the faint trail through the willows on the left (south). You'll still need to wade in water that may reach the hem of your shorts, but you'll avoid the deepest sections of the eastern bank. Once through the water, the grade mellows as you pedal through a wide basin that boxes at the eastern flanks of Mt. Champion and the northern slopes of French Mountain.
- **4.9** Yet another chance to soak your feet in a stream crossing.
- **5.6** A gate marks the end of the outbound ride. Several buildings left over from the mine's glory days are visible from this point. Take a moment and try to imagine enduring a winter at this site. Return along the same route.

Options: you can extend this ride by starting at any of the parking areas or campsites east of the Mount Elbert parking area. FSR 11 is very busy on weekends, however, and you should be prepared to share the road with motorized vehicles.

The Champion Mine

Twin Lakes

Roadies and summer tourists already know Twin Lakes as the gateway to Independence Pass, the high mountain pass that separates the Arkansas Valley from Aspen and the Roaring Fork Valley. What they may not know, however, is that this quiet and scenic village is also the gateway to some of the best single-track in the northern Arkansas Valley.

Most of the action happens on the two major trail systems that intersect the town, the Colorado Trail (COT) and the Continental Divide Trail (CDT). North of town, the COT surfs the eastern shoulder of Mount Elbert (14,433'), Colorado's tallest peak. The single-track line extends all the way to Halfmoon Road and Mt. Massive (14,421'), Colorado's second tallest peak.

South of CO Highway 82, the COT skirts the lakes then continues all the way to Clear Creek, offering several tasty single-track riding options along the way. The trail is skinny, smooth, and fast, but seldom ridden, and the only crowd you are likely to encounter is the one you bring.

The most notable section is the COT descent to Clear Creek. In summer 2007, trail crews re-directed the trail, the effort resulting in a sweet and fast downhill. Best of all, the new route won't leave you stranded at the bottom; the trail climbs almost as well as it descends!

The town's centerpiece trail, the Interlaken Loop, is a relatively easy but spectacular single-track that circumnavigates the lake and provides access to the historic Interlaken Resort Restoration Project. Widely regarded as the one of the best historic sites in the state, the only way to reach this once exclusive nineteenth-century resort is via this trail or by boat.

In addition to a couple US Forest Service campgrounds, there are several lodges and bed-and-breakfast style inns. While in town, stop by the visitor center (once the site of the notorious Red Rooster Tavern and Brothel) and have lunch or coffee at one of the cafes.

Interlaken Loop

Ride 10: Twin Lakes to Mount Massive Trailhead

39°07.314' N, 106°22.877' W WGS84

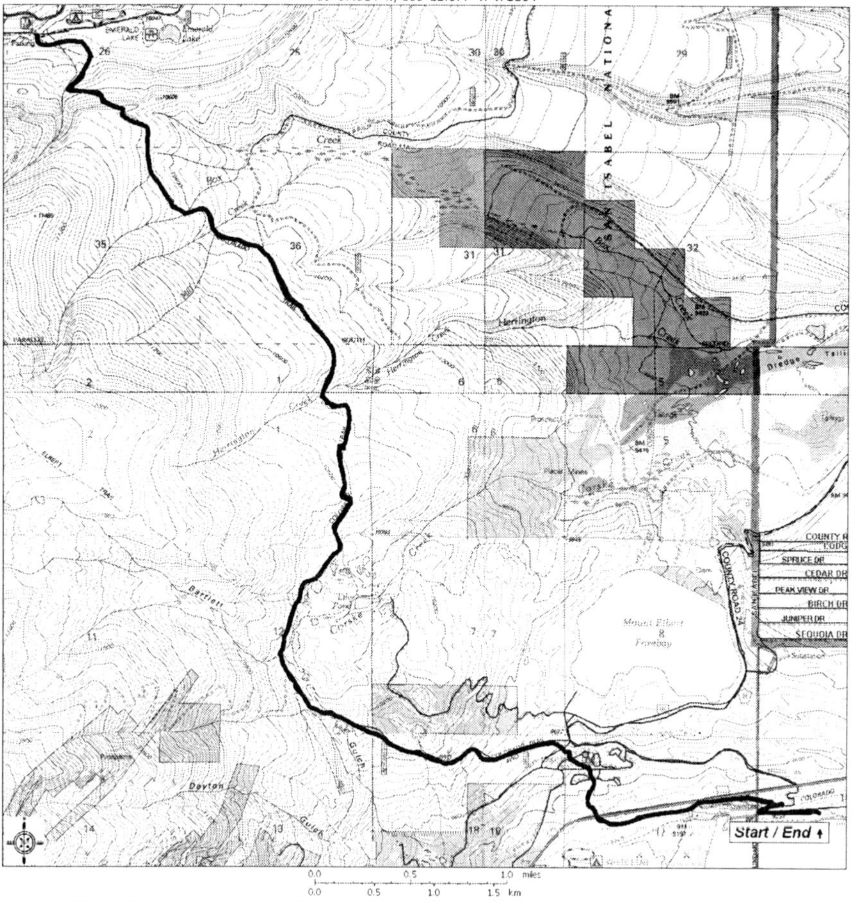

Map 10: Twin Lakes to Mt. Massive Trailhead (copyright National Geographic)

This route, a beautiful section of the Colorado Trail, reminds me of riding in the densely forested hills back East. After the initial lung-searing climb, the ride is a fast and smooth spin through thick stands of aspen. The big descent to Halfmoon Road is less technical than steep, but it will challenge even advanced riders.

Elevation profile:

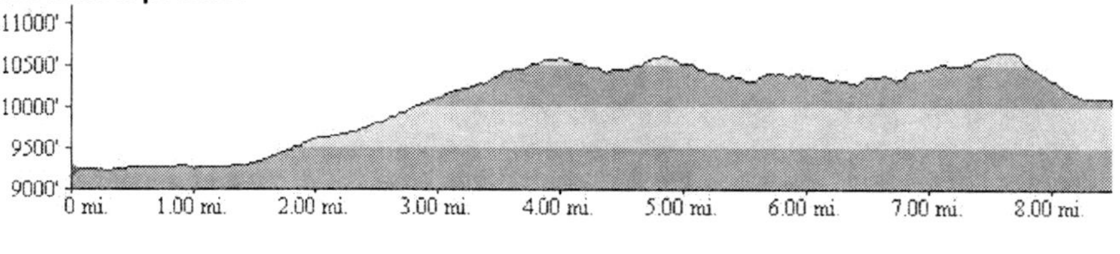

Ride length: 17.0 miles
Ride type: out-and-back
Riding time: 3.5 hours
Surface: single-track (13.2 miles); jeep road (3.8 miles)
Elevations: start/end 9,220'; max 10,670'; min 9,220'
Total climbing: gain/loss 3,320'

Aerobic level: strenuous (mucho climbing)
Technical level: 3 (one very steep section is a 4, but it can be easily walked)
Season: June through October
USGS Quadrangles: Granite, Mt. Elbert, Mt. Massive

Trailhead GPS coordinates: 39° 5.647' N; 106° 20.572' W

Getting there: from the intersection of US 24 and CO 82, drive 3.9 miles west on CO 82 to the intersection with CR 24C. Turn left onto CR 24C and drive 0.5 miles. Turn left at the "T" intersection and continue on CR 24C for 0.3 miles. Turn right and park in the "Mnt. Elbert" picnic area. The ride starts by the pit toilet.

The ride:

0.0 From the restrooms at the parking area, ride back to CR 24C and turn left.
0.3 Turn right up the paved road.
0.5 Look left for the entrance to the Colorado Trail. Turn left and start riding west on the single-track.
0.9 Cross the paved entrance to the power plant. Look for the Colorado Trail marker to help you find the next segment of the trail.
1.5 Stay left at the fork and head down through the tunnel under CO 82. The climb on the north side of the tunnel is slightly technical.
1.7 Cross another trail. Look for a marker on the right.
1.8 Cross a dirt road. The trail resumes on the other side of the road adjacent to the gate. 100 yards later, cross another dirt road. After crossing the second road and completing a short climb, the trail gets a little faint. Look slightly northwest and you'll notice a faint path in the pine needles leading the way.
1.9 Cross another dirt road.
2.0 Continue straight on the main trail. The trail on your right leads to the South Elbert Trail parking area. Continue for about another 50 yards until you reach another dirt road. Turn left onto the road; stay on this main road and avoid all spurs for the next 1.5 miles.
2.2 Continue straight, passing a spur on the left.
2.4 Bear right and pass a spur on the left.
2.8 Stay left, passing a spur on the right.
3.3 Stream crossing.
3.7 Turn right at the fork. Look for the Colorado Trail marker (as of May 2007, this marker was broken and on the ground). Another post is visible on the right side of the road about 50 feet from the intersection.
3.9 Cross a bridge and resume riding on single-track. About 50 yards after the bridge bear left at the fork marked by the Mount Elbert trail sign. Look for the Colorado Trail marker to confirm your route.
4.1 Bear right at the fork. (*Left is the South Mount Elbert Trail.*) 100 yards later, switchback to the left, following the Colorado Trail marker.
4.3 After passing above and to the left of what could arguably be biggest beaver pond I've ever seen, the trail may get faint. Stay right and sniff out the path on the forest floor.
5.8 Stream crossing. There are several stream crossings in the next 0.6

miles (*some may be seasonal*).

7.3 Continue straight through the intersection with the Mount Elbert Trail. (*The Mount Elbert trail switches back to your left.*)

8.2 Stream crossing after the raging downhill. 50 yards after crossing the stream, the Mount Elbert trail departs to your right; turn left, staying on the Colorado Trail.

8.5 Intersect the road. The Mount Massive trailhead is across the road on the left. Turn around and return the way you came.

Options: some people prefer to ride this as a one-way with shuttles. As to which way is better, north-to-south or south-to-north, you decide. North-to-south has a greater net downhill, but starts with a short, fiendish climb. South-to-north, on the other hand, has a 2.5-mile grunt uphill at the start, but the downhill at the end is a whole lot of fun.

To get to the Mount Massive trailhead, from the intersection of US 24/CO 82, drive 11 miles north on US 24. Turn left (west) on CO 300 and drive 0.8 miles to CR 11. Turn left (south) on CR 11 and drive 1.3 miles. Turn right, following the signs for Halfmoon Creek. Drive 5.5 miles to the Mount Massive trailhead parking area on the right (north) side of the road. The road is a little rough in sections, but should be okay for most passenger cars.

After the ride- Twin Lakes

Ride 11: Interlaken Loop

39°05.085' N, 106°20.994' W WGS84

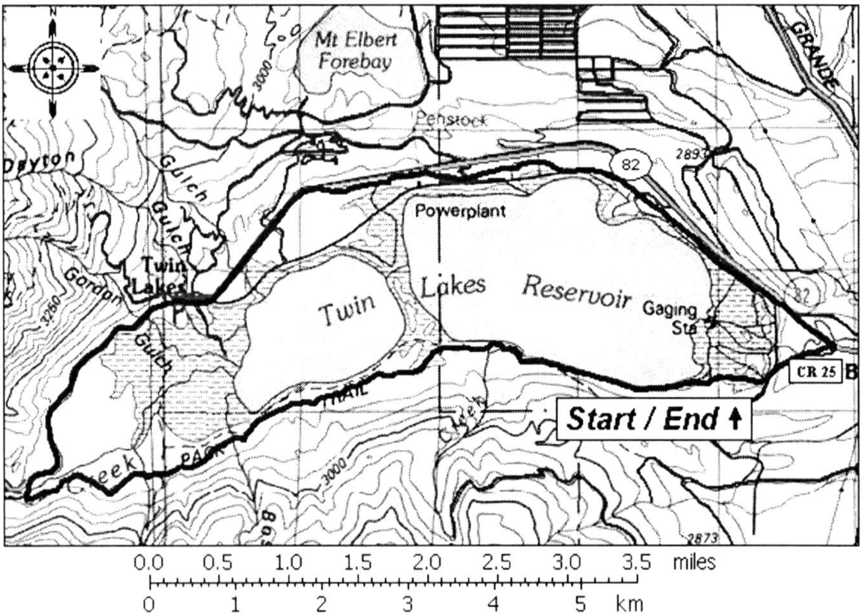

Map 11: Interlaken Loop (copyright National Geographic)

This beautiful and easy trail is a local favorite. The terrain is moderate, just easy enough for you to enjoy the magnificent scenery as you make your way around the lake. The trail also provides access to the historic Interlaken Resort—the only other way to get there is by boat!

This is a good ride for intrepid novice riders: the climbing is minimal with only a few tough, short sections (and those will challenge even hardened riders).

Start with some easy/moderate single-track that skirts the lake until you arrive at the Interlaken Restoration Project. A few difficult, short technical climbs come next, but before you know it, you're flying like a demon through Twin Lakes on CO 82. A fun stretch of easy single-track drops you less than a mile from the parking area and trailhead.

Warning! *Please be aware that security laws prohibit riding on or within 100 feet of the dam. Vigilant security officers are waiting and ready to intervene if you bypass the barriers!*

Elevation profile:

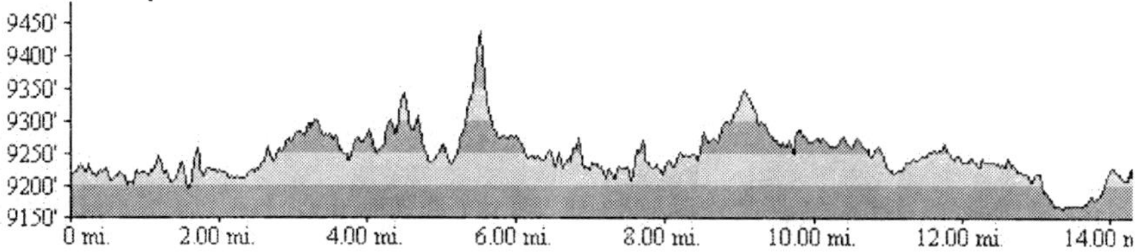

Ride length: 14.3 miles
Ride type: loop (clockwise)
Riding time: 2 hours
Surface: single-track (8.6 miles); pavement (3.8 miles); dirt road (1.9 miles)
Elevations: start/end 9,250'; max 9,410'; min 9,190'

Total climbing: gain/loss 535'
Aerobic level: easy
Technical level: 3 (a few sections may be 4, but they are easily walked)
Season: May through October
USGS Quadrangles: Granite, Mt. Elbert

Trailhead GPS coordinates: 39° 4.454' N; 106° 18.637' W

Getting there: from the intersection of US 24 and CO 82, drive 1.8 miles west on CO 82 to the intersection with CR 25. Turn left on CR 25 and drive 0.5 miles. Turn left at the "T" intersection and continue on CR 25, avoiding all spurs until you reach the trailhead parking area in 0.5 miles. The road is a tad rough, but should be okay for most passenger cars.

This ride has many potential starting points, but the trailhead on CR 25 gives you easy access to the lake and provides a great place to kickback after the ride.

The ride:

0.0 Start at the trailhead and map board at the entrance to the single-track.

1.2 Continue straight along the lake on the Continental Divide Trail. At this intersection, you'll see a post on your left with a "CD" marker and a Colorado Trail marker.

1.7 Cross a small bridge over a stream.

1.9 Enter the historic Interlaken Restoration Project. ***Note-*** *this project is sponsored by the US Forest Service with a number of partners and provides an interesting diversion. Take some time to read the interpretive signs along the way.*

3.7 Stream crossing. Use good judgment and caution when crossing. If water levels are high and the stream turbulent, consider turning back.

4.3 Cross a wide trail and continue on the single-track. You'll see a small log bridge ahead marking the way.

4.4 Several small stream crossings await you. Use the log bridges when possible, and be careful.

4.8 Nice, tough little climb. Things get a little rougher for the next 0.4 miles or so. Even though some of the crux moves are more advanced, intermediate riders should have few problems riding most of it. Do your best.

5.0 Pass the "Big and Little Willis" trail junction on your left.

5.4 Turn right at the "T" intersection with a wide, unmarked trail. Continue for approximately 75 yards and cross the bridge over Lake Creek. Turn right after the bridge and head out to CO 82. ***Note-*** *some people opt to* *turn around here and return to the trailhead along the same route.*

7.5 Enter Twin Lakes. Stop, have a look around, and treat yourself to some refreshments. There is a restroom at the visitors' center.

9.1 Cross a small bridge over the Colorado Trail and look right for the small, single-track connector to the Colorado Trail single-track. Take the connector and continue left (east) along the single-track. This provides a nice alternative to riding on CO 82 and the single-track is tight, fast and smooth.

9.7 Cross the driveway to the Mt. Elbert Pumped Storage Power Plant.

10.3 Cross CR 24C (unmarked, paved).

12.9 Go straight, following the Colorado Trail markers. Do not even think about crossing the dam. ***Note-*** *by the time you read this, trail crews will have finished the new connector segment between the road and trailhead. If so, just follow Colorado Trail markers back to the trailhead.*

13.3 Turn right onto CR 25 and stay on CR 25 until you return to your vehicle.

14.3 End at your car. Breakout the grill and beers, and spend the rest of the day relaxing lakeside.

Options: start the ride from the town of Twin Lakes; plenty of parking is available at the Visitors' Center across from the general store. If you stay at one of several Forest Service campgrounds, start the loop from there.

Or, do this ride as an out-and-back by turning around at mile 5.4 as described above.

Interlaken Loop

Ride 12: Twin Lakes to Clear Creek

39°02.879' N, 106°18.447' W WGS84

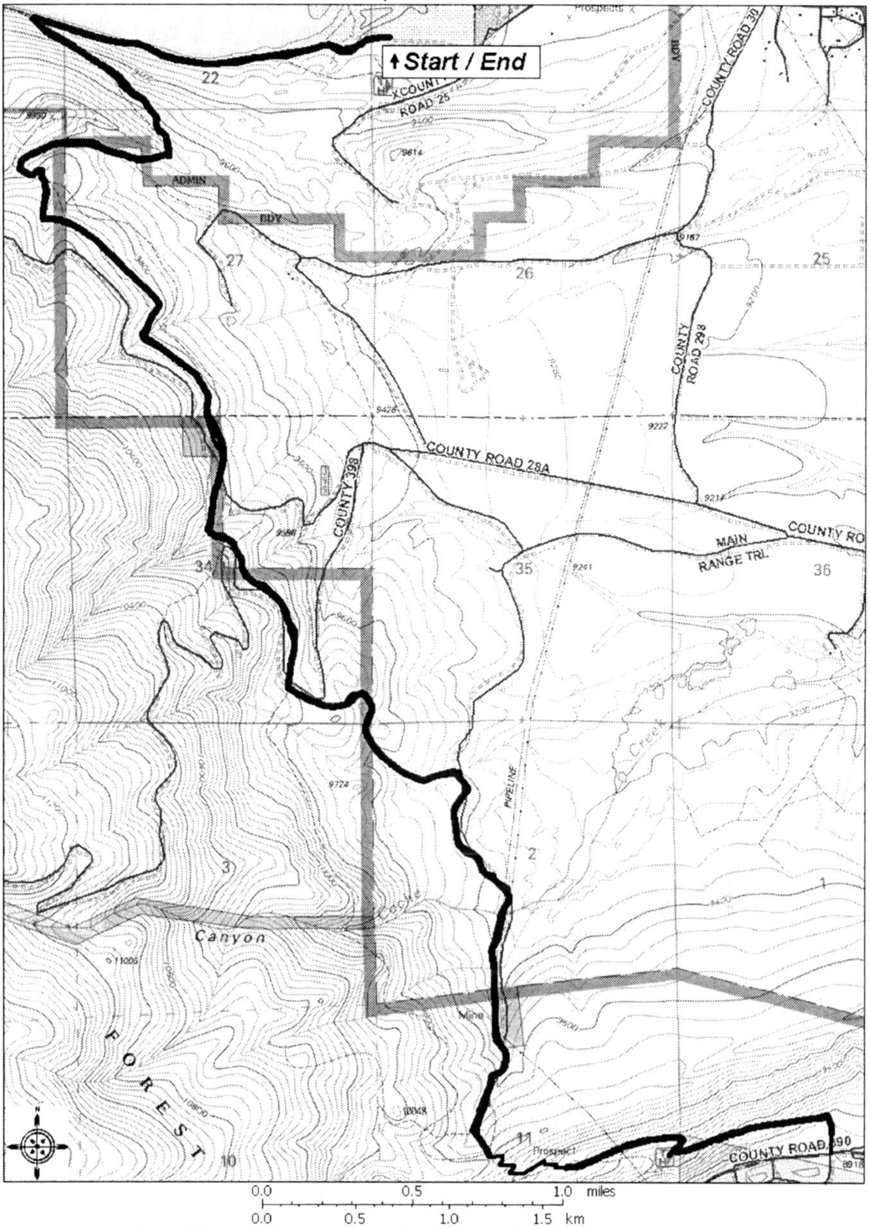

Map 12: Twin Lakes to Clear Creek (copyright National Geographic)

Yet another tasty slice of Colorado Trail to tempt you, and this section offers some of the best mountain biking in the Arkansas Valley. The single-track is narrow, well maintained, and very fast in sections. The descent into the Clear Creek valley is breathtaking and the new re-route of the trail is first-class. This gem is seldom ridden, but it won't remain overlooked for long: it's simply too good.

You start at the lake and it doesn't take long for the climbing to begin. Once you peak, however, the riding is fast and the miles fly by. The climb to the final ridge before Clear Creek might make your pulse race a bit, but it only prepares you for the amazing vistas from the top. Hang on tight as you rip down the trail. Watch out for the tight switchbacks!

Stop for a snack at the bottom, then turn around and return the way you came. Keep in mind that all those climbs on the way out will be blazing descents on the way back.

Elevation profile:

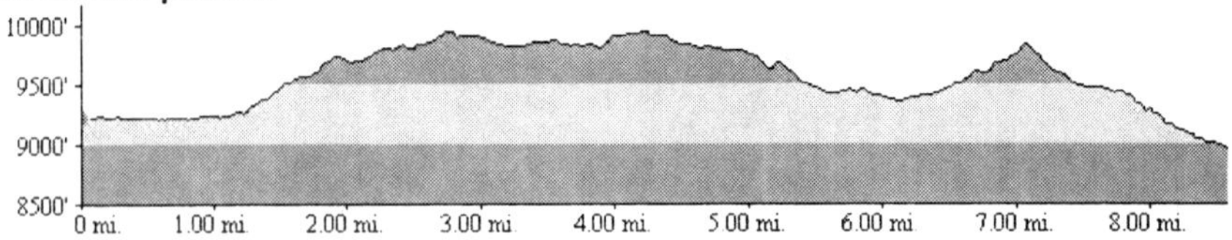

Ride length: 17.2 miles
Ride type: out-and-back
Riding time: 3 hours
Surface: single-track (13.2 miles); dirt road (4.0 miles)
Elevations: start/end 9,250'; max 9,950'; min 8,950'

Total climbing: gain/loss 3,230'
Aerobic level: strenuous (climbing)
Technical level: 3 (a few fast descents)
Season: May through October
USGS Quadrangle: Granite

Trailhead GPS coordinates: 39° 4.451' N; 106° 18.622' W

Getting there: from the intersection of US 24 and CO 82, drive 1.8 miles west on CO 82 to the intersection with CR 25. Turn left on CR 25 and drive 0.5 miles. Turn left at the "T" intersection and continue on CR 25 until you reach the trailhead and parking area in 0.5 miles. The road is a tad rough, but should be okay for most passenger cars.

The ride:

0.0 Start at the trailhead sign/maps at the entrance to the single-track.
1.2 Turn left at the "CD" / Colorado Trail marker post. This starts the first major climb of the ride.
1.9 Top-out and catch your breath.
2.0 At the bottom of a slightly rocky descent, turn right onto a jeep track. A large cairn on your left marks the intersection.
2.4 Turn left at the cairn. The single-track resumes as you depart the jeep trail.
2.5 Brace for another steep climb, but this one will be over before you know it.
2.8 Let it rip! You earned it. The trail is fast and smooth.
3.3 Cross a small stream on a rotted log bridge.
3.8 A small climb will bring you up to CR 399. Cross the road and resume climbing on the single-track. Look for the ruins of old log structures on your right and left.

4.6 Pop-out on CR 398 (Lost Canyon Road) and turn left (downhill). ***Note-*** *don't cross the road and continue on the faded single-track leading into the forest (the trail dead-ends after much tree fall).*

4.8 Turn right onto a small road leading into a clearing. Your speed will be up, but look for the Colorado Trail marker. Once on the road, look left for the next marker; it's about six feet up on a tree. Next, look left for the faint single-track heading left (east) into the grass. A couple trail markers will help you find your way. Let it rip, but watch for tree fall.

5.3 Cross a funky bridge and head left. Hop over the log and look left for the trail as it runs through the sage.

5.5 Intersect a faint jeep trail at a "T" and turn right, continuing downhill.

5.6 Continue straight as you cross an even more faded jeep track. Look for the Colorado Trail marker on the fat tree on your left.

5.8 Continue straight. Look for the trail post marker to guide you. Continue straight through the rock barrier.

6.0 Turn right at the intersection with the power line road and drop down to cross Cache Creek. A Colorado Trail marker tells you where to go.

6.3 Bear right on the double track and veer slightly away from the power lines. Several tracks intersect at this point, but you can't go wrong by staying on the most prominent line.

6.5 Bear right at the fork as the Colorado Trail and the power line road diverge. A trail marker leads the way.

6.8 Bear left and start your assault on the final ridge. A trail post marker and a tree marker let you know that you're on the right track.

7.1 The top. Wow!!! Check out that view! Get ready for some speed, but watch the switchbacks. You will descend almost 900' in a little over 1.5 miles. Don't let thoughts of climbing back up discourage you: because it's so well built and in such good condition, moderately strong riders will be able fly back up with little difficulty (yeah, right). ***Note-*** *if you're beat, turn around here and return along the same route.*

8.6 Cross the road and take a seat on one of the big boulders. Have a snack as you contemplate the return trip along the same route. Remember as you look back up at the ridge: pondering a task is often more daunting than the task itself!

Options: ride it as a one-way with shuttles. Leave a car at the intersection of the Colorado Trail and CR 390. From the intersection of CR 390 and US 24, drive about 2.1 miles west on CR 390. Look for the clearly marked trailhead designating the junctions of segments 11 and 12 of the Colorado Trail.

Ride 13: Cache Creek Loop

39°03.295' N, 106°18.994' W WGS84

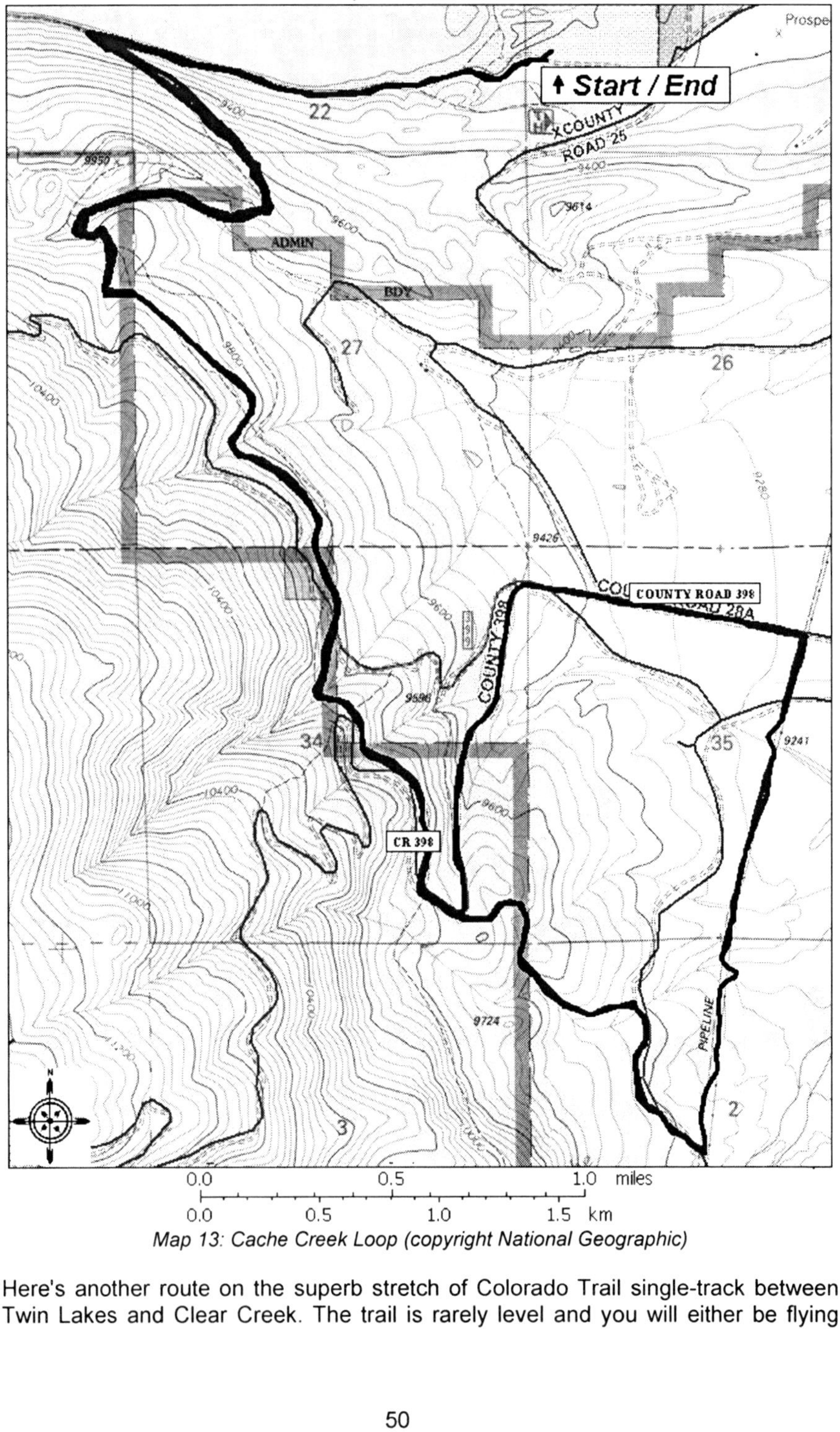

Map 13: Cache Creek Loop (copyright National Geographic)

Here's another route on the superb stretch of Colorado Trail single-track between Twin Lakes and Clear Creek. The trail is rarely level and you will either be flying downhill or cranking up hills. The climbing grades are somewhat steep but never sustained, and the constant transitions will keep you firing on all cylinders.

It starts with an easy glide along the edge of the lake. The first major climb will make you sweat, but the reward is some nice downhill on first-rate single-tack. A quick climb on the Lost Canyon Road brings you back to the Colorado Trail. A short stretch of climbing through lush forest precedes a blazing descent almost all the way back to the lake rim.

Elevation profile:

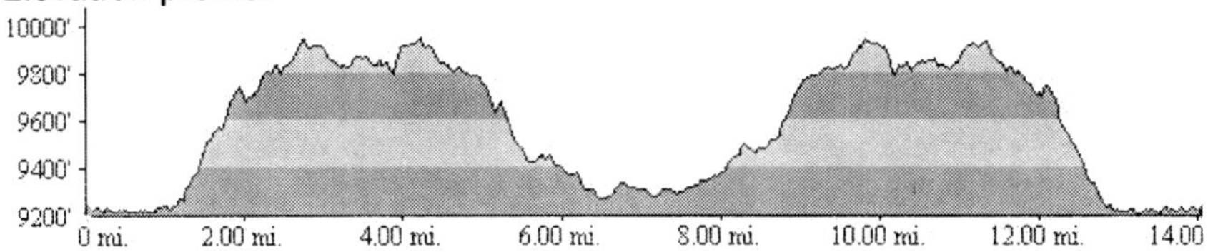

Ride length: 14.1 miles
Ride type: lollipop-loop (counter-clockwise)
Riding time: 2 hours
Surface: single-track (10.0 miles); dirt road (4.1 miles)
Elevations: start/end 9,250'; max 9,950'; min 9,190'

Total climbing: gain/loss 1,890'
Aerobic level: moderate (short, but steep climbs throughout the ride will keep your pulse up)
Technical level: 3 (a steep descent on an eroded slope)
Season: May through October
USGS Quadrangle: Granite

Trailhead GPS coordinates: 39° 4.451' N; 106° 18.622' W

Getting there: from the intersection of US 24 and CO 82, drive 1.8 miles west on CO 82 to the intersection with CR 25. Turn left on CR 25 and drive 0.5 miles. Turn left at the "T" intersection and continue on CR 25 until you reach the trailhead parking area in about 0.5 miles. The road is a tad rough, but should be okay for most passenger cars.

The ride:

- **0.0** Start at the trailhead sign at the entrance to the single-track.
- **1.2** Turn left at the "CD" / Colorado Trail post marker. This starts the first major, sustained climb of the ride.
- **1.9** Top-out and catch your breath.
- **2.0** At the bottom of a slightly rocky descent, turn right onto a jeep track. A large cairn on your left marks the intersection.
- **2.4** Turn left at the cairn. The single-track resumes as you depart the jeep trail.
- **2.5** Brace for another steep climb, but this one will be over before you know it.
- **2.8** Let it rip! You earned it. The trail is fast and smooth.
- **3.3** Cross a small stream on a rotted log bridge.
- **3.8** A small but steep climb will bring you up to CR 399. Cross the road and resume climbing on the single-track. Look for the remnants of old log structures on your right and left as you climb.
- **4.6** Pop-out on CR 398 (Lost Canyon Road) and turn left (downhill). ***Note-*** *don't cross the road and continue on the faded single-track leading into the forest. After crossing dozens of fallen tress, the trail dead-ends.*

4.8 Turn right onto a small road leading into a clearing. Your speed will be up, but look for the Colorado Trail marker. Once on the road, look left for the next marker; it's about 6 feet up on a tree. Next, look left for the faint single-track heading left (east) into the grass. There are a couple trail markers to help you find your way. Let it rip, but watch for tree fall.

5.3 Cross a funky bridge and head left. Hop over the log and look left for the trail (it runs through some sage).

5.5 Intersect a faint jeep trail at a "T" and turn right, continuing downhill.

5.6 Continue straight as you cross an even more faded jeep track. Look for the Colorado Trail marker on the fat tree on your left.

5.8 Continue straight. Look for the trail marker to guide you. Continue straight through the rock barrier.

6.0 Turn left at the intersection with the power line road. You are now leaving the Colorado Trail. ***Note-*** *the Colorado Trail continues right (south) past Cache Creek, toward the ridge in the distance.*

6.2 Go around the BLM gate.

7.2 Pass through another gate.

7.5 Turn left on CR 398 and start to climb.

8.3 Bear left at the fork with CR 398 and CR 399. Continue to climb on CR 398 toward the Gold Basin Mine. ***Note-*** *to shorten the ride, bear right at this fork and climb on CR 399. After climbing for about 0.75 miles, look for the Colorado Trail marker on your right. Turn right onto the Colorado Trail. This shortens the ride by about a mile and saves about 150' of climbing.*

9.1 Intersect the Colorado Trail to close the loop. Continue climbing on CR 398.

9.2 Look for the Colorado Trail marker on your right. Turn right and climb into the forest on the single-track.

10.1 Diagonally slash CR 398 as you blast downhill on the single-track. (*Stop to look for vehicles before crossing the road!*).

11.6 Turn right at the cairn and ride downhill on the jeep track.

12.0 Bear left at the cairn and climb the single-track. Look for the Colorado Trail marker on your left.

12.9 Intersect the lake loop and turn right, following the Colorado Trail.

14.1 Trailhead. Ride back to your car. Ditch the bike and hit the lake.

Colorado Trail

Granite

While it was once the Chaffee County seat, Granite is now a humble outpost (ghost town?) on the banks of the Arkansas River. This quiet site, however, was once the scene of a notorious scandal. According to local historians, when the citizens of Buena Vista voted in 1880 to make their town the Chaffee County seat, Granite residents refused to relinquish control of the county's documents. As the legend goes, a group of men from Buena Vista stole a locomotive and drove it to Granite. Once there, they smashed down the door of the Granite courthouse and started removing the records. When the sheriff arrived to investigate the commotion, the men held him at gunpoint until all of the paperwork and furniture was loaded onto the hijacked train.

Today, the most prominent landmark is the white public schoolhouse perched on the hillside overlooking the river and highway. Several other old structures and mine sites in the vicinity contribute to the town's ghost vibe.

As for mountain biking, east of town is a network of rarely used jeep trails and true double-track (think parallel single-track separated by tall grass) that border the Buffalo Peaks Wilderness Area. Wildlife abounds and you are likely to see deer, elk, and coyotes. Be aware, however, that this is also lion and bear habitat, and you may want to think twice about riding solo or at dusk and dawn.

Spring Creek descent

On the west side of US 24, you'll have easy access to one of the smoothest sections of Colorado Trail single-track. Spanning the distance between Twin Lakes and Clear Creek, this segment is fast, fun and seldom ridden.

The trophy ride of the area, however, is the Lost Canyon Road. This test piece serves as the crux climb and turn-around point of the Leadville 100 mountain bike racecourse. If you have the legs and lungs, it is possible to ride it up to a communications station located at the top of a 13,000' sub-peak.

If you visit, you'll agree that Granite is one of the best-kept MTB secrets in the Arkansas Valley.

Ride 14: Lost Canyon to Twin Lakes Loop

39°03.637' N, 106°18.610' W WGS84

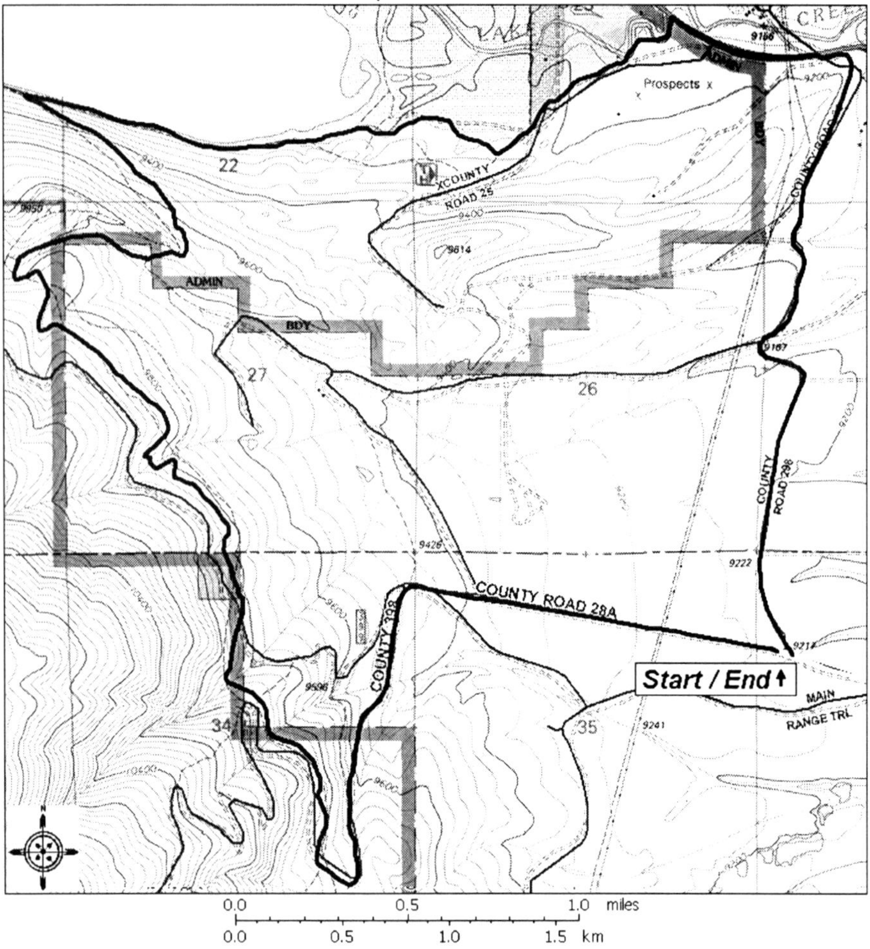

Map 14: Lost Canyon-Twin Lakes Loop (copyright National Geographic)

If this ride doesn't make you smile, you better check your pulse… you may be dead. Though short, the views are spectacular and the single-track sublime. Think of it as "concentrated happiness." While I rarely take breaks while riding, I always stop several times along this route to behold the views, especially when the aspen are in fall color.

The ride begins with a mild climb on easy graded roads. Once you get to the Colorado Trail single-track, however, the fun really begins. By the time you reach the lake, the charm of the ride will have you mesmerized. Finish with a fast and easy spin back to the car on well-graded county roads.

Elevation profile:

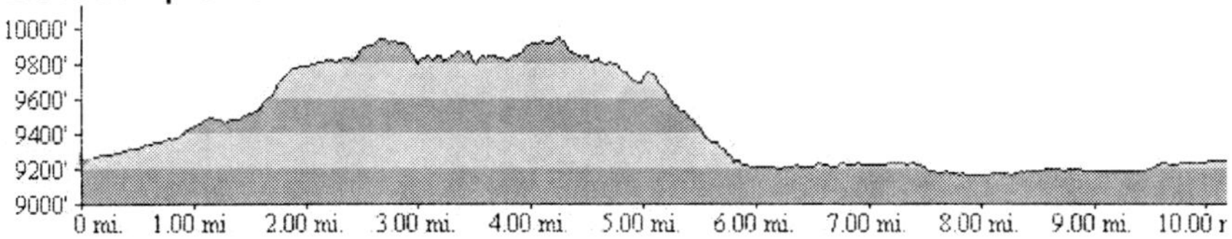

Ride length: 10.1 miles
Ride type: loop (clockwise)
Riding time: 1.5 hours
Surface: dirt road (5.1 miles); single-track (4.6 miles); pavement (0.4 miles)
Elevations: start/end 9,250'; max 9,950'; min 9,170'
Total climbing: gain/loss 1,060'
Aerobic level: moderate (some climbing)
Technical level: 3 (the descent to the lake is a little steep, so take it easy)
Season: May through October
USGS Quadrangle: Granite

Trailhead GPS coordinates: 39° 3.138' N; 106° 17.495' W

Getting there: from the intersection of US 24 and Main St. in Buena Vista (the only stoplight in Buena Vista), drive 16.6 miles north on US 24. Once in Granite, look for the entrance to Lost Canyon Road on your left. Turn left onto Lost Canyon Road (CR 398) and drive 1.7 miles to the triangular intersection with CR 398B on your right. There is no designated parking area, so park in the small clearing on the south shoulder of CR 398, just west of the intersection with CR 398B.

The ride:

0.0 From the car, ride west (uphill) on CR 398.

0.4 Continue straight on CR 398, passing the power line spur on the left.

1.1 Bear left at the fork to ride west on CR 398. ***Note-*** *right is CR 399. The Colorado Trail intersects it in approximately 0.8 miles. You can shorten the ride by about 1.0 mile and eliminate 150' of climbing by heading right at this intersection.*

1.9 Continue on the main road as you pass some campsite spurs on the left and an open meadow to your right. Continue climbing on CR 398 for another 0.2 miles. ***Note-*** *the Colorado Trail intersects the last campsite spur on your left and descends to Cache Creek.*

2.1 Look right for the post and a small cairn marking the entrance to the Colorado Trail single-track.

2.6 Cross an old jeep track and continue riding on the single-track.

2.8 Pass the remnants of old log buildings on your left and right. Slow down if you want to see them; you'll be flying fast down hill.

2.9 Slow down and look both ways for traffic before diagonally slicing across CR 399 and continuing on Colorado Trail single-track.

3.4 Cross the little stream on a rotting log bridge. After a short climb through a stand of aspen, stop to take in the magnificent views to the east.

3.9 Another stream crossing, but no bridge this time.

4.2 Turn right at the "T" intersection and cairn; continue east on jeep trail double-track.

4.6 Bear left at the fork with the cairn. The single-track resumes.

5.5 Intersect the Continental Divide Trail at the bottom of the hill. Turn right to continue along the Colorado Trail as it skirts the south shore of the lake. ***Note-*** *it's possible to extend the ride by turning left and riding the Interlaken Loop to CO 82.*

6.7 The single-track ends at the trailhead and parking area. Turn right (east) on CR 25 (unmarked). (*A hard left will take you a beach on the lake.*)

7.0 Stay right on the main road, following the Colorado Trail marker.

7.1 Turn right. After turning right, you will see a Colorado Trail marker on the left. ***Note-*** *no matter how tempted you get, do not ride on or approach the dam. It is very illegal to trespass on this strip of federal property. Trust me; you'll be sorry if you do.*

7.4 Turn left, following the Colorado Trail marker.

7.5 Look right for the next trail marker.

7.6 Ride through the fence maze. Watch the jersey-ripping barbed wire!

7.7 Turn right at the intersection with CO 82.

7.8 Stay on the highway as you pass CR 25 on your right.

8.1 Turn right at the gravel road (CR 30). Cross the cattle guard and turn left.

8.3 Continue straight on the main road.

9.1 Bear left, staying on the main road through an unmarked intersection.

9.3 Bear right, staying on the main road as you pass a driveway on the left.

9.8 Cross a cattle guard at the Lake County/Chaffee County boundary. CR 30 is now CR 398B.

10.1 Back at the car! How did that happen?

Options: park and start at the river access area across the highway from the Granite store. This adds about 3.5 miles and approximately 300' feet of additional climbing.

Ride 15: Lost Canyon Road

Did you ever wonder if you have what it takes to finish the Leadville 100 mountain bike race? Or, have you ever wanted to summit a 13er on your bike? Or, are you just a plain, old-fashioned masochist that delights in testing your pain threshold? If any of these apply, you'll want to try this ride.

The ride itself, the crux climb of the Leadville 100 racecourse, is not that bad. The first eight miles are, despite the tremendous gain in altitude, reasonably graded and easy to spin. Once you get above tree line things get a little tougher, but still manageable. The final half-mile push up to Point 13,130 is nothing short of insane and some hike-a-bike may be required.

If you need any consoling en route, just imagine how fast and fun the downhill will be. 'nuff said. Get out there!

Elevation profile:

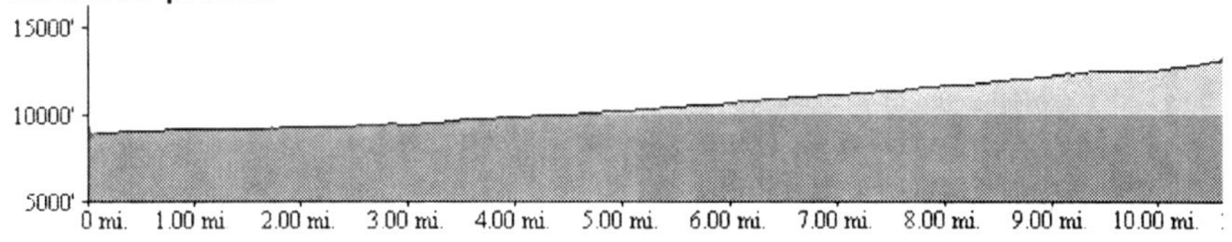

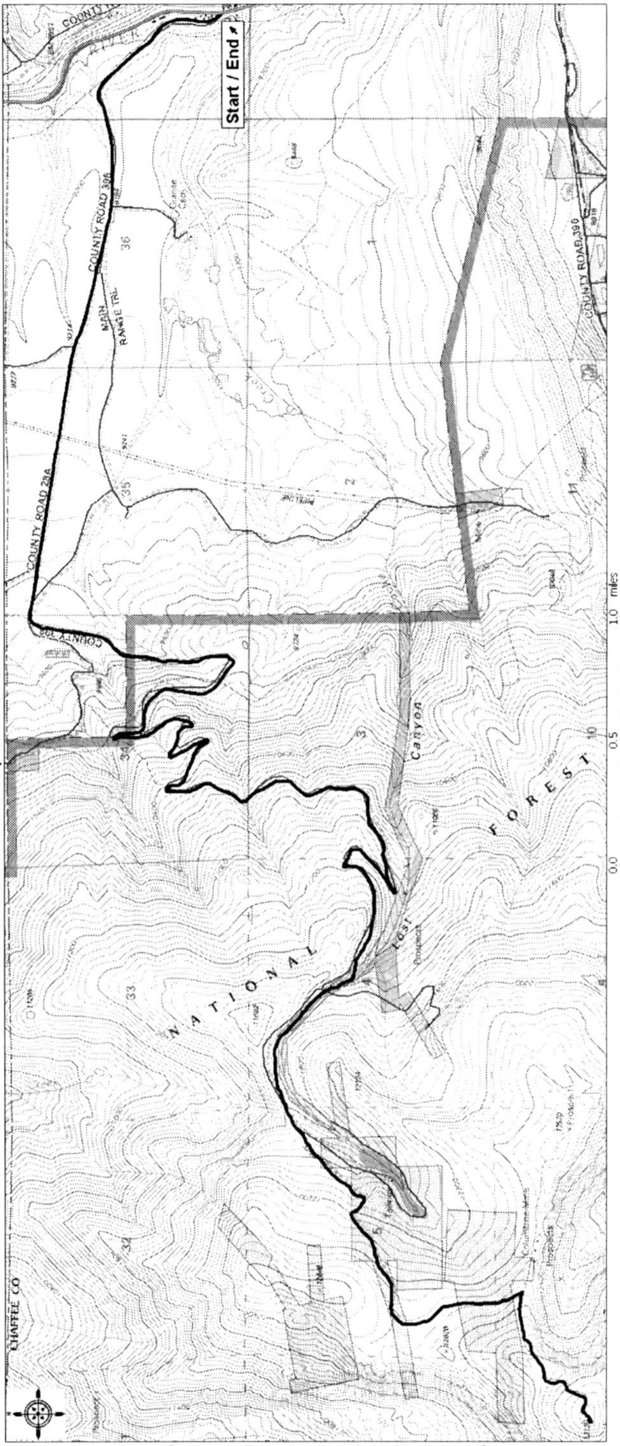

Map 15: Lost Canyon Road (copyright National Geographic)

Ride length: 21.4 miles
Ride type: out-and-back
Riding time: 3.5 hours
Surface: dirt road (rough and steep near the top)
Elevations: start/end 8,950'; max 13,130'; min 8,950'
Total climbing: gain/loss 4,130'

Aerobic level: strenuous (lot's o' climbing and the approach to the highpoint is scary steep)
Technical level: 3- (it's a little rough near the top)
Season: July through October
USGS Quadrangle: Granite

Trailhead GPS coordinates: 39° 2.61' N; 106° 15.985' W

Getting there: from the intersection of US 24 and Main St. in Buena Vista (the only stoplight in Buena Vista), drive 16.6 miles north on US 24. Once in Granite, turn right onto CR 397 and drive over the one-lane bridge. Turn right and park in the boat launch lot between the river and the railroad tracks. From the parking area, ride back across the bridge and carefully cross the highway. The ride starts at the intersection of US 24 and CR 398 (Lost Canyon Road). *Use caution when crossing the highway!*

The ride:

0.0 From the intersection of CR 398 and US 24, start climbing on CR 398. ***Note-*** *okay, let's get this out of the way. You won't need this guide until you approach the Gold Basin Mine above tree line. Almost the entire ride is on CR 398. The road is well marked and route finding will not be an issue. If you find you need a break, however, you can use the excuse that you need to check the guide. This will give you a few minutes to catch your breath as you fumble with your pack.*

1.1 Continue straight on CR 398, passing CR 398D on your left.

1.7 Bear left at the fork, staying on CR 398 as CR 398B peels away on your right.

2.1 Continue straight on CR 398, passing the power line road on your left.

2.8 Bear left, staying on CR 398 as CR 399 heads off to your right.

3.7 Pass some campsite spurs on your left. ***Note-*** *the Colorado Trail intersects the road on your left in about 100 yards.*

3.9 Pass the Colorado Trail single-track intersection on your right.

6.6 Continue on the main road as it switches back to the right. Pass the old garage.

7.7 Stay left on the main road as things get steeper and looser.

8.1 Continue straight on the main road as you pass a spur leading to the remnants of an old cabin on your right. As you look left up the valley, you will see the Gold Basin Mine.

8.2 Bear right at the fork. Continue along a steep and rough section for about 30 yards then bear right again at the second fork.

8.5 Continue straight on the main road, passing a spur on the right.

9.4 Bear left at the fork as you pedal along a high plateau.

10.0 Bear right at the fork and start the impossible climb. ***Note-*** *if you want to skip this ridiculous final section, head left to explore the Columbine Mine site. Enjoy the views of the 14ers (Oxford, Belford, Missouri, and Huron) across the valley. Few views anywhere are more spectacular than this!*

10.7 Whew! That was a bear of a climb. Okay. So, you have now climbed a 13,000' mountain on a bike. What's next? Oh yea, the killer descent!

Options: shorten your climb by driving as high as you want along CR 398. The road is passable for most vehicles for the fist 7 miles.

Ride 16: Spring Creek Short Loop

Have you ever ridden in the Fourmile Recreation Area and wished for a more tranquil (fewer ATVs) backcountry experience? This ride, a shorter version of the Spring Creek Loop, is an excellent alternative. Though open to jeeps, motorcycles, and ATVs, the area sees few visitors and you are very unlikely to suck dust and exhaust as you serenely spin this one. The riding surface is refreshingly bereft of tracks and nature is slowly narrowing the lines. Though the eastern side of the loop is technically double-track, the trail is overgrown and much of it rides like parallel lines of elegant single-track.

Cutting the traditional loop route short allows you to descend on a very aesthetic and steep jeep track back to CR 397.

Your chances of encountering wildlife on the trail are great (I unwittingly startled a lone coyote as I blasted through a stand of aspen at the start of the descent). This is lion and bear country, so think twice about riding this loop alone or riding it at dusk/dawn.

Elevation profile:

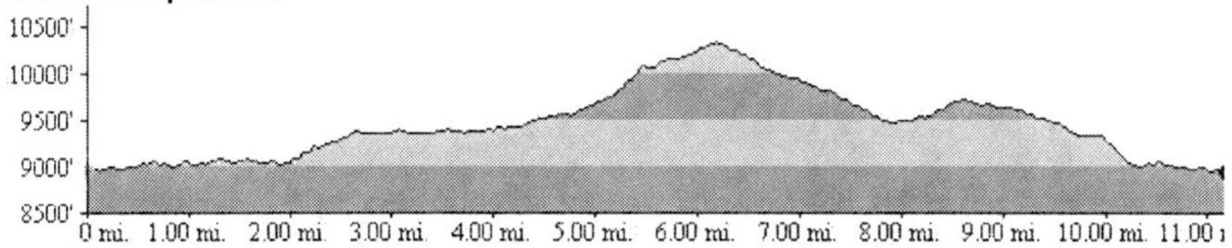

Ride length: 11.2 miles
Ride type: lollipop-loop (clockwise)
Riding time: 1.5-2 hours
Surface: dirt road/jeep trails
Elevations: start/end 8,950'; max 10,330'; min 8,950'
Total climbing: gain/loss 1,780'

Aerobic level: moderate (the climb approaching the highpoint is strenuous)
Technical level: 3+ (the final descent to CR 397 is intense)
Season: May through October
USGS Quadrangle: Granite

Trailhead GPS coordinates: 39° 2.6' N; 106° 15.917' W

Getting there: from the intersection of US 24 and Main St. in Buena Vista (the only stoplight in Buena Vista), drive 16.6 miles north on US 24. Once in Granite, turn right onto CR 397 and drive over the one-lane bridge. Turn right and park in the boat launch lot between the river and the railroad tracks. The ride starts from the parking area.

39°04.432' N, 106°15.903' W WGS84

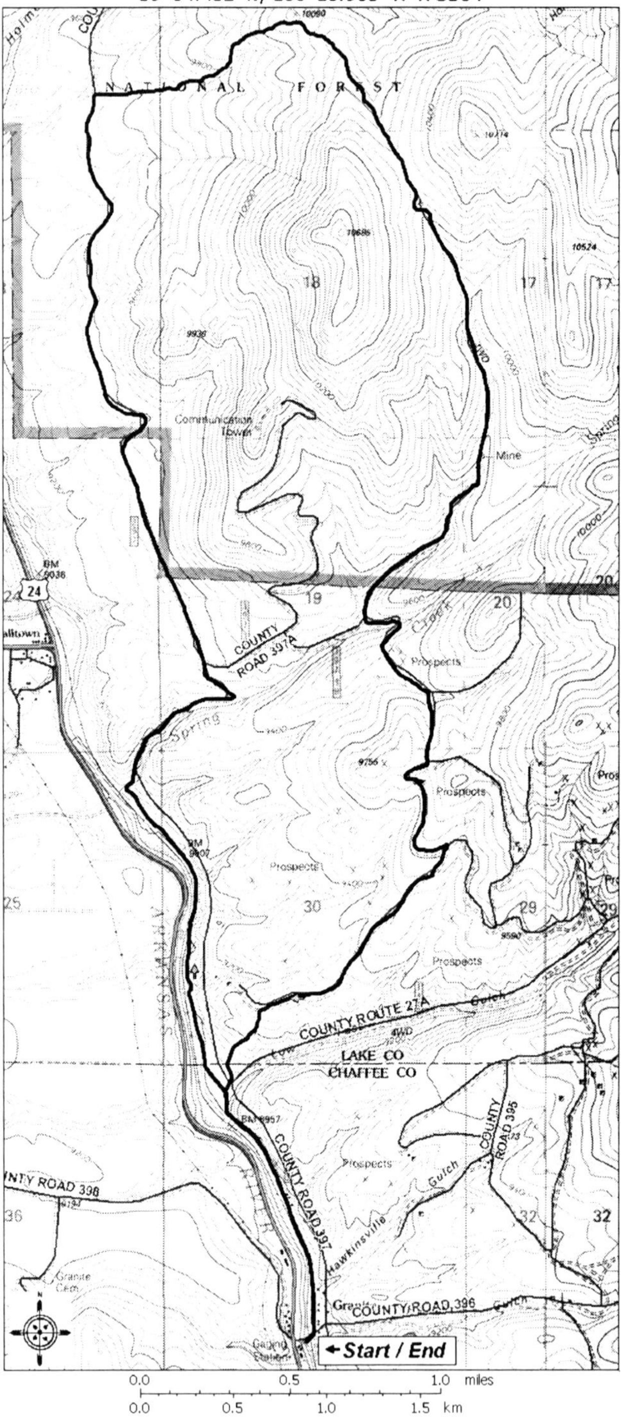

Map 16: Spring Creek Short Loop (copyright National Geographic)

The ride:

0.0 Turn right (east) from the parking area and cross the railroad tracks. At the intersection with CR 396, turn left (north) and ride parallel to the river on CR 397.

0.9 Continue straight on CR 397. (*The spur on the right is at the end of the final descent to this intersection.*)

1.9 Stay left on the main road.

2.6 Continue left through the forked intersection with CR 397A. What a beautiful place!

2.7 Stay left at the fork with CR 397B. Continue riding on CR 397.

3.6 Continue on the main road as a faint, unmarked jeep track heads right toward the hill.

4.9 Turn right on CR 397A.

5.4 Tough climb, huh.

5.7 The trail levels a bit as the crux of the killer climb becomes a memory.

6.1 Continue straight on the main trail through a stand of aspen. Several old and overgrown jeep tracks cross the route.

6.3 The trail bends right as a drainage line continues straight. The double-track here is sweet and the upcoming downhill is great. The trail gets a little thin; look ahead and ride the most obvious line.

6.6 Continue descending past an ascending spur.

8.0 After the descent, you'll approach a thick stand of brush along Spring Creek. Look left for an overgrown line of double-track that heads upstream. Take that left and ride it across the creek toward a stand of pine.

8.1 Stay right after crossing the creek. The next section is an ascent through the pines.

8.2 Crest a small rise and continue straight, passing a spur that heads right.

8.7 Crest another ridge after a slightly stiff climb. Descend through a switchback and stay left, avoiding the right spur in the turn. Next, descend past the remnants of an old mine site as the route crosses the tailings.

9.1 Take the hard right (effectively a switchback) that heads west. Get ready for some speed. ***Note-*** *the traditional loop continues straight into the pines before dropping into Low Pass Gulch.*

10.0 Things get radical here. Hang on! (Walk if it's too much for you.)

10.3 At the bottom of the white-knuckled descent, turn right and head toward the river and US 24.

10.4 Turn left at the intersection with CR 397. This intersection closes the loop as you coast back into Granite.

11.2 Arrive back in town and the parking area.

Options: explore the many spurs in the area or ride the full Spring Creek Loop by extending the ride to Hayden Gulch. Use a map to connect the numerous jeep trails and county roads.

Buena Vista

The town's name is Spanish for "good view" and one visit is all it takes to confirm the accuracy of that name. If the founding fathers (and mothers!) had a little foresight, however, they might have also added, "great rafting" and "awesome mountain biking" to their list of possible names.

Buena Vista is the geographic hub of the Valley and provides one of the best places to base your visit. Whatever you need, the town has it: restaurants, markets, motels, RV parks, an awesome little bike/outdoor gear shop, hot springs, and dozens of primitive campsites (free/no facilities). Best of all, the majority of the routes in this entire guide are within a thirty-minute drive from town.

Most of the rides in the Buena Vista area are in the Fourmile Recreation Area, a vast terrain playground just east and south of town. This is also an extremely popular motor sport area, so the routes are loaded with berms and "whoop-dee-doo" jumps. Because the riding surface is primarily hard-packed, crushed granite, things can get sandy in spots. This is especially true in late summer, after the sun bakes the ground dry and ATV treads stir it up. Tires with aggressive side lugs seem to grab best and enable you to carve hard turns on the downhills.

If you visit the Fourmile Recreation area, be sure to ride only on trails open to mountain bikes. Local advocacy groups are working hard to open more terrain. Riding illegal trails only hinders their progress.

Midland Railroad Grade

Ride 17: Castle Rock Gulch Loop

38°47.611' N, 105°57.719' W WGS84

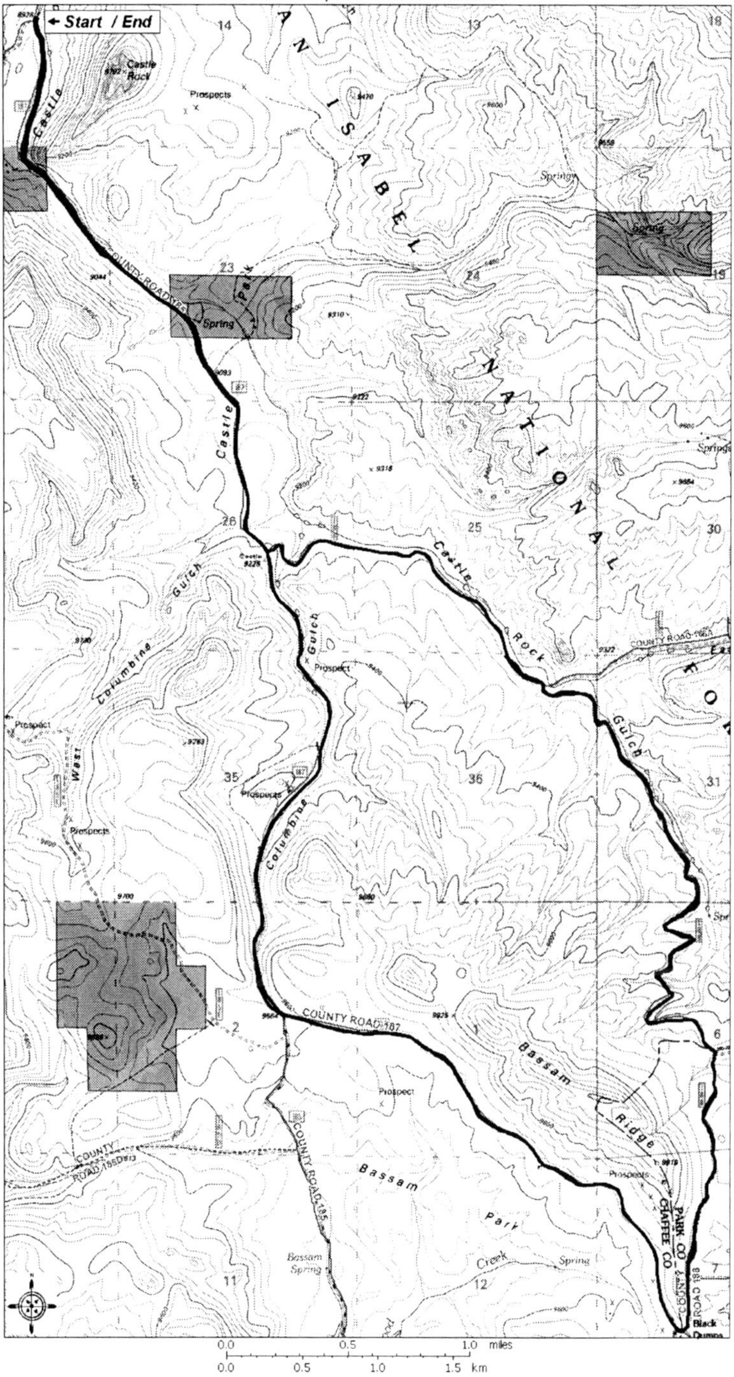

Map 17: Castlerock Gulch Loop (copyright National Geographic)

Someone once asked me whether a particular route was a "date ride." Well, this one certainly is. Pack a lunch and plan a leisurely outing through some of Colorado's most beautiful country.

The biggest question is whether to ride the loop clockwise or counter-clockwise. The climb is a little longer clockwise, but you'll be in shade for a good chunk of it. Counter-clockwise is a tiny bit steeper, but the road surface is slightly better. One thing to consider: while descending through trees may be more appealing to some, in the heat of summer I'd rather climb in shade.

This ride description here is clockwise; reverse the directions for a counter-clockwise ride on the loop.

Elevation profile:

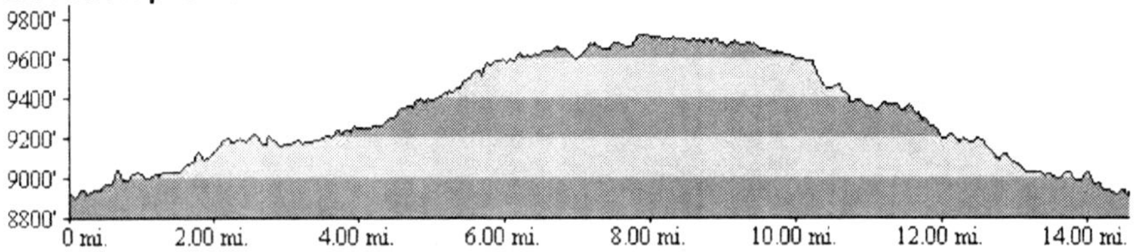

Ride length: 14.8 miles
Ride type: lollipop-loop (clockwise)
Riding time: 1.5 hours
Surface: dirt road
Elevations: start/end 8,900'; max 9,720'; min 8,900'
Total climbing: gain/loss 850'

Aerobic level: easy (some climbing, but not sustained or steep)
Technical level: 1
Season: April into November
USGS Quadrangle: Castle Rock Gulch

Trailhead GPS coordinates: 38° 49.88' N; 105° 59.234' W

Getting there: from the intersection of US 24 and Main St. in Buena Vista (the only stoplight in Buena Vista), drive 2.4 miles south on US 24 to the intersection with US 24/285. Turn left (east) on US 24/285 and drive 6.4 miles to the intersection with CR 307. Turn right on CR 307 and drive 1.6 miles to the intersection with CR 187. Turn right on CR 187 and drive 1.1 miles to the intersection with FSR 300 (not marked). Turn right onto FSR 300 and drive 50 yards to the large parking area. You'll see a Fourmile trailhead sign and a trail marker designating the jeep road (FSR 300) to Bald Mountain Gulch.

The ride:

0.0 Ride from the parking area back to CR 187 and turn right toward Bassam Park.
2.6 Turn left at the junction with FSR 188. Drop down a short downhill.
2.9 Look left. What a great spot for a picnic!
4.1 Continue straight on FSR 188. (*FSR 188a heads left.*) Rock climbers are bound to drool over the granite formations in the distance.
5.3 It gets steeper for a little more than a half-mile.
6.6 Bear right, continuing on FSR 188. (*FSR 189 heads left.*)
7.2 Continue straight on FSR 188 through the unmarked intersection.
7.8 Turn right at the intersection with CR 187. Check out the superb views of Mt. Antero, Mt. Princeton, Mt. Yale, and the Harvard/Columbia group

to the west.

10.1 Continue straight on CR 187 through the intersection with FSR 185. (*FSR 185 heads south to Aspen Ridge.*)

12.2 Continue straight on CR 187. Look familiar? FSR 188, the start of this loop, is on your right.

14.8 End at the junction with FSR 300. The parking area is uphill on your left.

Options: try it counter-clockwise to determine which direction you like best.

Ride 18: Bald Mountain Gulch Loop

Difficult yet fun. That's about all I can say about this one. The initial uphill grind is mild, but you may want to take it easy so that you have something left when the soup gets thick. Once you hit the jeep track, get ready for some technical terrain; some of the descents are steep with deep erosion ruts. Finish with a little climbing back to your vehicle on FSR 300.

Route finding gets a little tricky as you approach FSR 300 (between miles 7.0 and 9.2). In addition, this is a popular motor sports area, so watch for motorized traffic on the route.

Elevation profile:

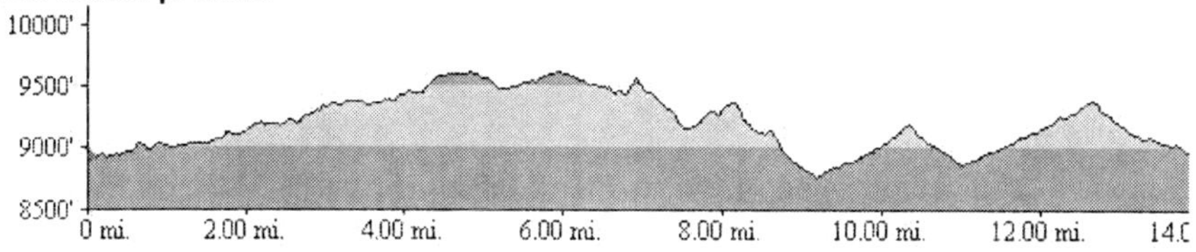

Ride length: 14.0 miles
Ride type: loop (clockwise)
Riding time: 2.5 hours
Surface: dirt road (5.3 miles); jeep trail (8.7 miles)
Elevations: start/end 8,930'; max 9,610'; min 8,775'
Total climbing: gain/loss 2,130'

Aerobic level: strenuous (climbing with some steeps)
Technical level: 4 (some of the descents on FSR 185D are steep and rutted)
Season: May into November
USGS Quadrangles: Castle Rock Gulch, Buena Vista East

Trailhead GPS coordinates: 38° 49.877' N; 105° 59.236' W

Getting there: from the intersection of US 24 and Main St. in Buena Vista (the only stoplight in Buena Vista), drive 2.4 miles south on US 24 to the intersection with US 24/285. Turn left (east) on US 24/285 and drive 6.4 miles to the intersection with CR 307. Turn right on CR 307 and drive 1.6 miles to the intersection with CR 187. Turn right on CR 187 and drive 1.1 miles to the intersection with FSR 300 (not marked). Turn right onto FSR 300 and drive 50 yards to the large parking area. You'll see a Fourmile trailhead sign and a trail sign designating the jeep road (FSR 300) to Bald Mountain Gulch.

38°47.851' N, 105°59.571' W WGS84

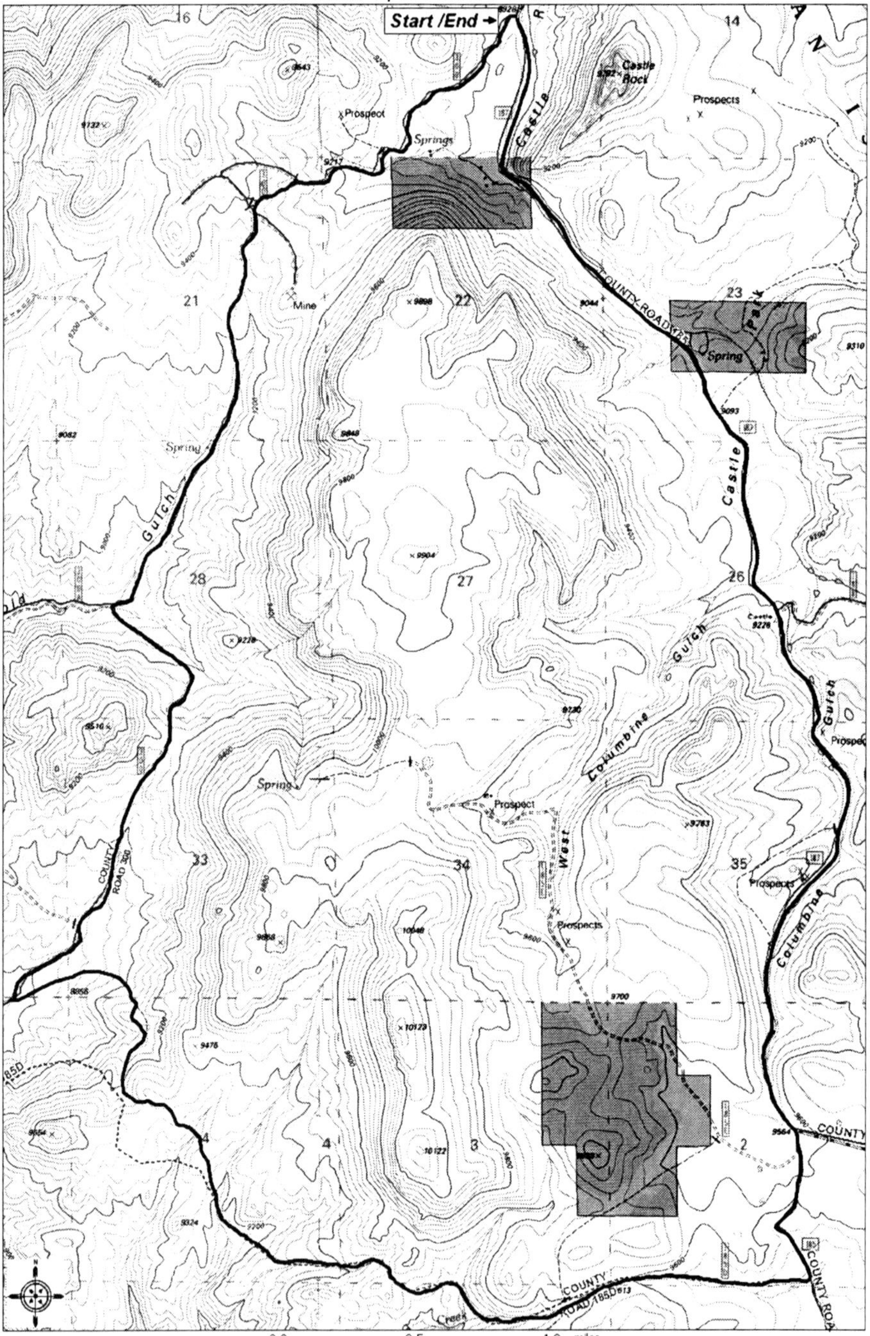

Map 18: Bald Mountain Gulch Loop (copyright National Geographic)

The ride:

0.0 Ride from the parking area back to CR 187 and turn right toward Bassam Park.
2.6 Continue straight on CR 187 at the intersection with FSR 188.
4.7 Turn right onto FSR 185, following the sign to Aspen Ridge.
4.8 Continue straight on FSR 185, passing intersection with FSR 185E on the right.
5.3 Turn right at the intersection with FSR 185D.
5.6 Pass through the seasonal closure gate.
6.1 Continue straight, passing an unmarked spur.
6.3 Continue straight on FSR 185D, passing TR 1434 on the left.
6.5 Pass through a gate. Be sure to close it.
7.0 Continue straight on FSR 185D, passing an unmarked spur on the left.
7.5 Bear right at the unmarked spur.
7.6 Cross a deep wash and start to climb.
8.4 Continue straight, avoiding the unmarked spur on your left.
9.2 Pass through the seasonal closure gate and turn right at the junction with FSR 300. Climb through a short sandy section.
10.4 Continue straight, passing an unmarked spur on the left.
11.0 Turn right at the parking area and continue on FSR 300. (*FSR 300A is the spur on the far left.*)
12.3 Continue straight (right) on FSR 300, passing TR 1423 on the left.
12.6 Continue straight through an unmarked intersection; stay on the main road.
13.2 Bear left at the unmarked intersection. The rock formation in the distance ahead of you is Castle Rock.
13.3 Bear right at an unmarked intersection. Continue pedaling toward Castle Rock.
14.0 Enter the parking area and trailhead.

Options: explore some of the multi-use trails in the area, but bring a map and compass so you don't get lost!

Midland 376A Loop

Ride 19: Davis Meadow Loop

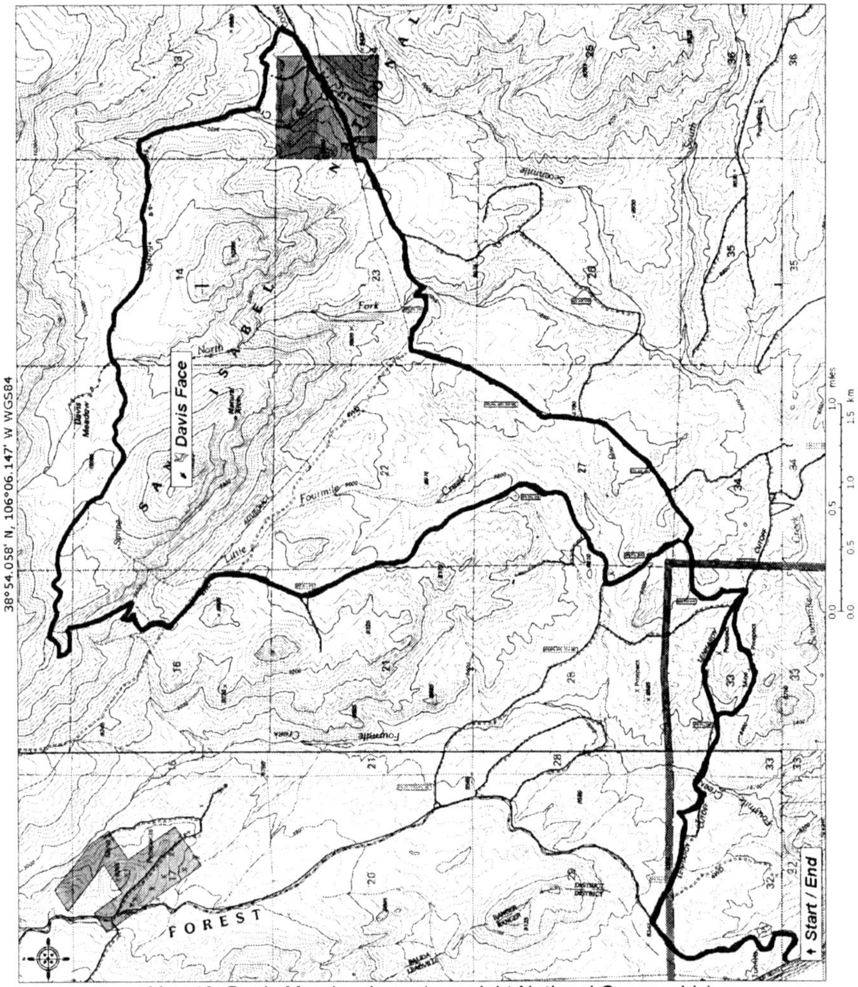

Map 19: Davis Meadow Loop (copyright National Geographic)

This little-known route will physically challenge you and test your route-finding skills. The goods, a nice stretch of downhill single-track, are difficult to reach and come only after a great deal of climbing and a couple miles of audacious bushwhacking deep in the backcountry. This one is solely for the adventurous at heart.

The ride starts by climbing up jeep roads. Then it continues climbing up jeep roads for what seems like an eternity. You'll eventually reach a difficult section of faint, overgrown single-track. Just when you think it can't get any tougher, you'll suddenly long for mosquito repellent and a machete as you plod your way through the marshy meadow. Ultimately, you'll reach the short-but-sweet downhill. The jeep tracks back to the start are fun, but several short climbs along the way will remind you that it was a long ride.

Warning! *Think twice about attempting this ride without high quality maps, a compass, and a GPS. You will greatly increase your risk of getting lost in very remote terrain if you aren't adequately prepared.*

Elevation profile:

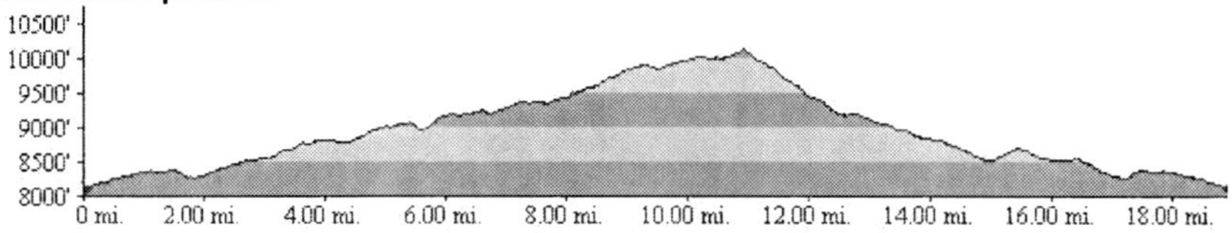

Ride length: 19.0 miles
Ride type: lollipop-loop (counter-clockwise)
Riding time: 3.5-4 hours
Surface: single-track (4.3 miles); jeep road (14.7 miles)
Elevations: start/end 8,130'; max 10,140'; min 8,130'

Total climbing: gain/loss 2,725'
Aerobic level: strenuous (climbing)
Technical level: 5 (very difficult route finding in remote wilderness; steep descents)
Season: June through October
USGS Quadrangles: Buena Vista West, Harvard Lakes, Marmot Peak

Trailhead GPS coordinates: 38° 52.478' N; 106° 8.596' W

Getting there: from the intersection of US 24 and Main St. in Buena Vista (the only stoplight in Buena Vista), drive 0.2 miles east on Main St. Turn left on N. Colorado Ave (CR 371) and drive 2.5 miles north to the intersection with CR 375 (just south of the tunnels). Turn right (east) and drive 0.1 miles to the large OHV parking area on your left. The ride starts at the Fourmile Area sign in the southeast corner of the parking area. If you need one, grab a Fourmile Recreation Area map from the dispenser attached to the sign (please bring additional maps as the one in the free pamphlet will not be sufficient).

The ride:

0.0	Head uphill on CR 375.
0.8	Pass the Turtle Rock camping area on your left.
1.0	Turn right onto FSR 376 (the Lenhardy Cutoff). Stay on FSR 376, passing all spurs for the next 1.9 miles. ***Note-*** *the prominent rock formation you'll see prior to turning, Split Rock, is another popular climbing crag.*
1.9	Cross Fourmile Creek. You will get your feet wet. Be prepared for tough climbing through about 0.4 miles of sand.
2.5	Bear right at the fork (*left is a dead end*). Continue uphill.
2.9	Pass the intersection with TR 6039 on your right. Continue on FSR 376 for another 100 yards then turn left onto FSR 311.
3.5	Bear right at the intersection with FSR 373, continuing on FSR 311.
3.8	After a quick downhill, continue straight on FSR 311, passing the unmarked spur on your right.
4.4	Continue on FSR 311 at the intersection with TR 1414.
5.4	Bear right at the fork with FSR 373 (*FSR 373 jug handles*), staying on FSR 311.
5.8	Cross a small stream just as your feet were about dry from the last stream crossing.
6.1	Bear right, staying on FSR 311 (*left is a dead end*).

6.3 Continue straight on FSR 311, passing a spur on the left.
6.6 Pass through the seasonal closure gate.
7.3 Turn left onto FSR 311D and continue climbing. After about 100 yards, bear left, passing a short spur on the right.
7.9 Arrive at the Davis Meadow trailhead (TR 1413). The single-track begins here.
8.0 As you pass through a gate, you may be wondering if you came to ride or mow the lawn. That's some deep grass you're riding through! From this point forward, the single-track is faint and may be very difficult to follow.
8.4 Cross Sevenmile Creek.
8.5 Keep your eyes open and look for any clues to help you follow the trail: cairns, cut branches, etc. Proceed with great caution, taking the time to observe and make note of your surroundings. You don't want to get lost back here!
9.6 Arrive at a marshy clearing and the vestiges of several log cabins. Look across the meadow between the cabins for the trail. The route may not be obvious at first, so take your time.
10.8 A trail marker let's you know that you are not lost.
11.0 The trail widens into a very rugged jeep road.
11.1 Depart right from the jeep road and resume riding on rough single-track. (*The road becomes a rutted gully filled with debris.*)
11.7 Another trail marker on the right to reassure you. Enjoy the hard-earned downhill.
12.2 After a little bit of rock hopping, pop-out at the TR 1413 trailhead on FSR 373. Climb up past the aqueduct vent and turn left. Enjoy the excellent descent that follows.
12.6 Bottom-out of the steep descent and look up at the Davis Face crag on your left. ***Note****- for you climbers out there, the crack up the center is a tasty, 4-pitch, 5.9 trad route with a crux roof on the second pitch.*
12.8 Continue straight past the FSR 373A trail marker then bear right at the top of a small rise on FSR 373.
15.2 Deep sand! Turn left and climb up the deeply rutted FSR 373. (*Straight is FSR 375A.*)
15.7 Turn right onto FSR 311 to close the loop.
16.3 Turn right onto FSR 376. Ride for about 0.1 miles, and then turn left onto TR 6039. (*If you've had enough, stay on FSR 376.*)
16.7 Bear right and stay on TR 6039. (*TR 6029 heads left.*)
17.0 Rejoin FSR 376 at the top of the sandy section. Turn left and plow through the sand as you descend to Fourmile Creek.
17.4 Cross Fourmile Creek and avoid all spurs until you reach CR 375.
18.3 Turn left onto CR 375. Not much left.
19.0 Find your car and drive into town for a shower and a malted shake.

Options: this is a long ride. Shorten it by starting at the junction of FSR 311 and FSR 311D. To do this, you'll need to drive to Trout Creek Pass. From the intersection of US 24 and Main St. in Buena Vista, drive 2.4 miles south and turn left at the intersection US 24/285. Drive approximately 12.7 miles east/north on US 24/285 to CR 311. Turn left onto CR 311 and continue driving on CR/FSR 311 until you reach the intersection with FSR 311D on your right in approximately 5.5 miles. Ride uphill on FSR 311D (mile 7.3 above). When you get to FSR 311 (mile 15.7 above), turn left and continue riding east on FSR 311 until you return to your vehicle.

Ride 20: Lenhardy Cutoff

38°51.163' N, 106°03.922' W WGS84

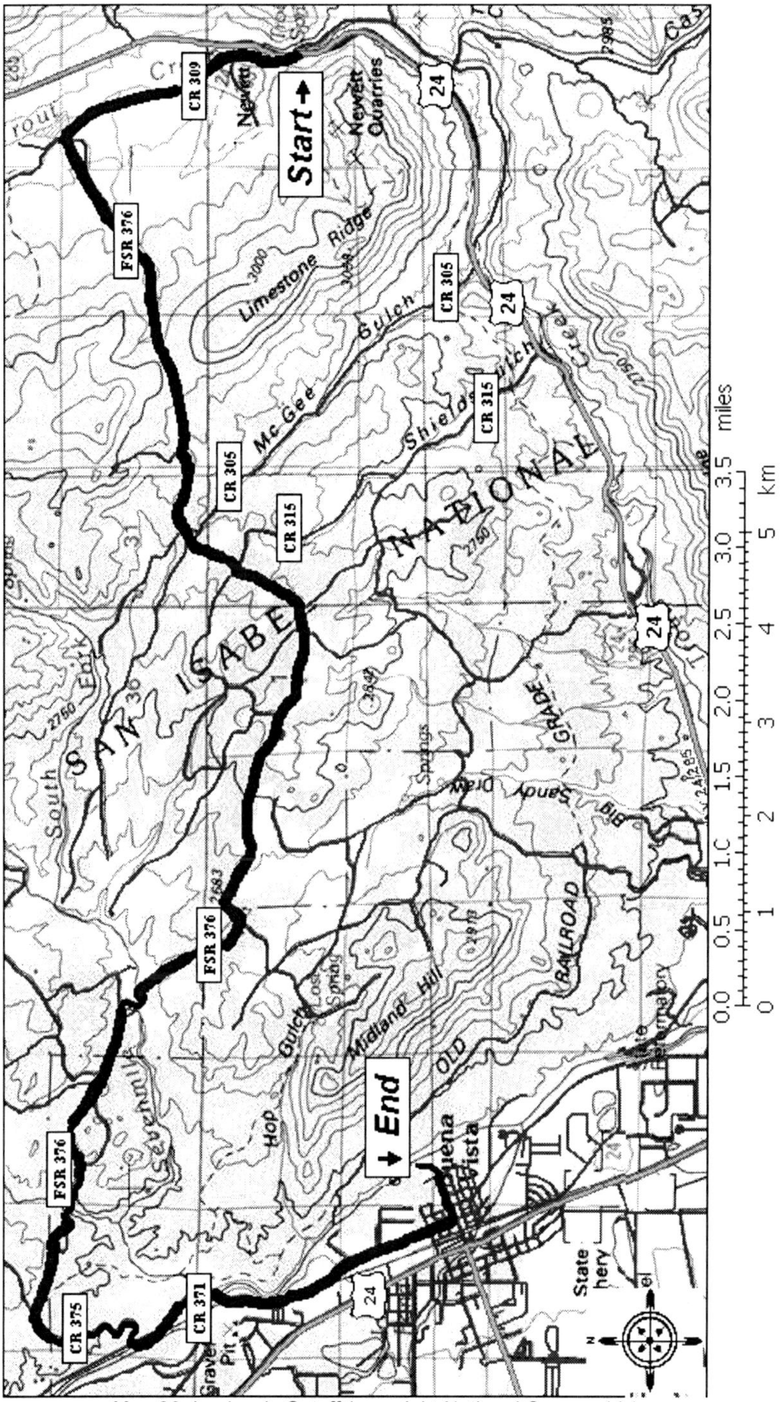

Map 20: Lenhardy Cutoff (copyright National Geographic)

What's Thanksgiving without turkey? Or July 4th without fireworks? The same as a Buena Vista mountain biking guide without the Lenhardy Cutoff!

This legendary ride starts with a brief climb on a county road. It then continues to climb into a pine forest before dropping into a screaming descent through the high desert terrain of the Fourmile Recreation Area. The long descent is especially fun, with fast miles of smooth jumps and bumps. The views of the Collegiate Peaks and Arkansas Valley are stunning. Finish with an easy pedal along the river as you return to town.

Be careful when you hit the sandy sections!

Elevation profile:

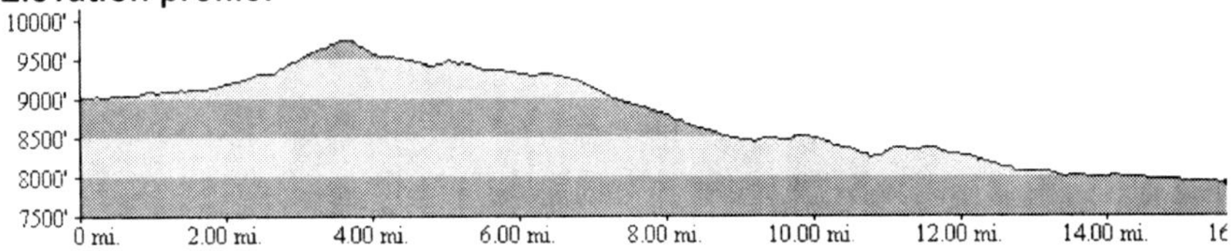

Ride length: 15.8 miles
Ride type: one-way with shuttle
Riding time: 2 hours
Surface: dirt road/jeep road
Elevations: start 9,030'; end 7,960'; max 9,760'; min 7,960'
Total climbing: gain 960' - loss 2,050' = total -1,090'
Aerobic level: easy (the climb and length make it slightly moderate)
Technical level: 2+ (short rocky sections on the climb, some sand during the descent)
Season: April into November
USGS Quadrangles: Castle Rock Gulch, Antero Reservoir, Marmot Peak, Buena Vista East, Harvard Lakes, Buena Vista West

Trailhead GPS coordinates: 38° 51.49' N; 105° 59.182' W

Getting there: leave a vehicle at the Buena Vista River Park. From the intersection of US 24 and Main St. in Buena Vista (the only stoplight in town), drive 0.5 miles east to end of Main St. Bear left into the Buena Vista River Park parking lot.

Take the other vehicle, riders and bikes to the trailhead. From the intersection of US 24 and Main St. in Buena Vista, drive approximately 2.4 miles south and turn left (east) at the intersection with US 24/285. Drive approximately 8.6 miles east/north on US 24/285 to the intersection with CR 309. There is a small parking area on the right (east) side of the highway, across from CR 309. The ride begins at the start of CR 309. *Use caution when crossing the highway!*

There is additional parking on CR 307 (8.7 miles from junction of US 24/285, turn right on CR 307).

The ride:

- **0.0** The ride starts at the west side of US 24/285 at CR 309. Ride uphill on CR 309.
- **1.8** Turn left on FSR 376. ***Note-*** *from here, the Lenhardy Cutoff overlaps the Midland Bike Trail for approximately 4 miles.*
- **2.7** Stay left on the main trail, passing a spur on your right.

3.6 Summit the ridge. Great views of the valley are your reward.
4.3 Pass a campsite spur.
4.5 Pass another the campsite.
4.8 Seasonal closure gate. Avoid all spurs for the next 100 yards. Continue straight on FSR 376 through the intersection with CR/FSR 305. ***Note-*** *there is a sign showing mileage to Buena Vista along this route (10 miles).*
4.9 Stay on FSR 376, passing the intersection with FSR 376B on your right.
5.8 Go straight, staying on FSR 376 through the intersection with CR/FSR 315. The sign says BV 9 miles. ***Note-*** *the Midland Bike Trail descends CR/FSR 315 (Shields Gulch).*
6.0 Continue straight on FSR 376, passing the intersection with FSR 376A on your left. The next downhill (2.4 miles) is mucho fun. Go for it!
8.4 The sand can get thick and loose here. Be careful.
9.3 A short climb provides a break in the action.
9.5 Stay on the main route, passing the spur on the left.
9.9 Stay on FSR 376 past the intersection with FSR 311 on your right. Next, pass the intersection with TR 6039 on your left.
10.4 More sand.
10.9 Cross Fourmile Creek. Your feet will get wet.
11.3 Stay on FSR 376, passing a couple multi-use trails on your right and left.
11.8 Turn left as you intersect CR 375 (*unmarked*) at a "T" intersection. CR 375 is well graded, but may be sandy in sections.
12.6 Stay on the main road, CR 375.
12.8 Turn left at the intersection with CR 371, the River Road.
13.3 Pavement begins.
15.3 Turn left at the intersection with Main St. in downtown Buena Vista. Continue east on Main St. until you reach the River Park.
15.8 Parking area and end of ride. Now go get your other car.

Options: the Fourmile Recreation Area has so many riding options that one local once said, "I've never done the same route twice." One could literally spend a week exploring the area. The possibilities are many. Just take a map and plan before you go.

To avoid the sand and 2.5 miles of pavement, at mile 6.0 try finishing on FSR 376A to the Midland trail.

Ride 21: Midland Bike Trail

38° 52.151' N, 106°02.914' W WGS84

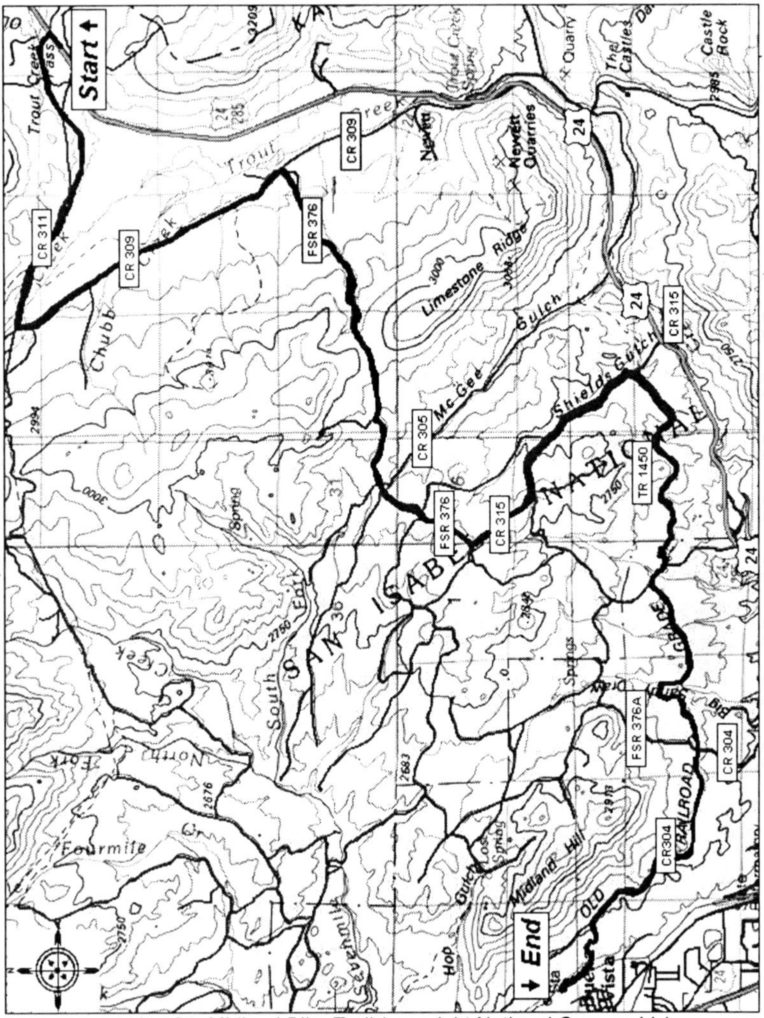

Map 21: Midland Bike Trail (copyright National Geographic)

This route provides a pleasant ride with terrific views. Not to be confused with the Midland Railroad Grade, this is the complete route from Trout Creek Pass to Buena Vista.

It starts with a gentle descent into the Chubb Park State Wildlife Management Area. Next, ascend through a pine forest to a ridge with sweeping vistas of the Collegiate Peaks and Arkansas Valley. A fast descent on CR/FSR 315 brings you to the single-track of the Midland Railroad Grade, where technical detours into gullies once spanned by rail trestles put even experienced riders on the edge of their saddles. The last mile returns you to Buena Vista along the serpentine single-track of the Barbara Whipple Trail.

Elevation profile:

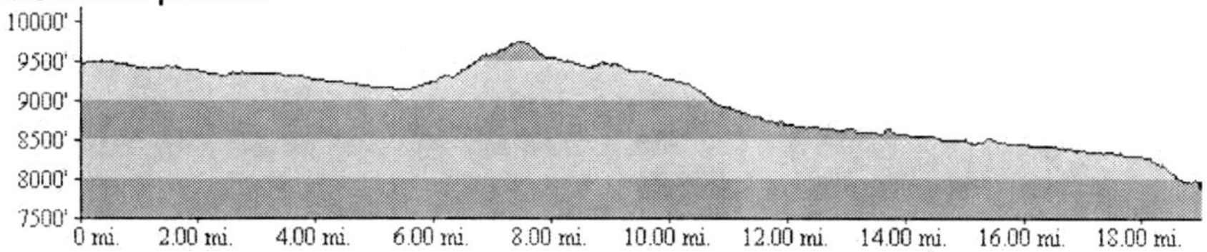

Ride length: 18.8 miles
Ride type: one-way with shuttle
Riding time: 2.5 hours
Surface: single-track (4.9 miles); dirt road (13.9 miles)
Elevations: start 9,480'; end 7,960'; max 9,750'; min 7,960'
Total climbing: gain 840' - loss 2,375' = total -1,535'
Aerobic level: easy (some climbing and the length make it somewhat moderate)
Technical level: 3 (the few technical sections are easily walked)
Season: April into November
USGS Quadrangles: Antero Reservoir, Marmot Peak, Buena Vista East

Trailhead GPS coordinates: 38° 54.652' N; 105° 58.661' W

Getting there: leave a vehicle at the Buena Vista River Park. From the intersection of US 24 and Main St. in Buena Vista (the only stoplight in town), drive 0.5 miles east to the end of Main St. Bear left into the Buena Vista River Park parking lot.

Take the other vehicle, loaded with riders and bikes, to the trailhead. From the intersection of US 24 and Main St. in Buena Vista, drive 2.4 miles south and turn left at the intersection with US 24/285. Drive 12.7 miles east/north on US 24/285 to CR 311. Turn left onto CR 311 and drive approximately 0.2 miles to the parking area and trailhead on the left.

The ride:

- **0.0** From the trailhead, turn left (west) on CR 311 to start the ride.
- **0.9** Cross the cattle guard and the seasonal closure gate.
- **1.5** Enter Chubb Park State Wildlife Management Area. Stay on the designated roads through this area.
- **2.6** Turn left at the intersection with CR 309.
- **3.3** Continue on the main road and avoid all spurs.
- **4.8** Cross the cattle guard and stay on CR 309.
- **5.2** Turn right on to FSR 376. This begins the main climb of the ride. ***Note-*** *from this point, the Midland Bike Trail overlaps the Lenhardy Cutoff for approximately 4 miles.*
- **6.0** Bear right, staying on the main road.
- **6.1** Continue on the main road, passing a spur on the right.
- **6.6** Keep going. Dominate the rocks!
- **7.2** The main climb is over and the trail rolls for the next few miles. Beautiful views will open on the horizon as you ride.
- **8.2** Pass through a seasonal closure gate. Avoid all spurs for the next 100 yards. At the junction with CR/FSR 305, continue straight on FSR 376. This intersection is marked with a mileage sign (*10 miles to Buena Vista*).
- **8.4** Stay on FSR 376, passing the intersection with FSR 376B on your right.
- **9.3** Turn left at the intersection with CR/FSR 315 (Shields Gulch). Enjoy

the views and fast descent. ***Note-*** *the Lenhardy Cutoff continues straight on FSR 376.*

11.5 Turn right at the intersection with TR 1450. There is a parking area and Fourmile signs designating the trailhead.

14.2 Continue straight on TR 1450. (*TR 1450A, part of the Gentlemen's Loop, heads uphill on the right.*)

14.8 Bear right, following the distinct trail.

15.7 Continue straight on FSR 376A.

15.8 Continue straight through the intersection to CR 304. (***Hint-*** *head toward the large "No Outlet" sign.)* Stay on CR 304 for about 2.1 miles, until you reach the intersection with the Barbara Whipple Trail on your left.

17.9 Look left for the Barbara Whipple Trail. This intersection is not well marked. Look for the Midland Bike Trail sign on the right of the single-track. ***Note-*** *TR 6032 (no bikes) heads uphill to your right.*

18.4 Continue straight, passing a trail on the right. In another 100 yards, you'll pass sheltered benches at a scenic viewpoint.

18.8 Cross the bridge and call it a success!

Options: the Fourmile Recreation area is packed with trails and riding options. One fun alternative to this ride is to take FSR 376 at mile 8.2. Continue on FSR 376 for approximately 0.2 miles, then turn left onto FSR 376A. Stay on 376A until you return to the Midland Bike Trail at mile 15.7 as documented in this ride.

Ride 22: Midland Railroad Grade

Okay. You've been to BV many times and you've ridden this one before. While easy to dismiss as "just another town trail," there is a great deal of charm to this route. Admit it: the Whipple Trail is nothing short of awesome and the "diversions" are a whole lot of fun. Nearly everyone loves this trail and it's a BV staple.

Start with a fun stretch of single-track along the Barbara Whipple Trail. After the climb, you reach spectacular views of the southern Arkansas Valley from the old Midland Railroad grade. Once you turn east, the trail returns to single-track that slices through narrow stone cuts and drops into diversions that wind down through gullies once spanned by rail trestles.

Elevation profile:

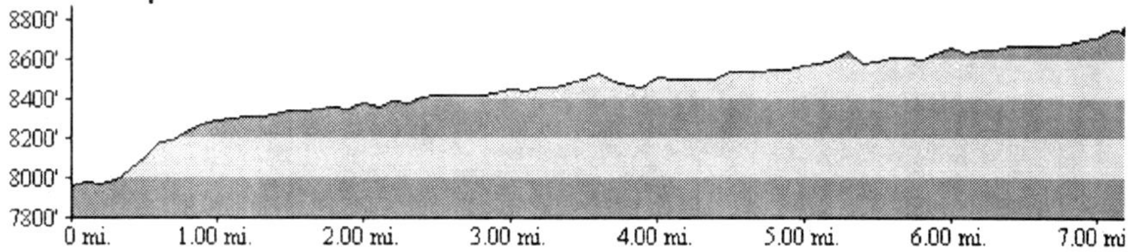

38°50.271' N, 106°04.520' W WGS84

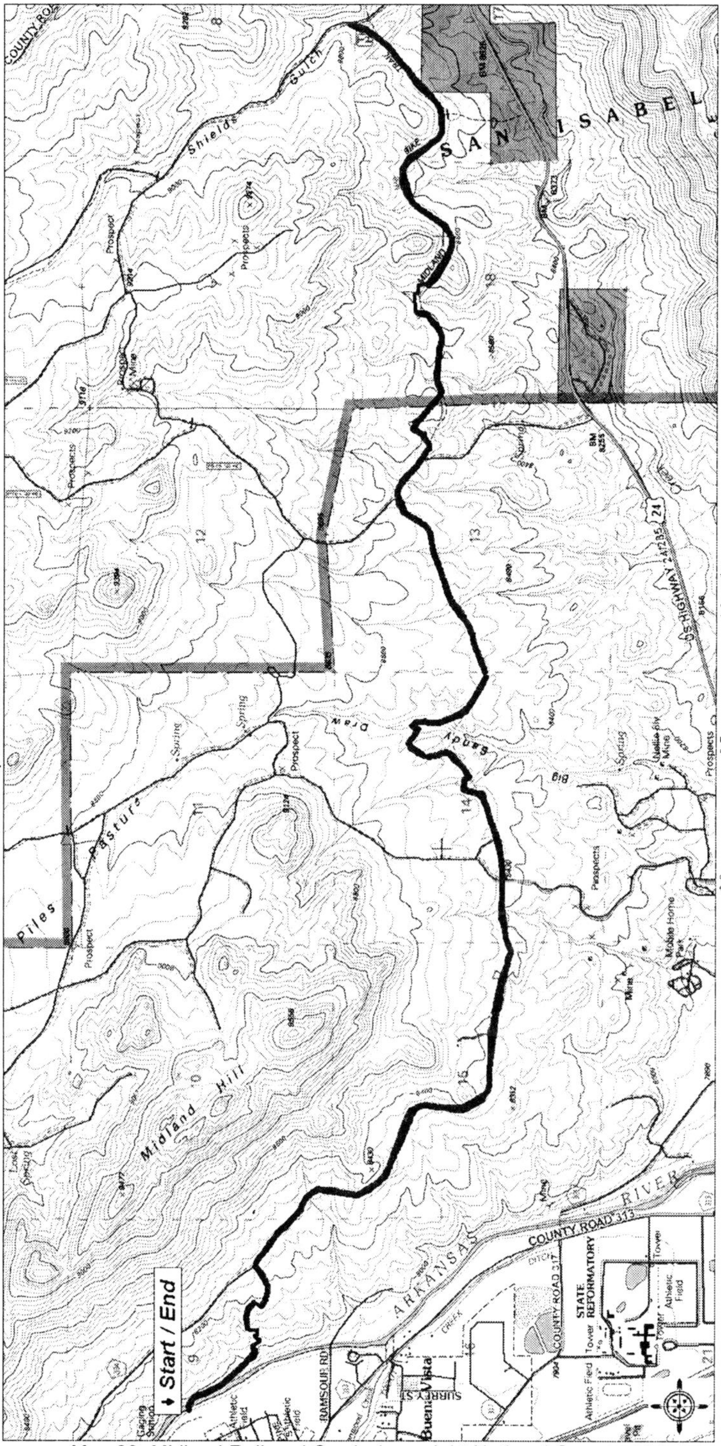

Map 22: Midland Railroad Grade (copyright National Geographic)

Ride length: 14.6 miles
Ride type: out-and-back
Riding time: 2 hours
Surface: single-track (9.8 miles); dirt road (4.8 miles)
Elevations: start/end 7,960'; max 8,750'; min 7,960'
Total climbing: gain/loss 1,015'

Aerobic level: easy (the 0.9-mile climb at the start is moderate)
Technical level: 3 (the short technical sections are easily walked)
Season: April through November (year-round when dry)
USGS Quadrangle: Buena Vista East

Trailhead GPS coordinates: 38° 50.821' N; 106° 7.323' W

Getting there: from the intersection of US 24 and Main St. in Buena Vista (the only stoplight in town), drive 0.5 miles east to the end of Main St. Bear left into the Buena Vista River Park parking lot. The ride starts at the west side (town side) of the footbridge over the river.

The ride:

0.0 Cross the bridge to start the ride. Enjoy the Whipple single-track. Pure fun.

0.1 Stay right at the split. The trail drops down a few feet and parallels the river. The line through the rocks is a little tricky.

0.2 Pass the shaded bench area with 4 interpretive signs. If you have the time, stop to read the signs and enjoy the view.

0.3 Stay right at the split.

0.9 Intersect CR 304 and turn right. There are amazing views of Mt. Princeton here. Stay on the road and avoid all spurs and driveways for the next 2 miles.

2.9 This is a slightly confusing 3-way split. Go straight along FSR 376A. You want to avoid the natural inclination to descend right on CR 304. FSR 376A is the middle fork just left (east) of the parking area and Fourmile sign.

3.3 Go straight onto TR 1450. (*FSR 376A heads left.*) The route is now single-track.

3.8 Cross a sandy wash at the bottom of the gully.

4.8 Continue straight along TR 1450. TR 1450 may not be marked at this junction, but TR 1450A is the spur on the left.

5.2 The trail heads left and drops into another gully. (*A faint foot trail goes straight to the base of the old trestle.*)

5.8 Another gully crossing.

7.3 Bear left and drop down to the well-marked trailhead at the intersection with CR/FSR 315. This is the turn-around. Return the way you came.

Options: for an easier, primarily downhill ride, leave a vehicle at the River Park and start the ride at the eastern trailhead (where the trail intersects CR 315). To get there, drive 2.4 miles south on US 24 from the intersection of Main St. and US 24 in Buena Vista. Turn left at the intersection with US 285/24 and drive 5.6 miles to CR 315. Turn left on to CR 315 and drive 0.5 miles to the trailhead and parking area on the left.

Ride 23: Midland 376A Loop (Shield's Gulch Loop)

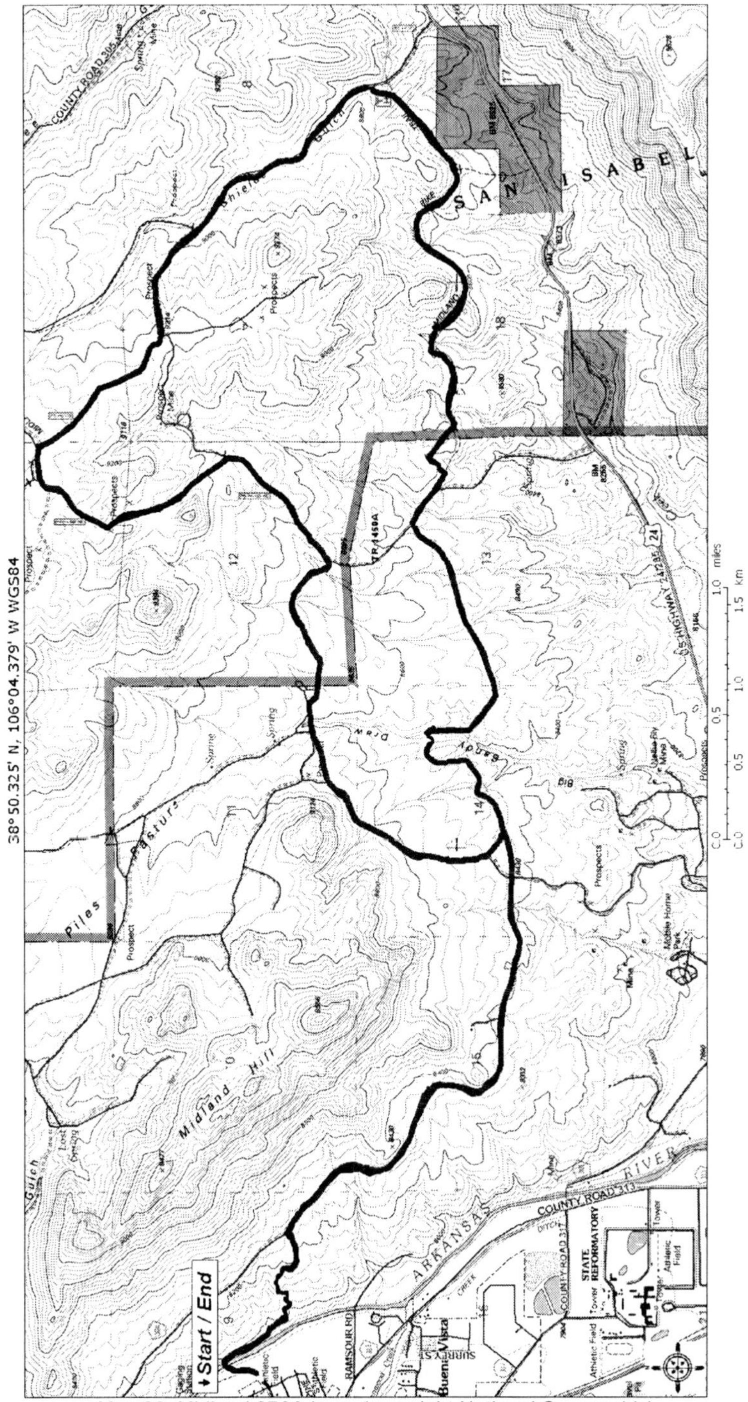

Map 23: Midland 376A Loop (copyright National Geographic)

This is one of the best rides in Buena Vista. Start by working your way up the Barbara Whipple Trail from the Buena Vista River Park. The next section, a spin on the Midland Railroad Grade, is fast and easy, but tight single-track diversions into gullies keep you working. The first 0.5 miles of the climb on CR/FSR 315 (Shields Gulch) can get sandy in summer, but the rest is a meditative spin that tops out with unsurpassed views of the southern Arkansas Valley and the Collegiate Peaks. The descent on CR 376A is fast, solid fun and is sure to make you smile. The Whipple Trail back to town provides a perfect ending.

Elevation profile:

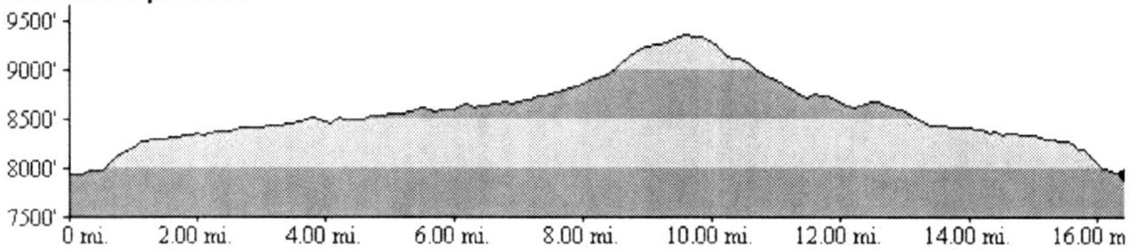

Ride length: 16.2 miles
Ride type: lollipop-loop (counter-clockwise)
Riding time: 2 hours
Surface: single-track (5.8 miles); jeep roads (10.4 miles)
Elevations: start/end 7,960'; max 9,365'; min 7,960'

Total climbing: gain/loss 1,650'
Aerobic level: moderate (climbing)
Technical level: 3 (short technical sections are easily walked)
Season: April through November (can be ridden all year when dry)
USGS Quadrangle: Buena Vista East

Trailhead GPS coordinates: 38° 50.795' N; 106° 7.342' W

Getting there: from the intersection of US 24 and Main St. in Buena Vista (the only stoplight in town), drive approximately 0.5 miles east to the end of Main St. Bear left into the Buena Vista River Park parking lot. The ride starts at the west side (town side) of the footbridge over the river.

The ride:

- **0.0** Cross the bridge to start the ride. Enjoy the single-track... gotta love it!
- **0.1** Stay right at the split. The trail drops down a few feet and parallels the river. The line through the rocks is a little tricky.
- **0.2** Pass the shaded bench area with 4 interpretive signs. If you have time, stop to read the signs and take in the scenery.
- **0.3** Stay right at the fork.
- **0.9** Go right at the intersection with CR 304. Take pleasure in the amazing views of Mt. Princeton and the lower valley. Stay on the road, avoiding all spurs and driveways for the next 2 miles.
- **2.9** Go straight on FSR 376A. This is a slightly confusing 3-way split. You want to avoid the natural inclination to descend right on CR 304. FSR 376A is the middle fork just left (east) of the parking area and Fourmile signs.
- **3.3** Go straight at TR 1450. (*FSR 376A heads left.*) The trail is now single track and closed to motorized traffic.
- **4.8** Continue straight along TR 1450. TR 1450 may not be marked at this junction, but TR 1450A is the spur on the left.
- **5.2** The trail heads left and drops into another gulch.

7.2 Bear left and drop down to CR/FSR 315. There is a parking area and trailhead sign at the bottom of the drop.

7.3 Turn left at the junction with CR/FSR 315 and start to climb on the sandy road. The sand will end in approximately 0.5 miles. Avoid all spurs, staying on CR/FSR 315 for approximately 2.2 miles.

7.8 Continue straight on CR/FSR 315, passing a spur on your right.

8.8 Avoid all campsite spurs. The scenery is big with excellent views.

9.5 Turn left at the junction with FSR 376. This ends the major climb of the ride. There is a large sign with mileage to Buena Vista (*9 miles via FSR 376*). Stay on the main road, passing numerous zigzagging spurs along the way.

9.7 Bear left onto FSR 376A at the fork. The next 1.5 miles are a blast: steeps, smooth surface, deep ruts, and slightly banked turns. Have fun! ***Note-*** *right at the fork returns you to Buena Vista via the Lenhardy Cutoff.*

10.2 Bear left at the fork. (*Right leads to an awesome campsite.*)

10.8 Pass all of the campsite spurs; keep bombing the downhill on the main road.

11.1 Bear right at the fork with TR 1450A. ***Note-*** *TR 1450A, part of the Gentleman's Loop, returns you to the Midland Railroad Grade at mile 4.8 of this route description.*

11.2 A short climb breaks the action. The route rolls for the next 1.2 miles.

11.8 Pass a spur on the right as you continue on the main road.

12.4 Turn left, passing the drive with the large gate. The descent is now on a well-maintained road.

12.7 Stay on the main road, avoiding all campsites.

13.1 Turn right to rejoin the Midland Railroad Grade back to Buena Vista.

13.2 Continue straight through the intersection to CR 304. (***Hint-*** *head toward the large "No Outlet" sign.)* Stay on CR 304 for about 2 miles, until you reach the intersection with the Barbara Whipple Trail on your left.

15.3 Look left for the Barbara Whipple Trail. This intersection is not well marked. Look for the Midland Bike Trail sign on the right of the single-track. ***Note-*** *TR 6032 (no bikes) heads uphill to your right.*

15.8 Continue the descent, passing the trail to your right.

16.2 Cross the bridge. Did you have fun?

Ride 24: Trout Creek Pass to Buena Vista

This route, connecting Trout Creek Pass to Buena Vista, is easier than the Midland Bike Trail and provides an excellent dirt alternative for touring off-road cyclists. With a little ingenuity, this route can be easily connected to dirt routes extending north to Fairplay or east to Hartsel.

It's also a fun and easy ride on its own. The climb is gentle, and once you crest the ridge separating Chubb Park and Buena Vista, the expansive views of the Collegiate Peaks and Arkansas Valley are magnificent. The descent is fast and smooth, with just the right amount of ruts and steeps to keep it interesting. Expect to slosh through about 0.5 miles of sand as you approach Fourmile Creek.

The route passes through dense stands of aspen and mid-September is a perfect time to ride it.

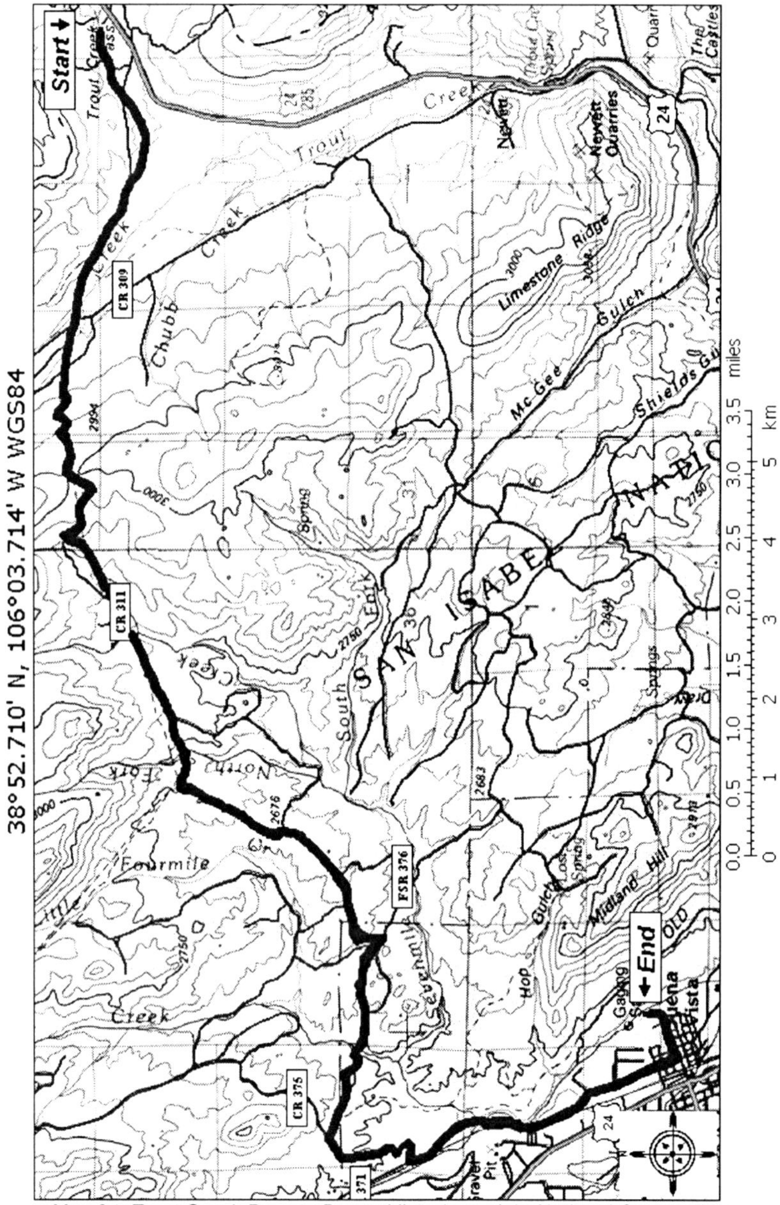

Map 24: Trout Creek Pass to Buena Vista (copyright National Geographic)

Elevation profile:

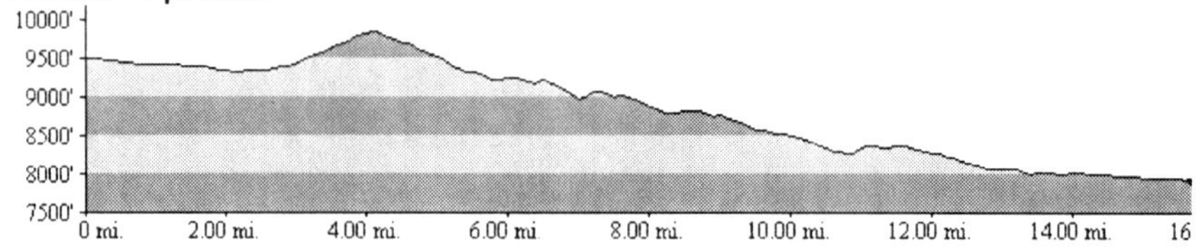

Ride length: 15.8 miles
Ride type: one-way with shuttle
Riding time: 1.5 hours
Surface: dirt/jeep road (13.3 miles); paved road (2.5 miles)
Elevations: start 9,480'; end 7,960'; max 9,840'; min 7,960'
Total climbing: gain 730' – loss 2,300' = total -1,570'
Aerobic level: easy (some climbing and a few short steeps)
Technical level: 2+ (some ruts, steeps, and a sandy section)
Season: April into November
USGS Quadrangles: Antero Reservoir, Marmot Peak, Harvard Lakes, Buena Vista East, Buena Vista West

Trailhead GPS coordinates: 38° 54.652' N; 105° 58.661' W

Getting there: leave a vehicle at the Buena Vista River Park. From the intersection of US 24 and Main St. in Buena Vista (the only stoplight in town), drive 0.5 miles east to the end of Main St. Bear left into the Buena Vista River Park parking lot.

Take the other vehicle, riders, and bikes to the trailhead. From the intersection of US 24 and Main St. in Buena Vista, drive approximately 2.4 miles south to the intersection with US 24/285. Turn left and drive approximately 12.7 miles east/north on US 24/285 to CR 311. Turn left onto CR 311 and drive approximately 0.2 miles to the parking area and trailhead on the left. The ride starts at your vehicle.

The ride:

0.0 From the trailhead, ride east on CR 311.

0.2 Continue on the main road as you pass spurs on the left and right.

0.9 Cross the cattle guard and the seasonal closure gate.

1.6 Enter Chubb Park State Wildlife Management Area. Stay on the designated roads through this area.

2.6 Continue straight (west) on CR 311 toward Sevenmile Creek as you pass the intersection with CR 309 on the left. Continue for fifty yards and pass the second intersection with CR 309 on the right. ***Note-*** *the Midland Bike Trail heads south on CR 309.*

2.8 Continue straight on CR 311 as you pass the intersection with CR 309A on the right.

4.1 Cross a cattle guard as you crest the summit of the route. Get ready for a fun descent into the Arkansas Valley. You'll pass through deep stands of aspen while treated to excellent views of the Collegiate Peaks and the town of Buena Vista.

5.5 Stay on the main road as you pass FSR 311D on the right.

5.8 The road becomes rutted as you pass the remnants of an old homestead on the left.

6.5 Stay on the main road as you pass an unmarked road on the right.

6.6 Continue straight on CR 311 as you pass the intersection with FSR 311E on your right.

6.7 Stay on CR 311 as you pass the fenced entrance to TR 1414 on the left.

7.0 Try to keep your feet dry as you cross the creek.

7.4 Bear left at the fork, continuing on CR 311 as you pass FSR 373 on the right. ***Note-*** *FSR 373 jug-handles and rejoins CR 311 at mile 9.3 of this description. It's a fun diversion and offers views of a natural arch adjacent to the Davis Face. The road is steep and may not be suitable for novice riders.*

8.4 Stay on CR 311 as you pass TR 1414 on the left.

8.7 Continue straight on CR 311 as you pass FSR 311F on the right.
9.3 Bear left at the fork, staying on CR 311 as FSR 373 intersects from the right.
9.8 Turn right as you merge with FSR 376 (*the Lenhardy Cutoff*).
9.9 Stay right on FSR 376 as an ATV trail (TR 6039) heads left.
10.3 Enter some soupy sand. Keep your weight slightly back and your front wheel straight. Pedal evenly and you will clean it.
10.8 The sand ends just before you cross Fourmile Creek.
11.2 Continue straight on FSR 376, past the intersections with TR 1415 and TR 6037.
11.7 Turn left as you intersect CR 375 (*unmarked*) at a "T" intersection. CR 375 is well graded but may be sandy in sections.
12.8 Turn left as you intersect CR 371 at a stop sign.
13.3 Pavement begins on CR 371.
15.0 Enter Buena Vista town limits. CR 371 is now N. Colorado Ave.
15.3 Turn left on E. Main St.
15.8 Enter the Buena Vista River Park. There are bathroom facilities and an outside spigot to refill water bottles.

Options: a couple rugged and fun ATV trails parallel this route. Take some time to explore, but expect to share summer weekends with motor sports enthusiasts.

Ride 25: Buena Vista River Road

Want a ride that is fun for the entire family? This is it. This route follows the old Midland Railroad grade along the banks of the Arkansas River and parallels one of the river's most popular whitewater runs, the Narrows. There are no hills and no technical obstacles, so this ride is appropriate for everyone.

During the summer, you're likely to see intrepid boaters on the water and local climbers on the rock outcroppings adjacent to the road. The real highlights of the ride, however, are the old railroad tunnels you'll pass through en route.

Though the tunnels are structurally safe, be sure to yield to auto traffic; it is difficult for drivers to see bikers in the tunnels.

Elevation profile:

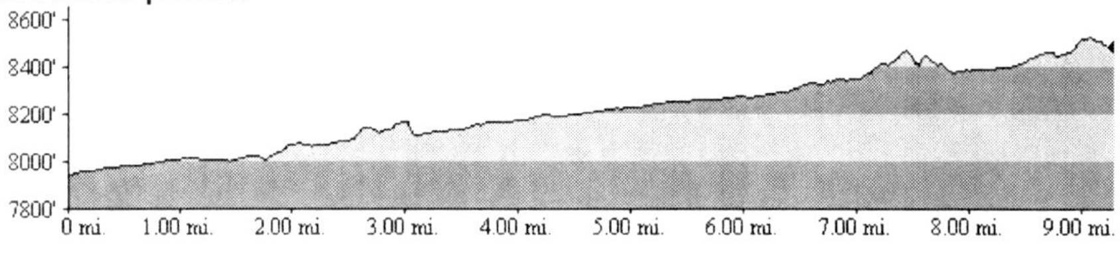

Ride length: 9.3 miles
Ride type: out-and-back
Riding time: 1-2 hours
Surface: dirt road
Elevations: start 7,950'; end 8,490'; max 8,520'; min 7,950'

Total climbing: gain/loss 550'
Aerobic level: easy
Technical level: 1
Season: all year
USGS Quadrangles: Harvard Lakes, Buena Vista West

Trailhead GPS coordinates: 38° 50.573' N; 106° 7.758' W

Getting there: park anywhere in downtown Buena Vista. The ride begins on N. Colorado Ave. at the intersection with E. Main St. (0.2 miles east of the only traffic light in town).

38°54.080' N, 106°09.639' W WGS84

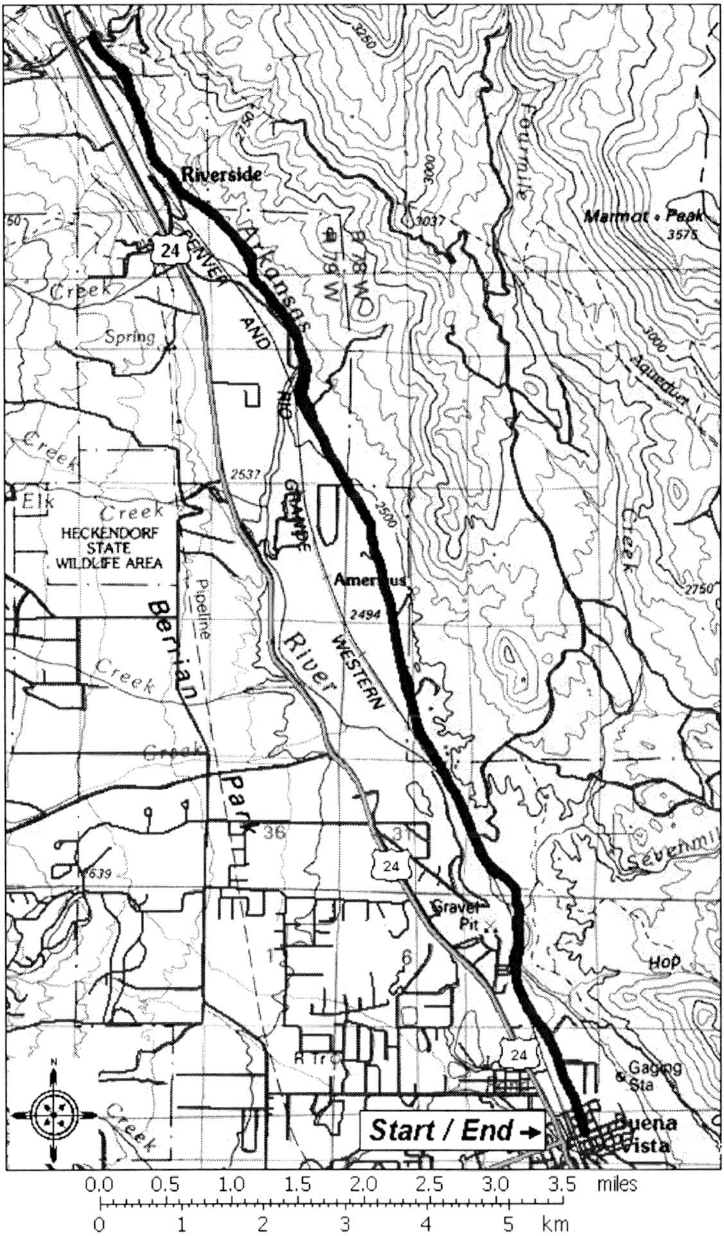

Map 25: Buena Vista River Road (copyright National Geographic)

The ride:

- **0.0** Ride north on N. Colorado Ave. from the intersection with E. Main St.
- **0.3** Buena Vista city limits. N. Colorado Ave. is now CR 371.
- **1.8** Cross a bridge over the river. Stop to watch the boaters pass beneath you. The road surface turns to dirt just after the bridge.
- **2.5** Pass the intersection with CR 375 on your right.
- **2.6** Enter the first tunnel. Watch for traffic!
- **3.0** Pass by two popular rock climbing areas, one (Bob's Rock) immediately on your right, the other (Elephant Rock) just ahead on your left.
- **6.2** Pass the Railroad Bridge recreation area on your left.
- **9.3** The ride ends when CR 371 turns left and crosses the river. Turn around and return the way you came. The return trip is faster and just a little more fun.

Options: if you aren't interested in exploring the entire length of the road, turn around whenever the mood strikes.

CR 375 is an interesting road to investigate, but be aware that it climbs aggressively and may not be suitable for everyone.

Ride 26: Frontier Ranch to South Cottonwood Creek

What could be better than skimming across the forested flanks of Mount Princeton's east slopes? This route, another tasty segment of the Colorado Trail, is probably the best trail in the Buena Vista area.

With the exception of the downhill to South Cottonwood Creek, the route is moderate. There are a few minor rock gardens and a few roots, but the toughest sections are the steep and sharp vertical transitions at the bottoms of seasonal drainage areas.

While the downhill to South Cottonwood Creek is not as smooth as the rest of the trail, strong intermediate cyclists should be able to ride most of it. Conversely, climbing up from the trailhead at CR 344 is not bad; strong intermediates should be able to pedal up 75% of it.

Since the best of this ride is the return ride from about mile 6.1 to the parking area, some may elect to turn around early, skipping the technical descent to CR 344.

Please be aware that FSR 345.2 connecting CR 345 to the trail is no longer open to bikes!

Elevation profile:

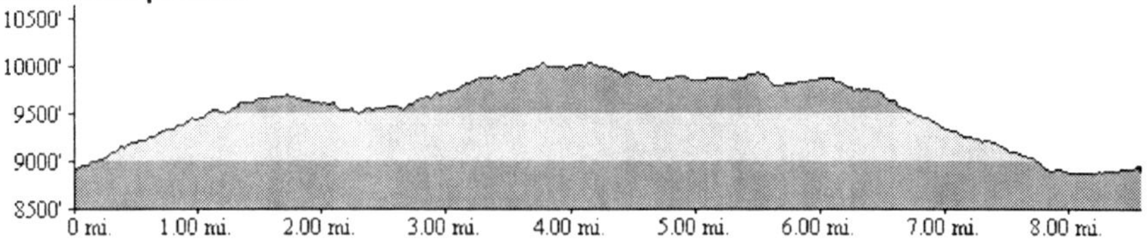

38°46.484' N, 106°12.388' W WGS84

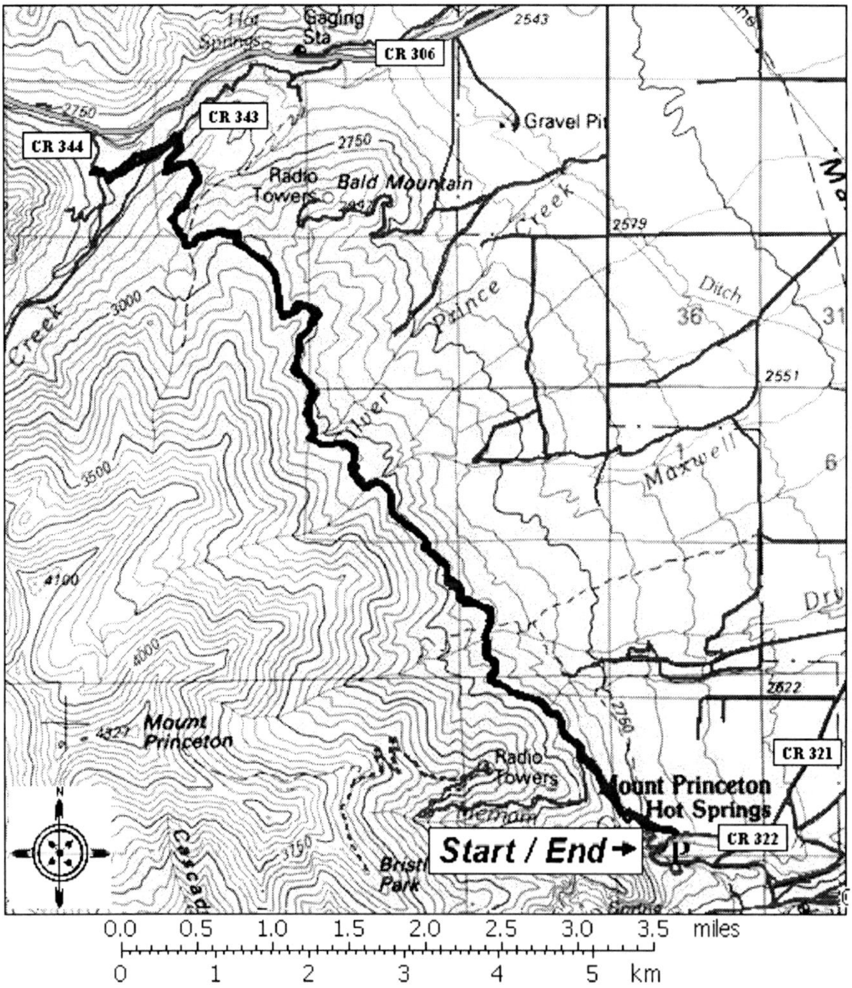

Map 26: Frontier Ranch to South Cottonwood (copyright National Geographic)

Ride length: 16.8 miles
Ride type: out-and-back
Riding time: 3 hours
Surface: single-track (14.6 miles); jeep road (2.2 miles)
Elevations: start/end 8,910'; max 10,030'; min 8,890'

Total climbing: gain/loss 3,100'
Aerobic level: strenuous (climbing)
Technical level: 4 (overall 3 with one steep and technical section)
Season: May through October
USGS Quadrangles: Mt. Antero, Buena Vista West

Trailhead GPS coordinates: 38° 44.391' N; 106° 10.539' W

Getting there: from the intersection of US 24 and Main St. in Buena Vista (the only stoplight in Buena Vista), drive 0.8 miles west on CR 306 to the intersection with CR 321 (Rodeo Road). Turn left on CR 321 and drive 6.8 miles to the intersection with CR 322. Turn right, following the sign to Frontier Ranch, and drive 0.9 miles to the fork. Turn right into the Mt. Princeton parking area. The ride starts from the west end of this parking lot.

The ride:

0.0 Head west and ride out of the parking lot. Take the right fork and start pedaling uphill.

0.4 Stay right through the switchback and stay on the main road. Do not cross the chained gate on the left.

1.1 Turn right onto the Colorado Trail singe-track. Let the fun begin.

2.2 Stream crossing.

2.4 Stay on the main trail, passing between two cairns. (*A faint trail heads east-west across the main trail.*)

3.5 Stream crossing.

6.1 Start the descent to Cottonwood Creek and CR 344. ***Note-*** *this is a good tum-around spot for those wishing to skip the climb back up from the creek and trailhead.*

8.0 Cross CR 343 and continue descending on the Colorado Trail single-track.

8.3 Cross South Cottonwood Creek on a good bridge.

8.4 South Cottonwood Trailhead parking area and CR 344. Turn around and return the way you came. Yee-haw!

Options: if you elect to ride this as a one-way with auto shuttles, I suggest starting at the South Cottonwood Trailhead and riding south to Frontier Ranch. This option puts the bulk of the hard work at the start of the ride and rewards you with an awesome romp on excellent single-track from the highpoint almost all the way to Frontier Ranch.

Leave a vehicle at Frontier Ranch and take the riders/bikes to the South Cottonwood Trailhead. From the intersection of US 24 and Main St. in Buena Vista, drive 6.8 miles west on CR 306 to the intersection with CR 344. Turn left on CR 344, drive about 0.25 miles; look for the small parking area on the left and Colorado Trail markers. The ride starts at the South Cottonwood Trail sign on the trail, about 30 yards southeast of the parking area.

Buena Vista River Park

Nathrop

The main draw to Nathrop has always been the natural hot springs that bubble up along the banks of Chalk Creek. The most popular, Mt. Princeton Hot Springs, features two large developed pools with decks as well as several primitive pools right at the edge of the creek.

In addition to the hot springs, Nathrop is the gateway to two popular Fourteeners: Mount Princeton (14,197') and Mount Antero (14,269'). Several US Forest Service campgrounds along the creek make it easy for you to get a dawn start for your attempts at their summits.

As for mountain biking, two of the Arkansas Valley's easiest rides are in this area. The Raspberry Gulch Loop is a short and smooth single-track loop that is ideal for beginners. The Cascade Railroad Grade is another easy route that is close to the hot springs and perfect for families.

Hammerheads will enjoy riding above the clouds on the Mount Princeton Road. This strenuous route runs from the Frontier Ranch to the shelter above tree line in Bristlecone Park (elev. 12,120'). To add a little extra challenge, some hardcore locals will ride their bikes to the end of the road then hike to the summit of Mt. Princeton, a stiff challenge for anyone.

Ride up and touch the sky- Mt. Princeton Road

Nathrop is also home to Yeti RPM Developmental Racing, hosts of the Chalk Creek Stampede mountain bike race. This annual event held on Yeti RPM's private courses, features dual slalom, mountain cross, and cross-country events. The race is a popular stage of the Mountain States Cup Championship race series and competitors appreciate the first-rate, spectator-friendly courses designed specifically for racing.

Ride 27: Mt. Princeton Road

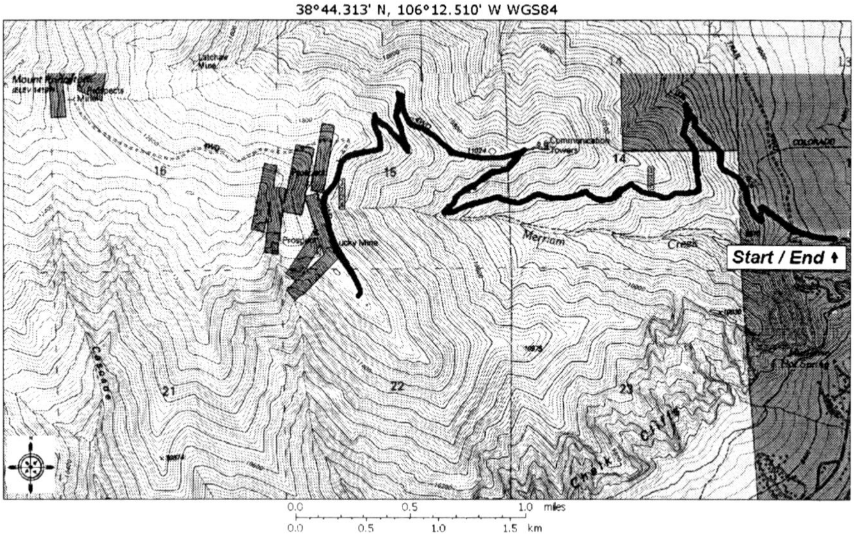

Map 27: Mt. Princeton Road (copyright National Geographic)

You feel strong and relish the challenge of a tough climb. Here's a good one.

This demanding route will take you above the trees on one of Colorado's most striking Fourteeners. Dominating Buena Vista's southwestern horizon, Mount Princeton (14,197') towers more than six thousand feet above the valley floor and serves as the dominant iconic feature of the area. Riding to the top of this road gives you an unrivaled appreciation of the sheer size of this commanding peak.

Elevation profile:

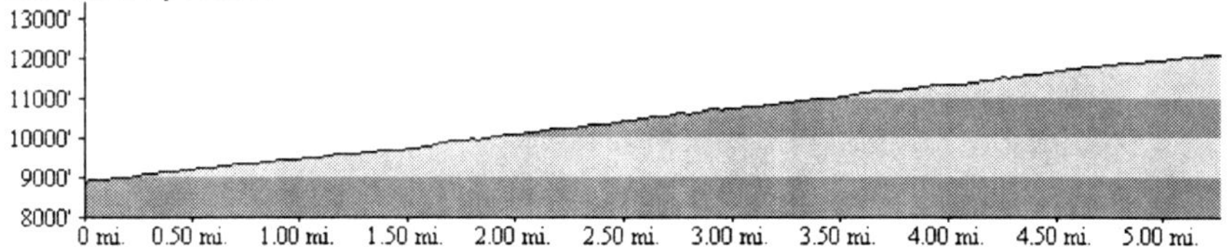

Ride length: 10.6 miles
Ride type: out-and-back
Riding time: 2 hours
Surface: jeep road
Elevations: start/end 8,910'; max 12,100'; min 8,910'
Total climbing: gain/loss 3,170'

Aerobic level: strenuous (climbing at altitude)
Technical level: 3+ (when you're sucking wind this hard, everything feels tough; fast descent over eroded, rocky terrain)
Season: June through October
USGS Quadrangles: Mt. Antero

Trailhead GPS coordinates: 38° 44.399' N; 106° 10.546' W

Getting there: from the intersection of US 24 and Main St. in Buena Vista (the only stoplight in Buena Vista), drive 0.8 miles west on CR 306 to the intersection with CR 321 (Rodeo Road). Turn left onto CR 321 and drive 6.8 miles to the intersection with CR 322. Turn right, following the sign to Frontier Ranch, and drive 0.9 miles to the fork. Turn right into the Mt. Princeton parking area. The ride starts from the west side of the parking lot.

The ride:

- **0.0** Head west and ride out of the parking lot. Take a right at the fork and start pedaling uphill.
- **0.4** Stay right through the switchback and stay on the main road. Do not cross the chained gate on the left.
- **1.1** Bear left, staying on the main road. (*The Colorado Trail singe-track heads right.*)
- **3.1** Turn left on FSR 322A. Communication towers are on your right.
- **4.6** The Mount Princeton summit trail is on the right. ***Note-*** *if you have some extra wind, why not summit the mountain? It's a 6-mile hike gaining/losing 3,200'. Stash your bikes and go for it.*
- **5.2** The road ends at a small parking lot. The Young Life hut is about 50 yards due south of the parking area. Scramble up the short hill to the Cross at the Mount Antero overlook. Look east to the valley for great views of Ruby Mountain and the Fourmile recreation area. When your heart rate and breathing return to acceptable levels, head back down the way you came.

Options: persuasive hedonists may be able to find someone willing to shuttle them to the top. If that's you, breakout your favorite downhill or all-mountain rig and let it rip. The first couple of miles of the descent are fast, chunky and loose, but those with the appropriate skills and nerve will eat it up. (*You need a high-clearance vehicle to make the drive to the top.*)

Colorado Trail- Raspberry Gulch

Ride 28: Raspberry Gulch Loop

38°41.801' N, 106°10.015' W WGS84

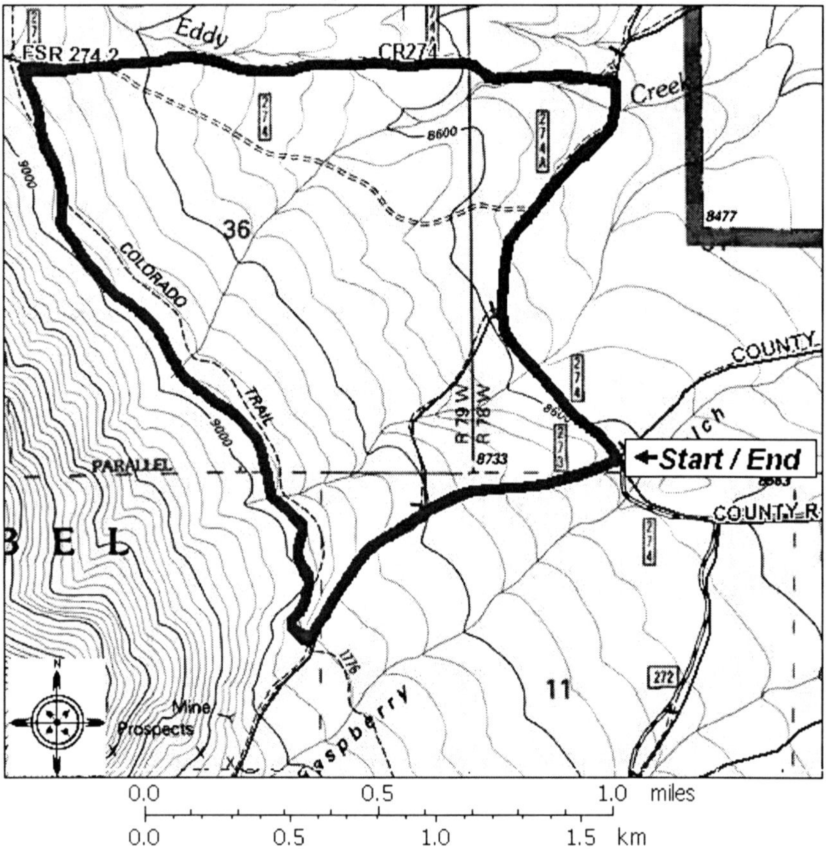

Map 28: Raspberry Gulch Loop (copyright National Geographic)

You are in the area with a friend, lover, or spouse who is new to riding and you want to introduce them to the joys of single-track. Where should you go?

This loop, incorporating a small, smooth section of the Colorado Trail in Raspberry Gulch, is the perfect place. The route provides a gentle, entry-level glimpse into the very best mountain biking has to offer. You'll roll into spectacular scenery on skinny single-track without any pain-inducing climbs, white-knuckled steeps, or brain-rattling rocks.

A gradual climb on a jeep road leads to a slightly steeper climb on single-track. Once at the top, the trail rolls through open meadows with sensational views of Mount Princeton's south slopes and the Chalk Cliffs. Once back on the road, you'll be treated a fun downhill on a double-track jeep trail. A gentle climb (gaining only 150' in under 1 mile) returns you to your vehicle.

There are a few established primitive campsites (free/no facilities) in the area, making this an excellent ride to start or end your day.

Elevation profile:

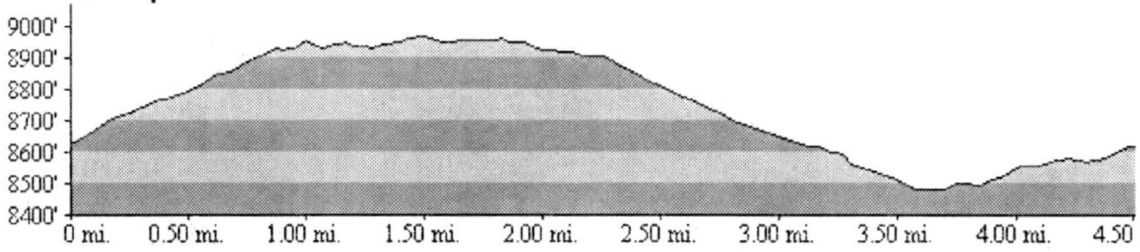

Ride length: 4.5 miles
Ride type: loop (clockwise)
Riding time: 1 hour (or less)
Surface: single-track (1.5 miles); jeep trail/double-track (3.0 miles)
Elevations: start/end 8,625'; max 8,970'; min 8,480'

Total climbing: gain/loss 490'
Aerobic level: easy (two small climbs)
Technical level: 2 (a little sand and a few rocks on the downhill)
Season: May through October
USGS Quadrangles: Mount Antero

Trailhead GPS coordinates: 38° 41.684' N; 106° 9.528' W

Getting there: from the junction of US 24/285 (2.4 miles south of Buena Vista), drive 8.9 miles south on US 285 to the intersection with CR 270. Turn right on CR 270 and drive 1.6 miles west to the intersection with CR 272. Continue straight on CR 272 (dirt) and drive 2.0 miles west to the intersection with FSR 274. Continue straight (west/northwest) on FSR 274 until you reach the intersection with FSR 273 on your left in 0.3 miles. Park in the pullout across from FSR 273. The ride starts at your vehicle.

The ride:

0.0 Ride uphill (southwest) on FSR 273.
0.8 Turn right onto the Colorado Trail single-track. The trail crosses the road just after you pass a small clearing and campsite on your right. Several trail markers on both sides of the road will help you find this intersection.
0.9 Reach the top of the toughest climb of the ride.
1.2 The transition at the bottom of the downhill is a little tricky.
1.8 Enter an open meadow with incredible views of Mount Princeton.
2.3 Turn right on FSR 274. Watch your speed as you approach FSR 274A in just over 0.1 miles!
2.4 Bear left at the fork with FSR 274A. You might encounter a little sand.
2.5 A few rocks, but nothing serious.
3.2 A slightly tricky section ahead! The route descends and twists over some ruts and rocks.
4.0 Turn left at the "T" intersection with FSR 274. A small climb awaits you.
4.5 Arrive back at your vehicle.

Options: extend your ride by exploring the Colorado Trail south of FSR 273 and north of FSR 274. Heading south, the trail gets somewhat technical and slightly strenuous beginning about 1.6 miles south of FSR 273. From that point, you'll encounter more than 1.5 miles of steady climbing through very rocky terrain before the trail settles into a smooth groove on the approach to Fourmile Creek.

North of FSR 274, the trail climbs steadily for 2.0 miles to the top of a very steep and extremely technical downhill leading to the Chalk Cliffs Trailhead.

Ride 29: Cascade Railroad Grade

38°42.530' N, 106°13.369' W WGS84

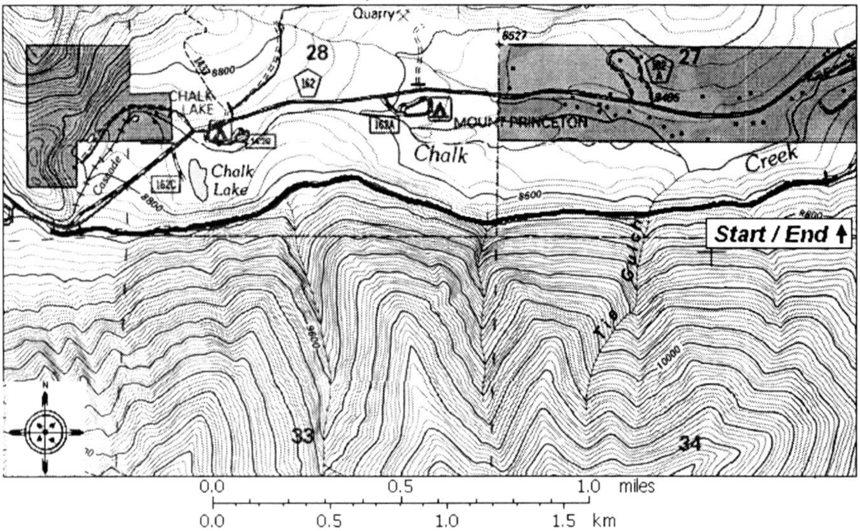

Map 29: Cascade Rail Grade (copyright National Geographic)

This gentle path, a former stretch of the Denver, South Park and Pacific Railroad grade, is an easy and scenic outing through the valley separating two massive mountains: Mount Princeton (north) and Mount Antero (south).

Suitable for riders of all abilities, this is a perfect ride for the whole family. The views of the Chalk Cliffs are majestic and, if you know where to look, you will see the false summit of Mount Princeton.

It may not be possible to get a kid carrier/trailer past the gates at either end of the trail. In addition, you'll need to lift your bike over a small barrier at the entrance gate.

Elevation profile:

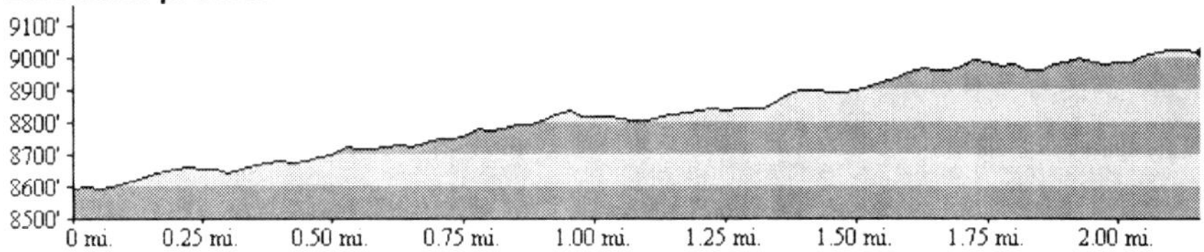

Ride length: 4.4 miles
Ride type: out-and-back
Riding time: 1 hour
Surface: wide dirt path
Elevations: start 8,600'; end 9,010'; max 9,030'; min 8,590'

Total climbing: gain/loss 490'
Aerobic level: easy
Technical level: 2- (some sand and brief rocky sections)
Season: May through October
USGS Quadrangles: Mount Antero

Trailhead GPS coordinates: 38° 42.671' N; 106° 12.168' W

Getting there: from the junction of US 24/285 (2.4 miles south of Buena Vista), drive 5.5 miles south on US 285 to the intersection with CR 162. Turn right and drive 5.6 miles west on CR 162 to the intersection with CR 189/190. Turn left on CR 189/190 and drive 0.2 miles to where CR 189 forks left from CR 190. Stay right on CR 190 and drive 1.4 miles to the parking area at the end of the road. The ride starts at your vehicle.

The ride:

- **0.0** From your vehicle, ride west 50 yards to the gate at the trailhead. You'll have to lift your bicycle over a low bar at the gate.
- **0.3** Look right at the Chalk Cliffs. Take note of the eroded sections where wind and water have hollowed shallow caves in the rock face. One interesting fact about this formation is that the cliffs are not comprised of chalk but of clay formed by geothermic water.
- **1.1** Encounter a rocky obstacle that may require you to dismount and push. Look up and to the right to catch a glimpse of Mount Princeton's false summit. Many hikers spend an hour working toward this goal only to find that the actual summit is still a fair distance beyond this prominent feature.
- **1.3** Pedal hard as you ride through approximately 10 yards of shallow sand. Dismount and push if you are uncomfortable riding through it.
- **1.4** Cross an old wooden bridge. Will it hold? Continue for another 50 yards and cross a stream. ***Hint-*** *look left for a footbridge if you don't want to get your feet wet.*
- **1.6** Cross a short rocky section of trail. Dismount if you have any doubts.
- **1.7** Look down. That's Chalk Lake, a popular fishing area, at the bottom of a steep talus slope.
- **2.0** Dismount to push your bike across about 50 feet of avalanche debris. Look around and take note of the broken trees and rocks that fill the gulch both above and below the trail. Imagine the power it took to sweep this much junk down the mountain.
- **2.1** Look across at the Cascade Falls of Chalk Creek.
- **2.2** After crossing the gate, the trail ends at CR 162. Turn around and enjoy an easy coast almost all the way back to the start of this ride.

Options: there are many ways to extend this ride. Use your imagination to add miles using CR 162, CR 189, or CR 190. Watch for traffic on these roads, especially on weekends. Please be aware that much of the land along these county roads is private. Respect area residents by parking only in designated public parking areas.

St. Elmo

Widely considered the best-preserved ghost town in Colorado, St. Elmo was founded as an outpost for the Mary Murphy and other mines in the area. Even though the founders strove to maintain unusually high moral standards for the town, the effort collapsed as the population swelled with young, single men drawn to the mines. The once orderly settlement quickly devolved into a place bustling with saloons, dance halls, and shady dens of an unsavory trade.

St. Elmo is unique because most of the buildings were well preserved and have not undergone major restoration efforts. In 2002, the St. Elmo schoolhouse and the site of the old town hall were donated to the Buena Vista Heritage Museum, and the recently renovated Schoolhouse Museum is now open for viewing during the summer.

Allie Belle Mine

The Alpine Tunnel, the first railroad tunnel built through the Continental Divide, opened rail passage between Denver and Gunnison via the Denver, South Park and Pacific Railroads. Taking almost eighteen months longer to construct than originally planned, the tunnel eventually opened in 1882. Unfortunately, a collapse in 1910 permanently closed it; by then the mining yields ebbed and the line deemed irrelevant because it didn't extend beyond Gunnison.

Today, the old railroad grade and ghost town provide an excellent setting for mountain bike adventures. Moreover, the section of the Continental Divide Trail leading to the tunnel's East Portal is one of the most scenic and popular rides in the area.

Ride 30: Alpine Tunnel

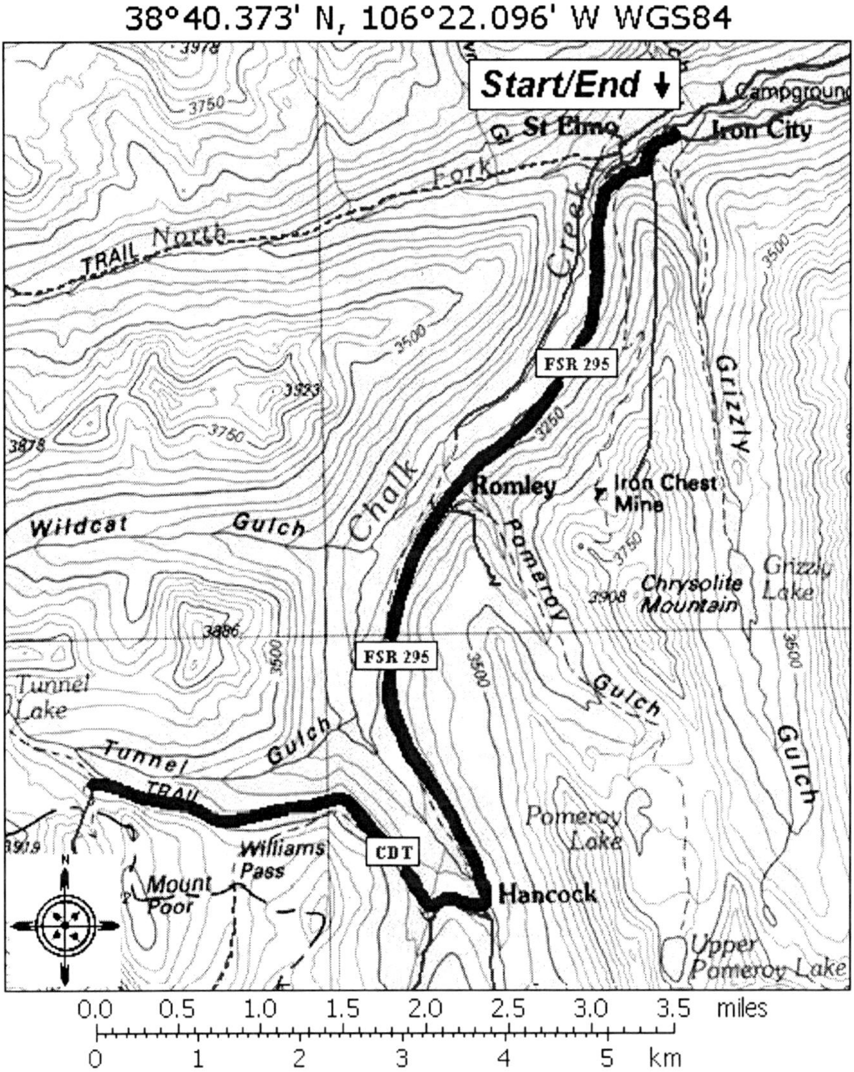

Map 30: Alpine Tunnel (copyright National Geographic)

This classic is suitable for most cyclists. It starts with a steady climb on FSR 295 to the Hancock town site. Along the way, you'll pass several mine sites as you work your toward the ghost town of Hancock. From there, you'll hop on the Continental Divide Trail (CDT) to the Alpine Tunnel East Portal. Some sections of the CDT are a bit bumpy as you roll over old railroad ties, but most novice riders should be able to pedal the lumps. The alpine valley of Tunnel Gulch is so spectacular that even the most hardened hammerhead will stop to take notice.

This is a popular area for ATVs, jeeps, and motorcycles. Be prepared to share the road on the way to the CDT, especially on the weekends.

Elevation profile:

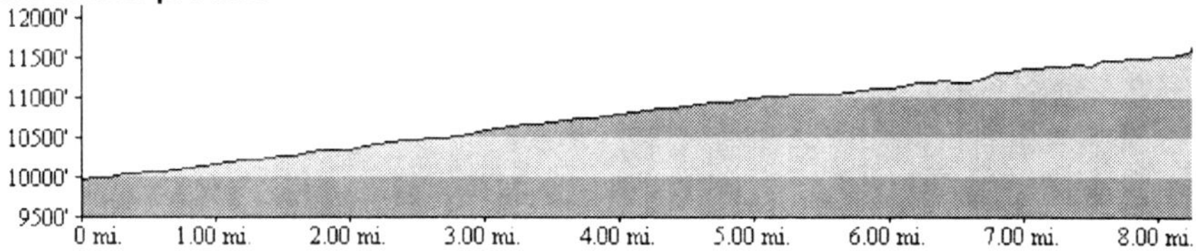

Ride length: 16.6 miles
Ride type: out-and-back
Riding time: 2 hours
Surface: jeep road (10.6 miles); wide trail (6.0 miles)
Elevations: start/end 9,980'; max 11,630'; min 9,980'
Total climbing: gain/loss 1,650'

Aerobic level: easy (mostly mid-ring; drop into the granny if altitude leaves you winded)
Technical level: 2+ (a few bumps and rocks; be careful on the downhill)
Season: July into October
USGS Quadrangles: St. Elmo, Cumberland Pass

Trailhead GPS coordinates: 38° 42.352' N; 106° 20.404' W

Getting there: from the intersection of US 285/24 (2.4 miles south of Buena Vista), drive 5.5 miles south on US 285 to the intersection with CR 162. Turn right on CR 162 and drive 15.4 miles west to the parking area on the left, just east of FSR 295. If this area is full, continue driving 0.5 miles west on CR 162 to the St. Elmo town site where parking is usually abundant. The ride starts at the intersection of CR 162 and FSR 295.

The ride:

0.0 At the intersection of CR 162 and FSR 295, ride up (southwest) FSR 295. Follow the sign to the Alpine Tunnel TR.

2.4 Bear right, staying on FSR 295.

2.6 After a slightly rough uphill, continue straight on FSR 295. ***Note-*** *the left, FSR 297.1, heads to the Mary Murphy Mine and Pomeroy Lake.*

4.3 Pass the Allie Belle Mine. The structure closest to the road appears to defy the laws of physics as it sits suspended over the road. Don't sneeze!

5.0 Enter the former Hancock town site.

5.1 Cross a bridge and bear right, following the signs to the Alpine Tunnel trailhead. (*Left leads to Hancock Pass.*)

5.2 Continue straight and ride toward the gate. Pass to the right of the gate.

5.3 Stop and sign the trail register on the right. You are now riding on the Continental Divide Trail (CDT).

5.5 Arrive at the interpretive history sign for the infamous Sawmill Curve. After riding through the tricky drop, stay right on the trail. (*On your left is the Williams Pass Road.*)

6.1 Another interpretive sign. ***Note-*** *if you stop to read the sign, look across the valley for the mine sites you passed on your approach to Hancock and the trailhead.*

7.4 Enjoy the postcard-perfect alpine valley to the right.

8.3 Leave the bike at the trail intersection and hike to the Alpine Tunnel East Portal. The tunnel entrance collapsed long ago, but a little imagination is all it takes to see it as it once was. Turn around and return along the same route. ***Note-*** *the CDT continues by climbing steeply on your left. It's possible to traverse the Divide to view the West Portal and historic train buildings on the other side, but getting bikes up the formidable grade of the trail isn't easy.*

Options: skip the ride up FSR 295 and park at the trailhead in Hancock. It'll be a short ride, but you'll avoid some jeep and ATV traffic on FSR 295.

Ride 31: Alpine Tunnel to Tin Cup Pass Road Loop

38°40.426' N, 106°23.473' W WGS84

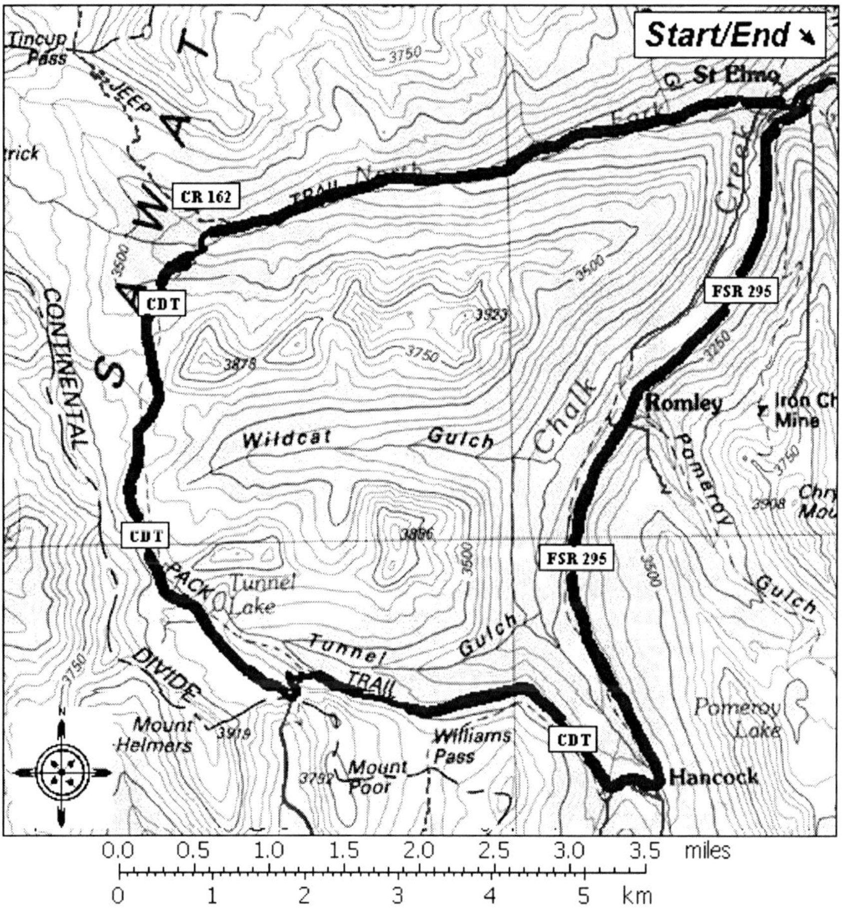

Map 31: Alpine Tunnel to Tin Cup Pass Road (copyright National Geographic)

To appreciate this ride more, think of it as two-thirds mountain biking and one-third adventure. Though there will be more hike-a-bike than you probably like, traversing the seldom-accessed span of the Continental Divide Trail to Tunnel Lake is a unique experience that few will know. Best of all, the reward for your effort, the descent through the pines, is solid gold.

It starts with an easy, scenic pedal up to the Alpine Tunnel. Along the way, you'll pass historic mining sites, interpretive signs, and stunning views of Tunnel Gulch. As you start the climb above the tunnel, however, the fun really begins. The next few miles will be a mix of hike-a-bike, route finding, and classic single-track riding. Once you pass the last ridge, the single-track downhill is pure bliss. End by zipping back to St. Elmo along the Tin Cup Pass Road, a rough jeep track with fast lines between the rocks.

This is a popular area for ATVs, jeeps, and motorcycles. Be prepared to share the road.

Elevation profile:

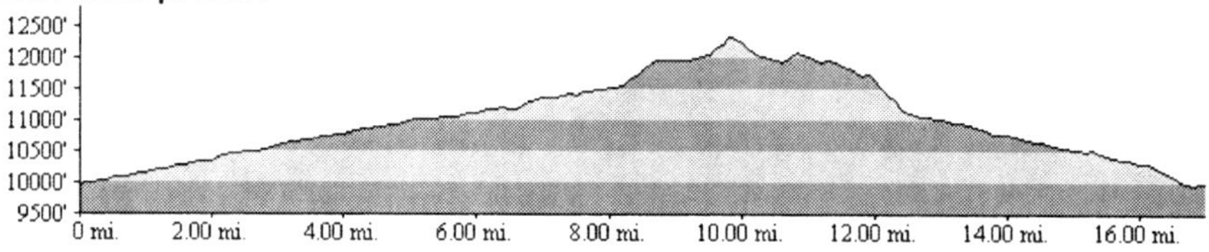

Ride length: 17.3 miles
Ride type: loop (clockwise)
Riding time: 3 hours
Surface: jeep road (9.9 miles); single-track (4.4 miles); wide trail (3.0 miles)
Elevations: start/end 9,980'; max 12,340'; min 9,980'
Total climbing: gain/loss 2,500'

Aerobic level: moderate (the climbs you will ride are easy, the rest you'll probably walk; if you can clean the steeps, then everything is easy for you!)
Technical level: 4 (some rocks, ruts, and roots; expect some walking)
Season: July into October
USGS Quadrangles: St. Elmo, Cumberland Pass

Trailhead GPS coordinates: 38° 42.352' N; 106° 20.404' W

Getting there: from the intersection of US 285/24 (2.4 miles south of Buena Vista), drive 5.5 miles south on US 285 to the intersection with CR 162. Turn right on CR 162 and drive 15.4 miles west to the parking area on the left, just east of FSR 295. If this area is full, continue driving 0.5 miles west on CR 162 to the St. Elmo town site where parking is usually abundant. The ride starts at the intersection of CR 162 and FSR 295.

The ride:

0.0 At the intersection of CR 162 and FSR 295, ride up (southwest) FSR 295. Follow the sign to the Alpine Tunnel TR.

2.4 Bear right and stay on FSR 295.

2.6 After a slightly rough uphill, continue straight on FSR 295. ***Note-*** *the left, FSR 297.1, heads to Mary Murphy Mine and Pomeroy Lake.*

4.3 Pass the Allie Belle Mine. The structure closest to the road appears to defy the laws of physics as it sits suspended over the road. Don't sneeze!

5.0 Enter the former Hancock town site.

5.1 Cross a bridge and bear right, following the signs to the Alpine Tunnel trailhead. (*Left leads to Hancock Pass.*)

5.2 Continue straight and ride toward the gate. Pass to the right of the gate.

5.3 Stop and sign the trail register on the right. You are now riding on the Continental Divide Trail (CDT).

5.5 Arrive at the interpretive history sign for the infamous Sawmill Curve. After riding the tricky dip at the curve site, stay right, passing Williams Pass Road on your left.

6.1 Another interpretive sign. ***Note-*** *look across the valley for the crumbling mine sites you passed on your approach to Hancock and the trailhead.*

7.4 Enjoy the picture-perfect alpine and sub-alpine valley to the right. ***Note-*** *this route eventually crosses the ridge at the western end of the valley.*

8.3 Turn left and climb the burly grade of the CDT. A sign marks the way. If you can ride it cleanly, consider turning pro. Do your best and walk the rest.

8.6 Turn right at the sign, following the CDT to the Tunnel Lake. (*Straight leads to the Alpine Tunnel West Portal.*)

8.8 The next 0.5 miles are classic alpine single-track. Ride it!

9.4 Arrive at Tunnel Lake. This portion of the trail sees little use and route finding may prove difficult. Watch for cairns and follow the sometimes-faint line that meanders toward the ridge to the north.

9.8 Top-out on the big ridge. The trail is now very faint. Look for cairns and take your time.

10.8 Top-out on the next ridge.

11.3 The quality of the trail improves dramatically from this point forward. Get ready for some classic fat-tire fun. (*Tin Cup Pass Road is now visible in the distance.*)

11.8 Enter the pines. Let it rip! Single-track does not get much better than this!

12.4 Wow! Was that excellent or what? Cross some cool little bridges.

12.5 Stay right, passing small single-track spurs on the left.

12.7 Merge onto the Tin Cup Pass Road. Turn right and stay on this road until you reach the St. Elmo town site. Fast and fun here, but watch for traffic.

16.7 Pass the Poplar Gulch trailhead on your left.

16.8 Enter St. Elmo. Continue straight.

16.9 Turn right and cross the bridge. Turn left on the main street of St. Elmo.

17.3 Arrive back at your car. A soak in a hot spring would be nice.

Poncha Springs

Often referred to as the "Crossroads of the Rockies," Poncha Springs is the gateway to some of the Arkansas Valley's hottest mountain biking. While known to most as simply a shuttle point for the Monarch Crest rides, its close proximity to both the Rainbow Trail and Colorado Trail makes it a noteworthy mountain biking destination of its own.

Originally called *Poncho* Springs, Poncho being the Spanish word for "cape," the town acquired its name from its proximity to nearby hot springs. While historians debate whether Kit Carson or Zebulon Pike was the first US citizen to bathe in those springs, Chief Shavano discovered the healing powers of the waters long before any white men set foot in the region.

In an interesting turn of events, a 1935 WPA project capped the town's namesake hot springs and diverted the water to Salida. You can access the site of the former hot springs by riding up CR 115 from the center of town. The area is now a Scout Camp, but the ride is an interesting diversion to a few historic buildings that serve as a reminder of the site's former glory.

As for riding, the Rainbow Trail intersects US 285 about five miles south of town. West of the highway, the trail is fast and smooth with at least two primary riding options. *A little exploration and imagination always yields more!* On the east side, the trail climbs aggressively and is probably more fun ridden from east to west.

The Colorado Trail intersects US 50 less than nine miles west of town and offers an amazing twenty-mile stretch of single-track that runs north all the way to Nathrop. The south side is a fun out-and-back through lush forest.

Silver Creek aspens

So, as the old song says, head down to the Crossroads, but don't fall down on your knees. Just hammer away and don't let anyone pass you by.

Ride 32: Colorado Trail: US 50 to Chalk Creek

38°37.847' N, 106°12.711' W WGS84

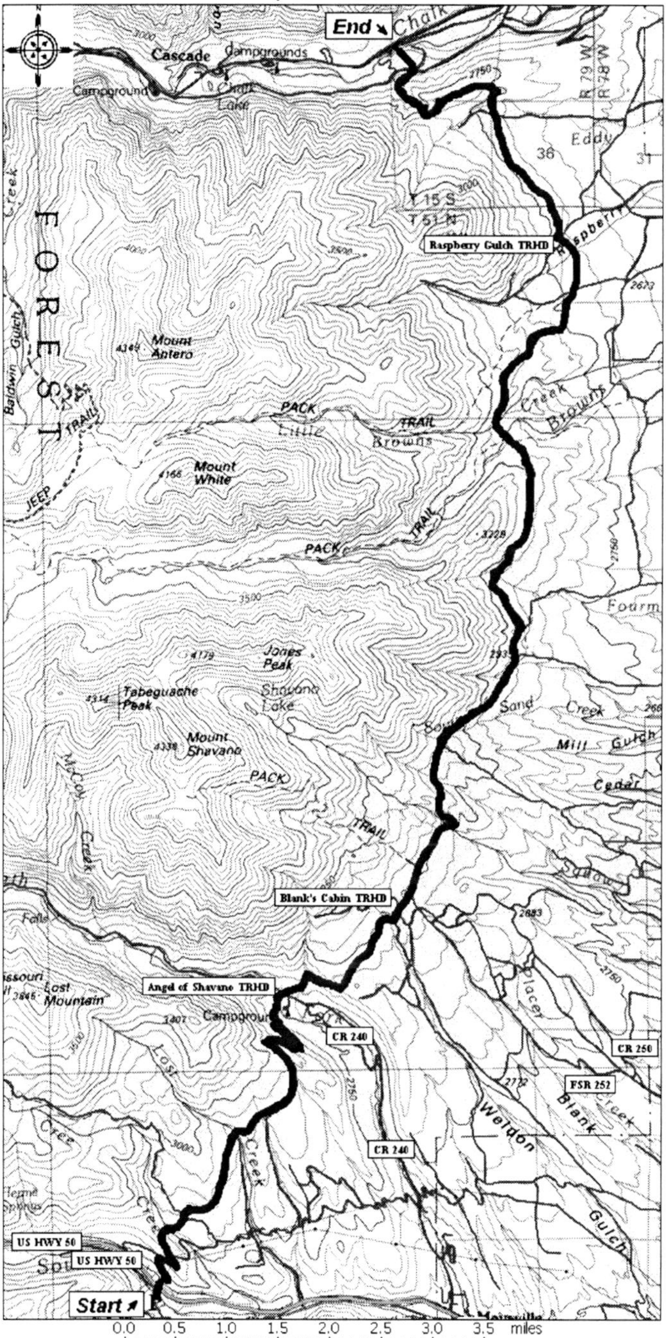

Map 32: US 50 to Chalk Creek (copyright National Geographic)

Well, if you are going to go, go big. After a couple months of recon riding this segment of the Colorado Trail, I feel the best way to access these somewhat remote, yet very sweet single-track lines is to sweep the whole thing from south to north. You will work a little for it, but the reward is one of the valley's longest stretches of continuous single-track.

The ride begins with a stiff climb up from US 50 and ends with an insanely steep, technical descent to the Chalk Creek Trailhead. In between is an endless roller coaster of sometimes smooth, sometimes technical, trail through deep stands of aspen and pine.

So, pack a lunch, bring plenty of water, and go for it!

Please be aware that this ride is physically strenuous with few bailout points.

Elevation profile:

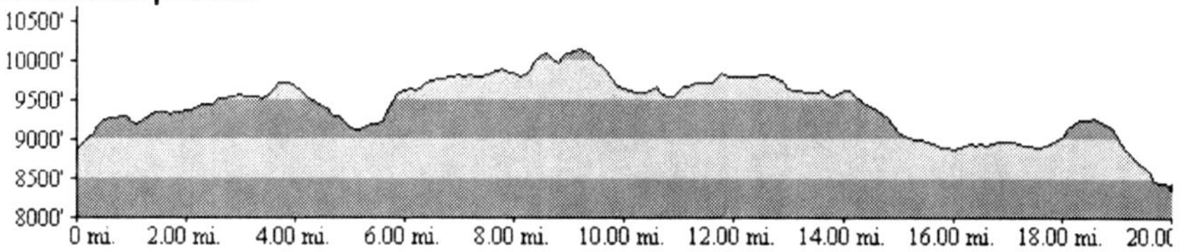

Ride length: 20.1 miles
Ride type: one-way with shuttle
Riding time: 4 hours
Surface: single-track
Elevations: start 8,870'; max 10,160'; min 8,390'; end 8,390'
Total climbing: gain 3,130' - loss 3,600' = total -470'

Aerobic level: strenuous (long ride with lots of ups and downs)
Technical level: 4 (steeps with rocks; the final descent is a 5)
Season: June through October
USGS Quadrangles: Maysville, Mount Antero

Trailhead GPS coordinates: 38° 32.625' N; 106° 14.573' W

Getting there: leave a drop vehicle at the Chalk Creek Trailhead. From the intersection of US 24/285 (2.4 miles south of Buena Vista), drive 5.5 miles south on US 285 to the intersection with CR 162. Turn right and drive 6.8 miles west on CR 162 to the intersection with CR 291. Turn left on CR 291 and drive about 50 yards to the trailhead and parking area.

Take the riders and bikes to the trailhead on US 50. From the intersection of US 50 and US 285 (where US 285 joins US 50 from the north), drive 9.2 miles west on US 50 to the intersection with CR 225. There is a large pullout on the left (south) side of the highway at the intersection. Park there. The ride begins at your vehicle.

The ride:

- **0.0** Carefully cross the highway and look for the Colorado Trail marker at the start of the single-track. Start climbing. In about 100 yards, the trail crosses a double-track and continues climbing.
- **0.5** Turn right (east) and continue climbing up on the double-track.
- **0.8** Pass under the steel power tower and continue riding straight along the single-track into the pines. (*A double-track spur heads east.*)

1.1 Cross a small stream on a log bridge.
1.4 Cross a dirt road and continue riding the single-track line on the other side.
1.5 After riding clockwise around a meadow, join a double track and ride east for about 20 yards. Look left for the single-track and the Colorado Trail marker about eight feet up on a pine tree. Head left on the single-track.
2.4 Cross an old jeep track and continue along the single-track through the aspen.
2.6 Enter a new growth forest and enjoy the view.
3.8 Get ready for a nice downhill. Watch for lateral erosion, rocks, and downed trees.
5.1 Cross a stream on a good bridge, then head left on the main trail along the fence line. (*A small single-track line scoots right.*)
5.3 Cross CR 240 and continue on the single-track. The intersection is signed and well marked.
5.4 Arrive at the Angel of Shavano Trailhead. Continue riding along the trail as it skirts the parking area. Please register at the trailhead. Brace for a steep climb. ***Note-*** *to avoid the steep climb up from US 50, you may want to start the ride here. Maysville and US 50 are approximately four miles downhill on CR 240.*
6.0 The trail levels a bit and the crux of this climb is now history.
6.9 Cross a jeep track and continue on the single-track.
7.3 Continue straight as you pass a single-track spur on your right. Ride parallel to the timber fence. ***Note-*** *this spur leads to the Shavano/Tabeguache trailhead at Blank's Cabin. This is another possible shuttle point for this ride.*
7.7 Continue straight on the Colorado trail as the Shavano/Tabeguache hiking trail peels off to the left (west).
8.0 A Colorado Trail sign provides some useful info. Ride ahead for another fifty yards then sign the trail register.
8.6 Yet another steep climb is now behind you.
10.5 Stay on the single-track as you pass a jeep trail on the right.
13.2 Continue straight on the Colorado Trail as the Wagon Loop Trail intersects and joins this route from the right.
13.5 Cross Browns Creek on a nice bridge.
13.6 Cross another bridge.
13.7 Turn right at the "T", following the Colorado Trail. (*The Browns Creek trail heads left.*)
13.9 Head left and uphill at the fork. The trail is very rocky here.
14.2 Turn right at the "T" as the Little Browns Creek Trail (#1430) heads left.
15.5 Cross the double-track. This is fun!
15.9 A small water crossing in the heart of Raspberry Gulch.
16.1 Cross FSR 273 (unmarked). Continue on the single-track as it begins to climb a ridge. ***Note-*** *this is an alternate place to end to this ride if you want to avoid the gnarly downhill to Chalk Creek. Leave your shuttle at the bottom of FSR 273.*
17.6 Cross FSR 274 and continue on the single-track.
17.9 Stay left on the main trail. Look for a Colorado Trail marker for assistance.
18.6 Here it is... are you ready? Hold on through a steep, loose, and extremely technical downhill. If in doubt, walk.
19.7 Turn right (east) on CR 290. Ride about 30 yards and look left for the

Colorado Trail single-track just shy of gated CR 290A. Look for the Colorado Trail marker.

20.0 Pass the Bootleg Campsite spur on your right.

20.1 Cross the bridge and arrive at the Chalk Creek Trailhead.

Options: there are two additional starting points for this ride. The first, avoiding the strenuous climb up from US 50, starts at the Angel of Shavano Trailhead. To get there, from the intersection of US 285 and US 50 (from US 285 north), drive 6.2 miles west on US 50 to CR 240. Turn right on CR 240 and drive 3.8 miles to the trailhead.

To start this ride from the Blank's Cabin Trailhead: from the intersection of US 285 and US 50 (from US 285), drive approximately 2.3 miles west on US 50 to the intersection with CR 250. Turn right on CR 250 and drive 4.7 miles on CR 250 to the junction with CR 252. Bear left, following the sign to the Shavano/Tabeguache trailhead, and drive 2.9 miles to the trailhead parking area. Start the ride on the Shavano/Tabeguache trail; it joins the Colorado Trail in about 0.1 miles.

Riding the final descent to Chalk Creek is strictly for experts. To avoid this section, end the ride at Raspberry Gulch. To leave a car here, drive to the intersection of CR 270 and US 285 (about 3 miles south of Nathrop). Drive 1.5 miles west on CR 270 to the intersection with CR 272. Drive 2.1 miles west on CR 272 to the intersection with CR/FSR 274. Drive 0.4 miles northwest on CR/FSR 274 to the intersection with FSR 273. Park at the right side of the intersection. The Colorado Trail crosses FSR 273 about 0.8 miles southwest (uphill) from this intersection.

A true classic

Ride 33: Marshall Pass to Silver Creek Loop

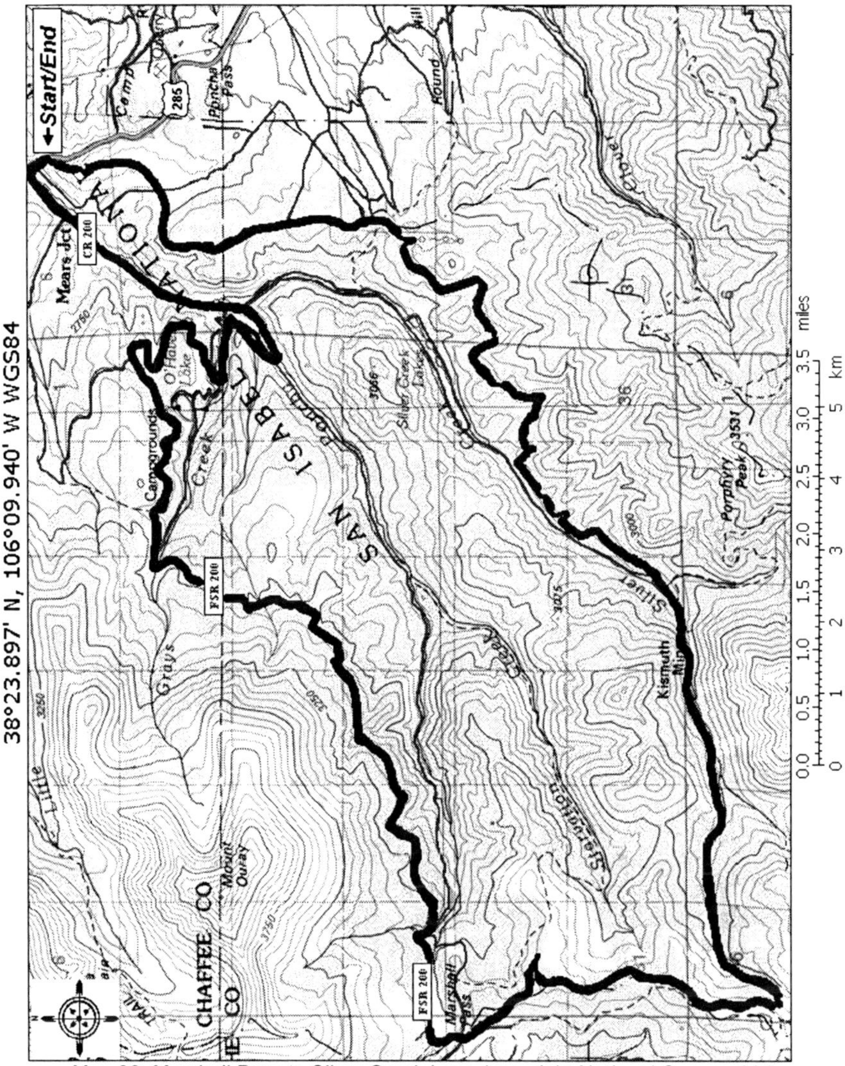

Map 33: Marshall Pass to Silver Creek Loop (copyright National Geographic)

This is an ambitious ride with lots of everything mountain bikers love: many miles of sweet single-track, high elevations, sweeping vistas, and a healthy climb. It's also one of the few routes to incorporate long sections of the Rainbow Trail without a shuttle.

Before attempting on this one, be sure you have plenty of water, food, some extra clothing layers, and good weather. You will be out for a while, far from your car, and retreat will not be easy or fast.

Elevation profile:

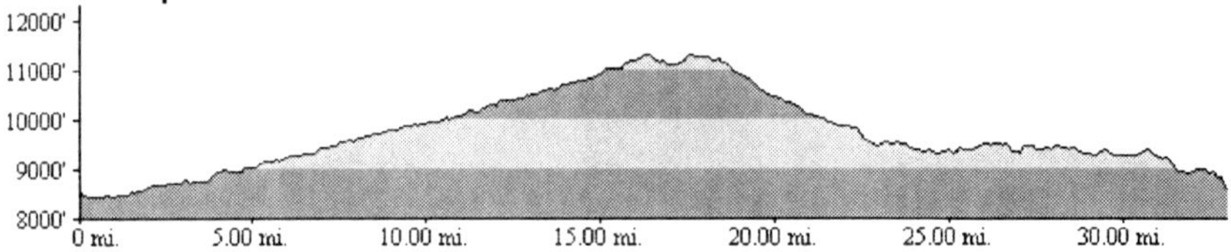

Ride length: 32.5 miles
Ride type: loop (counter-clockwise)
Riding time: 5 hours
Surface: paved road (0.2 miles); dirt road (14.9 miles); single-track (17.4 miles)
Elevations: start/end 8,550'; max 11,300'; min 8,440'
Total climbing: gain/loss 4,510'
Aerobic level: strenuous (it's a long ride)
Technical level: 4+ (steeps with loose rocks; laterally eroded side-cuts; tight vertical transitions on single-track)
Season: July through October
USGS Quadrangles: Poncha Pass, Mount Ouray, Bonanza

Trailhead GPS coordinates: 38° 26.748' N; 106° 6.328' W

Getting there: from the intersection of US 50 and US 285 (5 miles west of Salida on US 50), turn left on US 285. Drive 5.2 miles south on US 285 to the large parking turnout adjacent to the Rainbow Trail sign on the right. Park here. *This area is approximately 0.2 miles south of the intersection of CR 200 and US 285 (designated by signs to O'Haver Lake and Marshall Pass).*

The ride:

0.0 From your car, ride north (downhill) on US 285.
0.2 Turn left (west/southwest) on CR 200.
2.5 Continue straight on FSR 200, passing a turn-off for the O'Haver Lake Campground on your right.
2.7 Turn right and continue on FSR 200 at the intersection with FSR 201. Follow the signs to Marshall Pass and Poncha Creek. ***Note-*** *the Shirley Site is on your left, distinguished by a large parking area with pit toilets.*
3.2 Cross the bridge over Poncha Creek then turn right at the "T" intersection to continue on FSR 200 (Marshall Pass Road).
3.4 Continue straight on FSR 200, passing a spur on the left.
4.3 Continue straight on FSR 200 through the intersection with FSR 202. Note the sign: Marshall Pass 10 Miles.
6.2 Continue on FSR 200 past the intersection with FSR 204 on your right; follow the sign to Marshall Pass.
7.0 Stay on the main road.
11.4 Pass over Tent Creek. Is this a long climb or what?
13.6 Pass over Ouray Creek. Yes, it's a long climb.
14.5 Stay on the main road. You're almost there!
14.6 Pass the entrance to the Colorado Trail on the right. Pedal a little more and you will arrive at the top of Marshall Pass... finally! Pit toilets are available at the parking area on the left.
14.7 Continue on FSR 200, passing a trailhead on the left.
14.8 Bear left on FSR 203 toward a small rise. Continue until you reach a 4-way split. From there, take the route that's about 45 degrees right of your front wheel. This is poorly marked and slightly confusing. The left-most spur is FSR 203 (this leads to the junction of FSR 200 and 203

below O'Haver Lake). The next option on the left is unmarked and leads to a campsite. ***The third option, the Colorado Trail, is about 45 degrees right of your front wheel; take this one.*** The fourth option, a hard right, is unmarked and leads back to FSR 200.

14.9 Depart left from the road and ride toward the single-track, the Colorado Trail/Continental Divide Trail (TR 486). A large message board marks the entrance to the trail. Follow the sign to Silver Creek (3 miles). (*Do not ride on TR 243.3H!*)

15.5 Cross an open meadow. Nice trail.

15.9 Ignore the Colorado Trail marker and broken sign at the switchback. Stay on the main trail, following the switchback right.

17.0 Turn left at the intersection marked by the sign "Silver Creek 1." Climb.

17.3 Stay on the main trail. Look for the Colorado Trail/Continental Divide Trail marker.

17.5 Stay straight on the main trail, ignoring all the various tracks. Follow the orange blazes on the trees.

18.0 Turn left on the Silver Creek Trail (#1407). The downhill begins in earnest. (*The Colorado Trail continues straight to Saguache.*)

21.8 Enter private property and prepare for lots of loose rocks ahead. ***Watch for a big drop as the trail gets increasingly technical!***

22.1 Cross Silver Creek on a bridge. Prepare to get your feet wet as the trail becomes the creek for the next 150 yards.

22.2 Stay left on FSR 201. Do not climb up Toll Road Gulch.

22.4 Leave FSR 201 to enter the Rainbow Trail at the Silver Creek Trailhead on your right. There is a prominent sign about 20 yards southwest of the trail entrance. Be sure to sign the trail register. ***Note-*** *if you've had enough, stay on FSR 201 and return to FSR 200 at the Shirley Angler Site. US 285 is an easy 7.6 miles ahead on this route. The descent is gentle, but expect a couple wet stream crossings.*

22.5 Stream crossing and some mud. You won't get wet feet, but each little stream crossing ahead comes with a tight downhill/uphill transition. There are several more.

28.7 Cross an unmarked road and continue straight on the trail through the opening in the fence.

31.2 Continue straight on the single-track through a meadow.

32.5 After a steep descent to US 285, you are finished. And so is the ride. Crawl into your car and take a nap.

Options: there are several options for decreasing the intensity of this ride. First, you can do this as a shuttle ride by leaving a car on US 285 and driving the bikes to Marshall Pass.

The next option is to descend FSR 203 from Marshall Pass. This rocky jeep road is easier and faster than descending via the single-track.

Finally, you can opt out of the final 10 miles of Silver Creek single-track by descending along FSR 201. This option is much easier and faster than the single-track.

Ride 34: Silver Creek Loop

38°24.393' N, 106°07.743' W WGS84

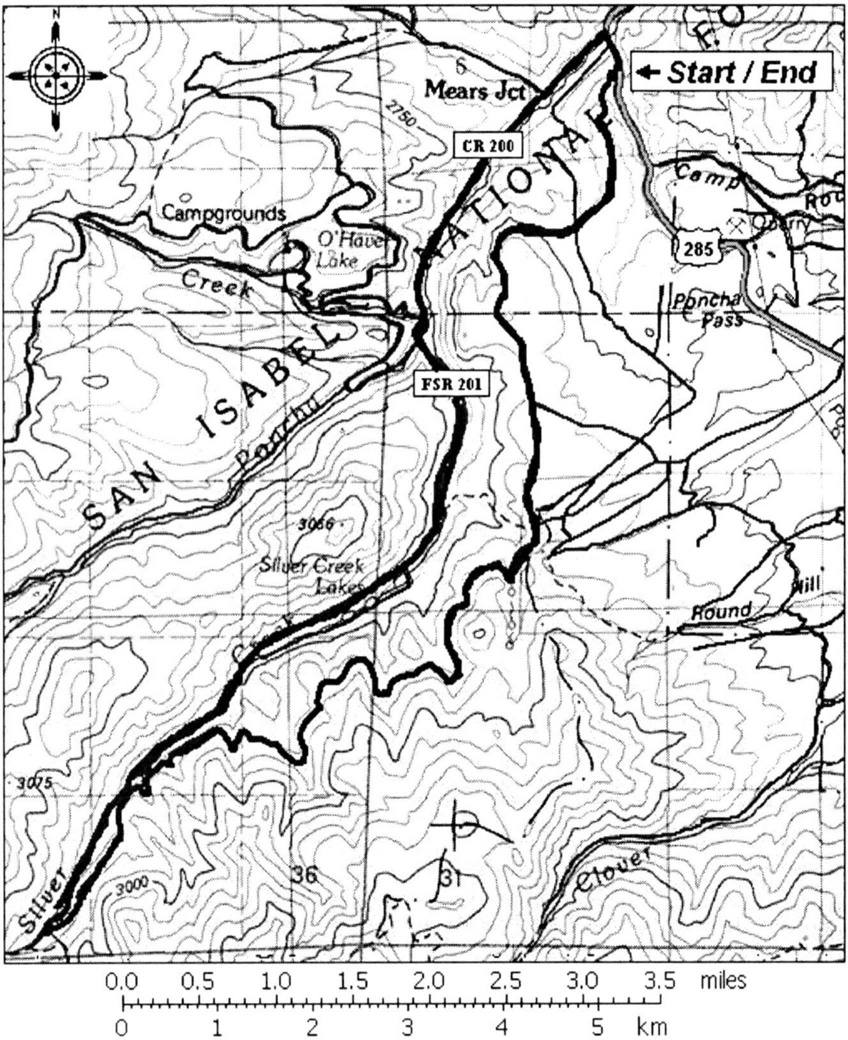

Map 34: Silver Creek Loop (copyright National Geographic)

Friends who know me well will say that I claim every great trail as one of the best I've ever ridden. If that's true, here I go again.

The climb out is on an easy yet extremely scenic road. The single-track that comes next is some of the best in the Valley: the narrow dirt vein ahead of you just keeps going and going and going and the bliss seems to never end. Moreover, the views of nearby Mount Ouray and distant Mount Shavano will make you leap out of your shoes.

Elevation profile:

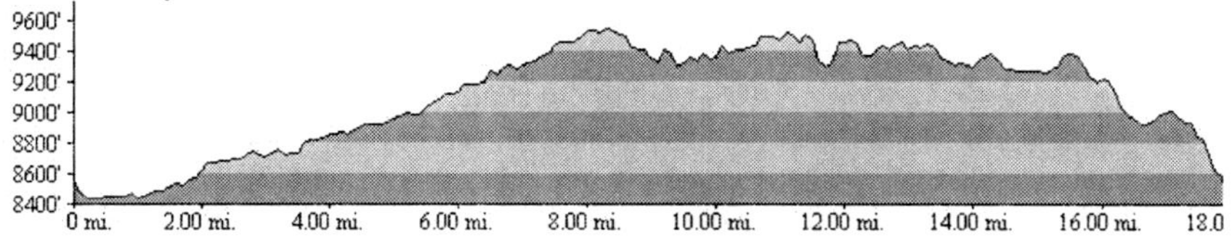

Ride length: 17.9 miles
Ride type: loop (counter-clockwise)
Riding time: 2.5 hours
Surface: paved road (0.2 miles); dirt road (7.6 miles); single-track (10.1 miles)
Elevations: start/end 8,550'; max 9,550'; min 8,440'
Total climbing: gain/loss 2,040'

Aerobic level: moderate (moderate climbing throughout the route)
Technical level: 3+ (rocks and laterally eroded side-cuts; the descent to US 285 is steep)
Season: May through October
USGS Quadrangles: Poncha Pass, Mount Ouray, Bonanza

Trailhead GPS coordinates: 38° 26.721' N; 106° 6.318' W

Getting there: from the intersection of US 50 and US 285 (5 miles west of Salida on US 50), turn left on US 285. Drive 5.2 miles south on US 285 to the large parking turnout adjacent to a Rainbow Trail sign on the right. Park here. *This area is approximately 0.2 miles south of the intersection of CR 200 and US 285 (designated by signs to O'Haver Lake and Marshall Pass).*

The ride:

0.0 From your car, ride north (downhill) on US 285.
0.2 Turn left (west/south-west) on CR 200.
2.5 Continue straight on FSR 200 past the turn-off for O'Haver Lake Campground on your right.
2.7 Continue straight on FSR 201. (*Do not turn right on FSR 200 to Marshall Pass and Poncha Creek.*) Unless you need a bio-break, pass the parking lot for the Shirley Site Trailhead on the left. (*Last chance. I warned you.*)
4.4 Stay right, climbing on FSR 201. You will soon see lakes on your left.
5.7 Continue straight on the main road, passing a road on the left.
5.8 Break out the waders and make your way upstream. Overachieving beavers at it again. (*As of June 2007, a few eager rodents diverted Silver Creek so that during high flows, the road serves as the creek's channel for about 100 yards.*)
7.8 Take a hard left at the Silver Creek Trailhead entrance to the Rainbow Trail. The single-track starts here. There is a prominent Silver Creek Trailhead sign about 20 yards southwest of the trail entrance. Register your party at the box provided about 20 yards from the trail entrance.
7.9 Stream crossing and some mud. You won't get wet feet, but each crossing comes with a tight downhill/uphill transition. Several more of these await you.
14.1 Cross an unmarked road and continue straight on the trail through the opening in the fence.
16.6 Stay on the Rainbow Trail as you ride through a meadow.
17.9 That's it. Now go get a burrito in Salida.

Monarch Crest

Hands-down, this is the best the Arkansas Valley has to offer. Not only is it critically acclaimed as one of the finest trails in all of Colorado, it's also regarded as one of the best trails in the United States. The quality of the ride and unsurpassed views just can't be beat. Officially, the Monarch Crest Trail is a stretch of the Continental Divide Trail from Monarch Pass to Marshall Pass. Unofficially, the ride also includes any of several descent routes, accessed either from Marshall Pass or from one of the intersecting trails along the way.

One popular myth is the misconception that these rides are entirely downhill. As you will see from the elevation profiles, there will be some climbing, especially on the classic Silver Creek descent route. Don't let that discourage you, however, since the net loss in elevation is much greater than the net gains on almost every option.

Because of this area's popularity, it is especially important to obey the rules of the trail. Please yield to hikers and ride within the trail boundaries. Your behavior on this trail has a great impact on the status of this treasured area.

Also, since much of the Crest trail is above tree line, you'll want to get an early start to avoid getting caught in afternoon storms.

Monarch Crest Trail

Note- *the High Valley Center in Poncha Springs (just south of the intersection of US 50/US 285) shuttles bikes and riders to the top of Monarch Pass for about $20/person. Shuttles leave daily at regularly scheduled intervals, or by reserved, special arrangements. Please call for more information. (719)539-6089 / (800)871-5145*

Ride 35: Monarch Crest Trail

38°26.690' N, 106°17.199' W WGS84

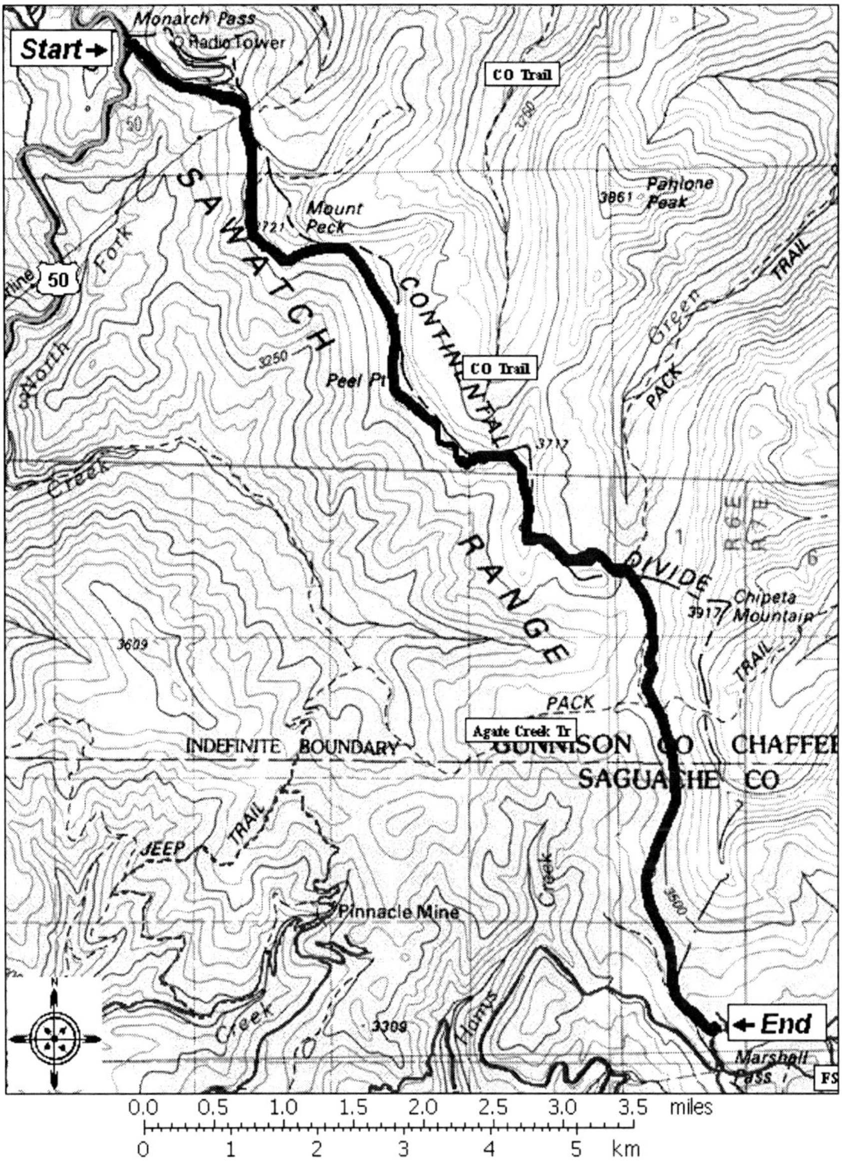

Map 35: Monarch Crest Trail (copyright National Geographic)

This route description is for the ride between Monarch and Marshall Passes. Included elsewhere in this guide are descriptions for some of the more popular descent routes.

Elevation profile:

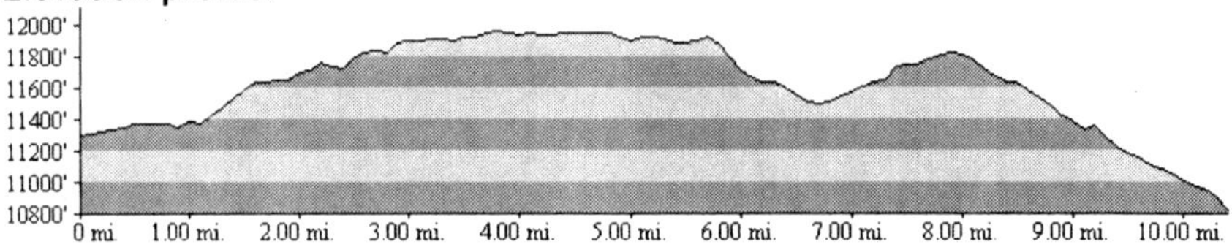

Ride length: 20.8 miles
Ride type: out-and-back
Riding time: 3 hours
Surface: jeep road (4.8 miles); single-track (16.0 miles)
Elevations: start/end 11,300'; max 11,960'; min 10,830'
Total climbing: gain/loss 2,460'

Aerobic level: moderate (the climbs are easy, but the altitude can make them feel tough)
Technical level: 3 (some rocks and roots, but the overall line is clean and built for speed)
Season: July through October
USGS Quadrangles: Pahlone Peak, Mount Ouray

Trailhead GPS coordinates: 38° 29.784' N; 106° 19.541' W

Getting there: from the intersection of US 50 and US 285 (5 miles west of Salida on US 50), turn right (north/west) on US 285/US 50. Drive18.0 miles west on US 50 to the summit of Monarch Pass. Park in the large lot by the store and tram ride.

Note- *you can leave a shuttle at Marshall Pass, making this a one-way ride of 10.4 miles. The dirt road leading to the pass (CR/FSR 200) is well graded and suitable for passenger vehicles. To get there, drive 5.0 miles south from the intersection of US 50/US 285 in Poncha Springs. Turn right on to CR 200 and follow it to the summit of Marshall Pass. The road is well marked; avoid all unmarked intersections (those without distinct "200" signs).*

The ride:

0.0 From your car, ride up the paved drive leading to the tram.
0.3 Bear right onto the Continental Divide Trail. The single-track looks awesome, but don't forget to sign the trail register!
1.0 Pass under some power lines then bear right onto the jeep track leading uphill.
1.5 Bear right and leave the jeep track for another helping of single-track. Trail markers a map board lead the way.
1.8 Check out the views!
2.7 More amazing views! Can it get any better?
2.8 Pass the sign marking Middle Fooses Creek on your left.
4.7 Round a big bend and Mount Ouray comes into prominent view.
5.0 Continue straight past the intersection with the South Fooses Creek descent route (Colorado Trail) on your left. (*This is an awesome descent back to US 50 and the route intersects the highway approximately 8.4 miles below the summit of Monarch Pass*). From this point forward, the Colorado Trail overlaps the Continental Divide Trail.
5.7 Get ready for some speed.
6.0 Drop into forest cover on some slightly technical terrain.
6.6 Pass the Greens Creek spur and the backpackers' shelter on your left. Continue straight on the CDT/COT into the woods.
7.3 The climbing gets a little steep here, but nothing you can't handle.

7.7 Continue straight on the main trail. Pass the Little Cochetopa trail on your left.

7.8 Stay on the main trail. The Agate Creek Trail (TR 484) intersects to your right.

8.3 Cross a small talus slope.

8.8 The single-track becomes a fast jeep trail. Let it rip, but watch for hikers and traffic.

10.2 Pop-out onto Marshall Pass Road (FSR 200). Turn right and ride toward the parking lot and pit toilet.

10.4 That was excellent, but now what? If you are riding without a shuttle, turn back and return to Monarch Pass along the same route. If you have a shuttle vehicle at Marshall Pass, you are done.

Options: if you shuttled from Poncha Springs, you can descend along the Marshall Pass Road, FSR 200 (easy). You can also descend along FSR 203, Poncha Creek Road (moderate). Or... the classic descent line follows the CDT/COT to the Silver Creek portion of the Rainbow Trail (advanced) for almost 18 additional miles of single-track! Find these routes in the pages ahead.

Silver Creek Road

Ride 36: Monarch Crest descending Marshall Pass Road

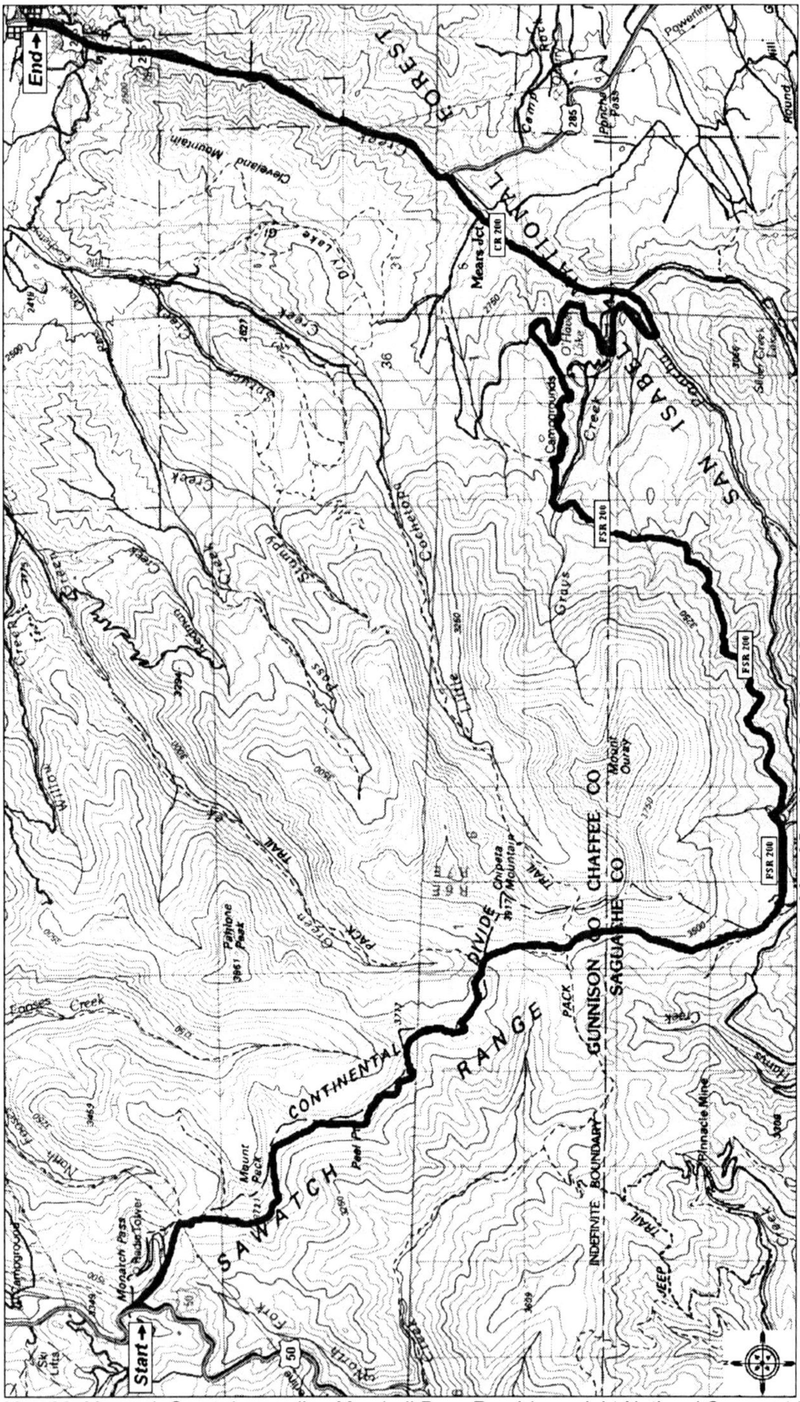

38°27.311' N, 106°12.507' W WGS84

Map 36: Monarch Crest descending Marshall Pass Road (copyright National Geographic)

This is the least technical descent from Marshall Pass. After riding the amazing Crest line, some may want to finish with an easy glide back to Poncha Springs. Better yet, take the first shuttle from the High Valley Center, hustle down this route, eat lunch, and then catch another shuttle for a second run on a different descent line.

Elevation profile:

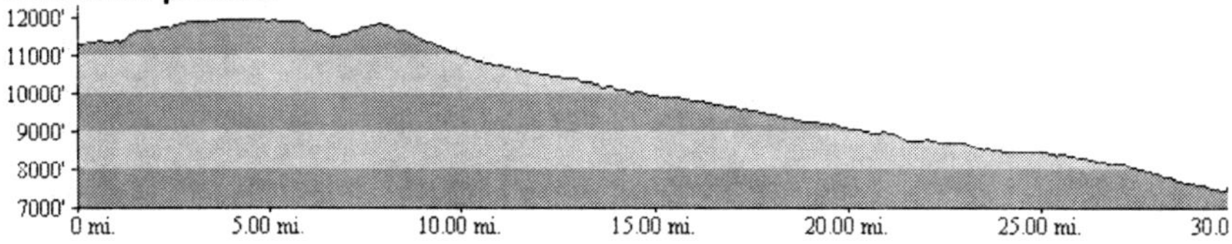

Ride length: 29.7 miles
Ride type: one-way with shuttle
Riding time: 3 hours
Surface: single-track (8.0 miles); dirt road (16.7 miles); paved road (5.0 miles)
Elevations: start 11,300'; end 7,480'; max 11,960'; min 7,480'
Total climbing: gain 1,200' – loss 5,020' = total -3,820'

Aerobic level: moderate (easy climbs, but altitude might make them feel tough)
Technical level: 3 (some rocks and roots)
Season: July through October
USGS Quadrangles: Pahlone Peak, Mount Ouray, Poncha Pass, Salida West

Trailhead GPS coordinates: 38° 29.784' N; 106° 19.541' W

Getting there: from the intersection of US 50 and US 285 (5 miles west of Salida on US 50), turn left on US 285 and drive about 0.25 miles south. Leave a vehicle in the open parking area on the left, just north of the High Valley Center in Poncha Springs.

Take the bikes and riders to the top of Monarch Pass. From the parking area in Poncha Springs, turn right (north) on US 285/US 50 and drive approximately 18.2 miles west on US 50 to the summit of Monarch Pass. Park in the large lot by the store and tram ride.

The ride:

0.0 From your car, ride up the paved drive leading to the tram.
0.3 Bear right onto the Continental Divide Trail. The single-track looks awesome, but don't forget to sign the trail register!
1.0 Pass under some power lines then bear right onto the jeep track leading uphill.
1.5 Bear right and leave the jeep track for another helping of single-track. Trail markers a map board lead the way.
1.8 Check out the views!
2.7 More amazing views! Can it get any better?
2.8 Pass the sign marking Middle Fooses Creek on your left.
4.7 Round a big bend and Mount Ouray comes into prominent view.
5.0 Continue straight past the intersection with the South Fooses Creek descent route (Colorado Trail) on your left.
5.7 Get ready for some speed.
6.0 Drop into some forest cover for some slightly technical terrain.

6.6 Pass the Greens Creek spur and the backpackers' shelter on your left. Continue straight on the CDT/COT into the woods.
7.3 Steep climbing here, but nothing you can't handle.
7.7 Continue straight on the main trail. Pass the Little Cochetopa trail on your left.
7.8 Stay on the main trail. The Agate Creek Trail (FSTR 484) intersects to your right.
8.3 Cross a small talus slope.
8.8 The single-track becomes a fast jeep trail. Let it rip, but watch for traffic and hikers.
10.2 Pop-out onto Marshall Pass Road (FSR 200). If you need to use the pit toilet, turn right and ride toward the parking lot. Otherwise, turn left and start the descent.
10.3 Stay on the main road.
11.2 Pass over Ouray Creek.
13.4 Pass over Tent Creek.
17.8 Stay on the main road.
18.6 Pass the intersection with FSR 204 on your left. Stay on FSR 200.
20.5 Continue straight through the intersection of FSR 200 and FSR 202. Stay on FSR 200.
21.4 Continue straight on FSR 200, passing the spur on the right.
21.6 Turn left at the "T" intersection, staying on FSR 200 (Marshall Pass Road), then cross the bridge over Poncha Creek.
22.1 Turn left at the intersection with FSR 200 and FSR 201. The Shirley Site is on your right, distinguished by a large parking area with pit toilets. Continue rolling down FSR/CR 200.
22.3 Continue straight past the turn-off for O'Haver Lake Campground on your left.
24.8 Intersect US 285. Carefully cross then turn left (north) on US 285.
29.9 Arrive at the car. Awesome! Go get a cold drink and something to eat at the High Valley Center.

Ride 37: Monarch Crest descending Poncha Creek Road

38°27.153' N, 106°12.544' W WGS84

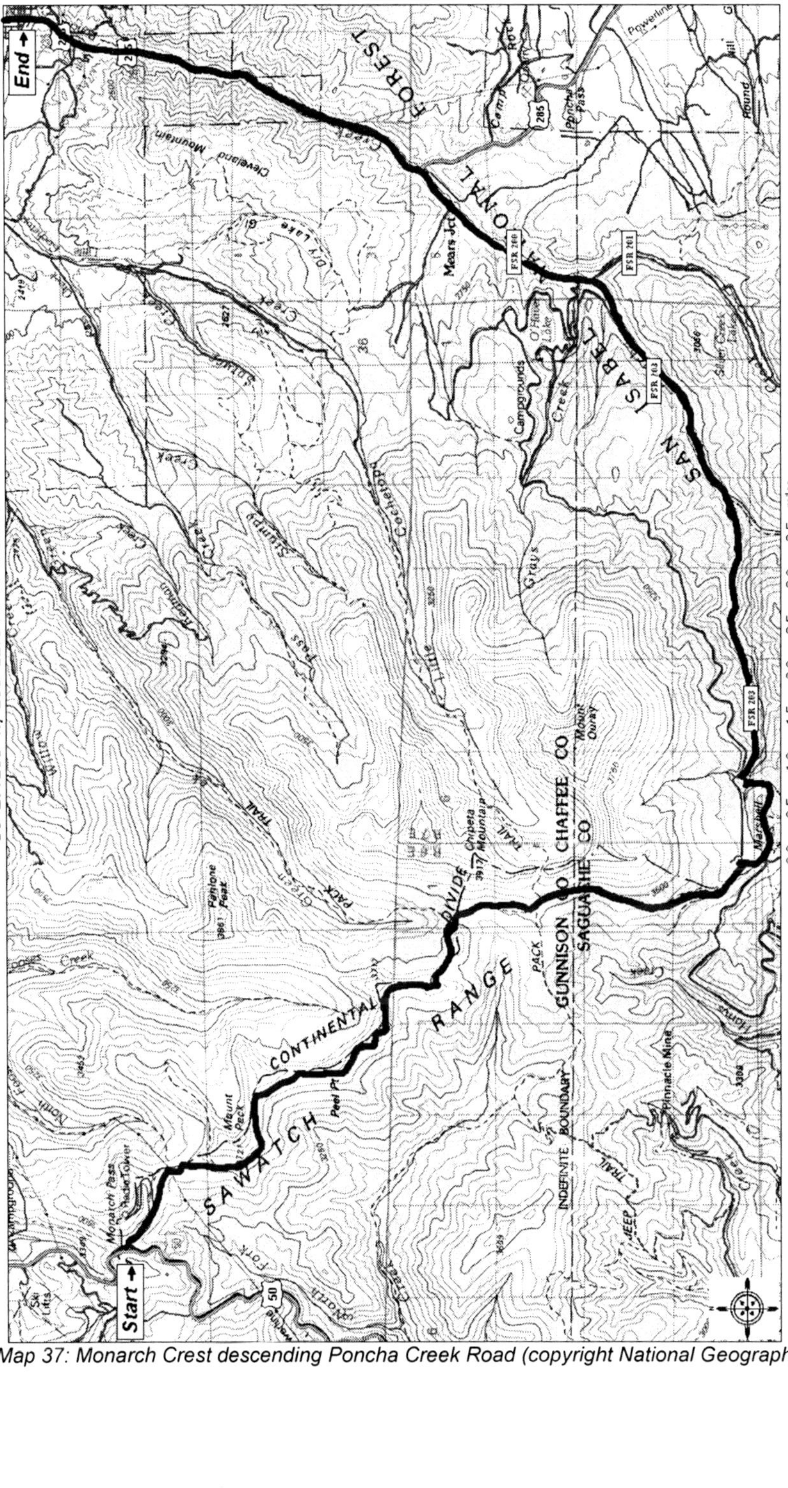

Map 37: Monarch Crest descending Poncha Creek Road (copyright National Geographic)

This route provides a slightly more technical descent from Marshall Pass than the Marshall Pass Road. Though somewhat rocky, the descent line is fast and very fun.

Elevation profile:

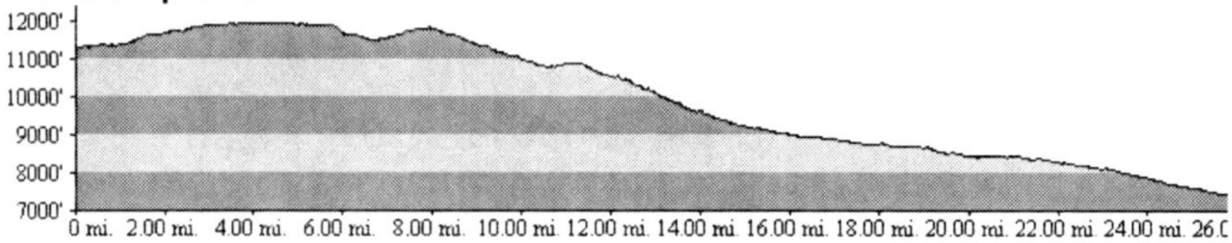

Ride length: 26.0 miles
Ride type: one-way with shuttle
Riding time: 2.5-3 hours
Surface: dirt/jeep road (12.9 miles); single-track (8.0 miles); paved road (5.1 miles)
Elevations: start 11,300'; end 7,480'; max 11,960'; min 7,480'
Total climbing: gain 1,095' – loss 4,910' = total -3,815'

Aerobic level: moderate (easy climbs, but altitude can make them feel tough)
Technical level: 3 (roots and rocks; the upper portion of Poncha Creek Road is rocky)
Season: July through October
USGS Quadrangles: Pahlone Peak, Mount Ouray, Poncha Pass, Salida West

Trailhead GPS coordinates: 38° 29.784' N; 106° 19.541' W

Getting there: from the intersection of US 50 and US 285 (5 miles west of Salida on US 50), turn left on US 285 and drive about 0.25 miles south. Leave a vehicle in the open parking area on the left, just north of the High Valley Center in Poncha Springs.

Take the bikes and riders to the top of Monarch Pass. From the parking area in Poncha Springs, turn right (north) on US 285/US 50 and drive approximately 18.2 miles west on US 50 to the summit of Monarch Pass. Park in the large lot by the store and tram ride.

The ride:

0.0 From your car, ride up the paved drive leading to the tram. The surface quickly turns to dirt. Continue climbing.
0.3 Bear right onto the Continental Divide Trail. The single-track looks awesome, but don't forget to sign the trail register!
1.0 Pass under some power lines then bear right onto the jeep track leading uphill.
1.5 Bear right and leave the jeep track for another helping of single-track. Trail markers a map board lead the way.
1.8 Check out the views!
2.7 More amazing views! Can it get any better?
2.8 Pass the sign marking Middle Fooses Creek on your left.
4.7 Round a big bend and Mount Ouray comes into prominent view.
5.0 Continue straight past the intersection with the South Fooses Creek descent route (Colorado Trail) on your left.
5.7 Get ready for some speed.
6.0 Drop into forest cover and some slightly technical terrain.
6.6 Pass the Greens Creek spur and the backpackers' shelter on your left. Continue straight on the CDT/COT into the woods.

7.3 A little steep climbing, but nothing you can't handle.
7.7 Continue straight on the main trail. Pass the Little Cochetopa trail on your left.
7.8 Stay on the main trail. The Agate Creek Trail (FSTR 484) intersects to your right.
8.3 Cross a small talus slope.
8.8 The single-track becomes a fast jeep trail. Let it rip, but watch for traffic.
10.2 Pop-out onto Marshall Pass Road (FSR 200). Turn right and ride toward the parking lot and pit toilet. If you don't need to stop, continue south on FSR 200 past the open meadow.
10.4 Bear left onto FSR 203. This road is slightly rougher and climbs a bit.
10.5 Approach a 4-way intersection. Take the left-most option, Poncha Creek Road (FSR 203).
11.1 Continue straight on FSR 203 as you pass Starvation Creek Road (203A) on the right. A sign will inform you that the Shirley Site is 7 miles ahead.
11.9 Pass over Poncha Creek. Just in case you didn't notice, the terrain is a little rocky.
13.1 Keep descending on the main road.
13.9 Stay on the main road.
14.3 A ruptured drainage pipe may make the going a little wet here.
15.4 Pass the Starvation Creek trailhead on the right.
16.4 Stay on the main road.
17.9 Turn right at the "T" intersection and descend on FSR/CR 200.
18.5 Turn left at the intersection with FSR 201 at the Shirley Site. Continue downhill on FSR/CR 200.
18.6 Continue downhill on FSR/CR 200, passing a road leading to O'Haver lake on your left.
20.9 Cross US 285 (*be careful!*) then turn left (downhill) on the pavement toward Poncha Springs.
26.0 Find your car, pack your bikes, and plan your next adventure.

Poncha Creek Road

Ride 38: Monarch Crest descending Silver Creek

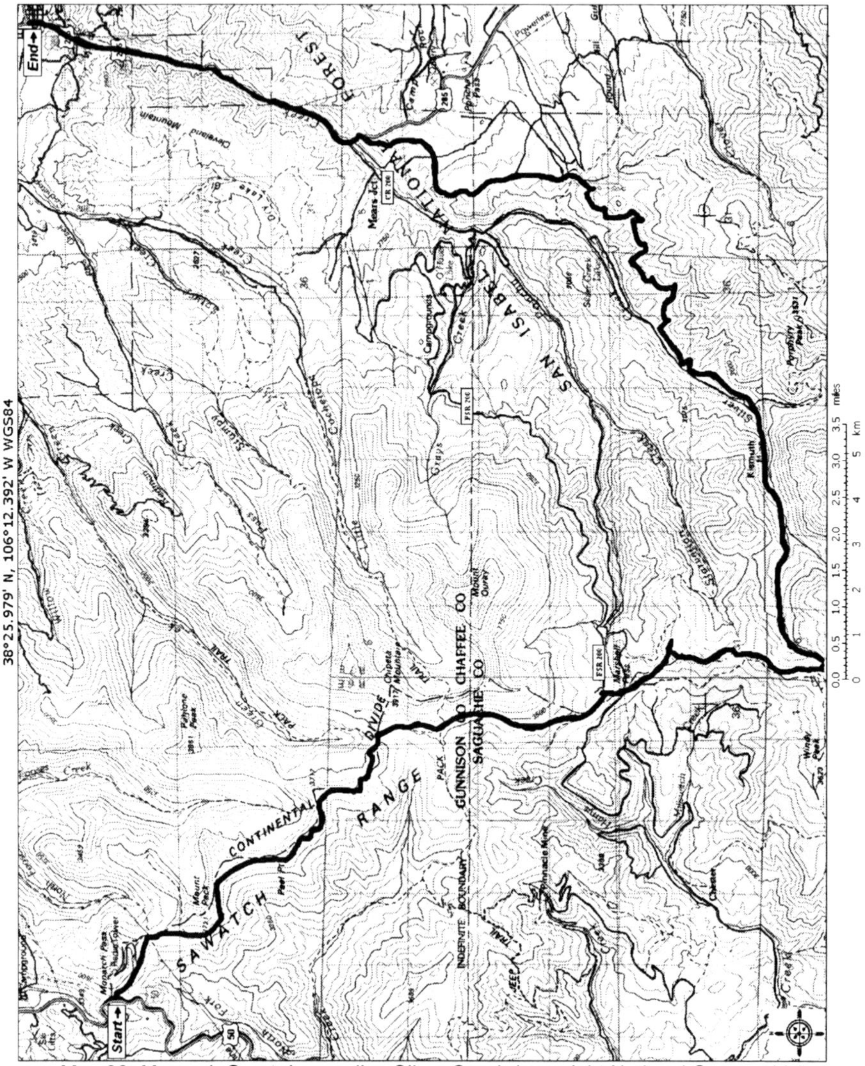

Map 38: Monarch Crest descending Silver Creek (copyright National Geographic)

You've seen it: your friends just got back from riding the "Monarch Crest" and they have this odd, dreamy expression on their faces. They rave about endless single-track and epic scenery. You can tell by their glazed eyes that they wish they were still there. That's a typical reaction to this route. This is *the* classic ride Front Range mountain bikers return to each summer like disciples on a pilgrimage. Few rides anywhere offer as much.

Please bear in mind that this is a strenuous and technically demanding route. The stretch from Marshall Pass to US 285 is much more demanding than the initial ride to Marshall Pass, and some intermediate riders will find it above their skill level. Have fun, but be smart and use good judgment.

Elevation profile:

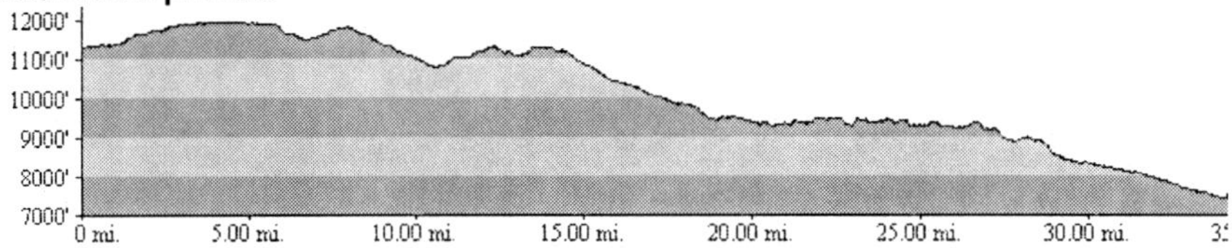

Ride length: 33.2 miles
Ride type: one-way with shuttle
Riding time: 4.5 hours
Surface: dirt/jeep road (2.8 miles); single-track (26.4 miles); paved road (5.0 miles)
Elevations: start 11,300'; end 7,480'; max 11,960'; min 7,480'
Total climbing: gain 3,260' – loss 7,080' = total -3,820'

Aerobic level: strenuous (lots of ups and downs)
Technical level: 4+ (roots, rocks, and steeps)
Season: July through October
USGS Quadrangles: Pahlone Peak, Mount Ouray, Bonanza, Poncha Pass, Salida West

Trailhead GPS coordinates: 38° 29.784' N; 106° 19.541' W

Getting there: from the intersection of US 50 and US 285 (5 miles west of Salida on US 50), turn left on US 285 and drive about 0.25 miles south. Leave a vehicle in the open parking area on the left, just north of the High Valley Center in Poncha Springs.

Take the bikes and riders to the top of Monarch Pass. From the parking area in Poncha Springs, turn right (north) on US 285/US 50 and drive approximately 18.2 miles west on US 50 to the summit of Monarch Pass. Park in the large lot by the store and tram ride.

The ride:

- **0.0** From your car, ride up the paved drive leading to the tram. The route quickly turns to a dirt road. Continue climbing.
- **0.3** Bear right onto the Continental Divide Trail. The single-track looks awesome, but don't forget to sign the trail register!
- **1.0** Pass under some power lines then bear right onto the jeep track leading uphill.
- **1.5** Bear right and leave the jeep track for another helping of single-track. Trail markers a map board lead the way.
- **1.8** Check out the views!
- **2.7** More amazing views! Can it get any better?
- **2.8** Pass the sign marking Middle Fooses Creek on your left.
- **4.7** Round a big bend and Mount Ouray comes into prominent view.
- **5.0** Continue straight past the intersection with the South Fooses Creek descent route (Colorado Trail) on your left.
- **5.7** Get ready for some speed.
- **6.0** Drop into some forest cover for some slightly technical terrain.
- **6.6** Pass the Greens Creek spur and the backpackers' shelter on your left. Continue straight on the CDT/COT into the woods.
- **7.3** The climb gets a little steep, but nothing you can't handle.
- **7.7** Continue straight on the main trail. Pass the Little Cochetopa trail on your left.

7.8 Stay on the main trail. The Agate Creek Trail (FSTR 484) intersects to your right.
8.3 Cross a small talus slope.
8.8 The single-track becomes a fast jeep trail. Let it rip, but watch for traffic.
10.2 Pop-out onto Marshall Pass Road (FSR 200). Turn right and ride toward the parking lot and pit toilet. If you don't need to stop, continue south on FSR 200 past the open meadow.
10.4 Bear left on FSR 203 and ride toward a small rise. Continue until you reach a 4-way split. From there, take the route that's about 45 degrees right of your front wheel. This is poorly marked and slightly confusing. The left-most spur is FSR 203. The next option on the left is unmarked and leads to a campsite. ***The third option, the Colorado Trail, is about 45 degrees right of your front wheel; take this one.*** The fourth option, a hard right, is unmarked and leads back to FSR 200.
10.6 Depart left from the road and ride toward the single-track, the Colorado Trail/Continental Divide Trail (TR 486). A large message board marks the entrance to the trail. Follow the sign to Silver Creek (*3 miles*). (*Do not ride on TR 243.3H!*)
11.2 Cross an open meadow. Nice trail.
11.6 Ignore the Colorado Trail marker and broken sign at the switchback. Stay on the main trail and take the switchback right.
12.7 Turn left at the intersection marked by the sign "Silver Creek 1." Climb.
13.0 Stay on the main trail. Look for the Colorado Trail/Continental Divide Trail marker.
13.2 Continue straight on the main trail, passing various tracks. Use the orange blazes on trees to help guide you.
13.7 Turn left on the Silver Creek Trail (#1407). The downhill begins in earnest. (*The Colorado Trail continues straight to Saguache.*)
14.8 Pass a sign. (What did it say?)
17.5 Enter private property and prepare for lots of loose rocks ahead. ***Watch for a big drop as the trail gets increasingly technical!***
17.8 Cross Silver Creek on a bridge. Prepare to get your feet wet, as the trail becomes the creek for the next 150 yards.
17.9 Stay left on FSR 201. Do not climb up Toll Road Gulch.
18.1 Turn right to enter the Silver Creek Trailhead for the Rainbow Trail. (There is a prominent Silver Creek Trailhead sign about 20 yards southwest of the trail entrance.) Register your party at the box about 20 yards from the trail entrance. ***Note-*** *if you've had enough, stay on FSR 201 to FSR 200; US 285 is an easy 7.6 miles ahead along this route, but a couple stream crossings will refresh your drying shoes.*
18.2 Stream crossing and some mud. You won't get wet feet, but each little stream crossing comes with a tight downhill/uphill transition. There are several more ahead.
24.4 Cross an unmarked road and continue straight on the trail through the opening in the fence.
26.9 Continue straight on the single-track through the meadow.
28.2 After a steep, technical descent, carefully cross US 285 and turn left to coast into Poncha Springs.
33.2 Arrive back at your car. Yes!!!

Ride 39: Monarch Crest descending South Fooses Creek

38°30.213' N, 106°17.096' W WGS84

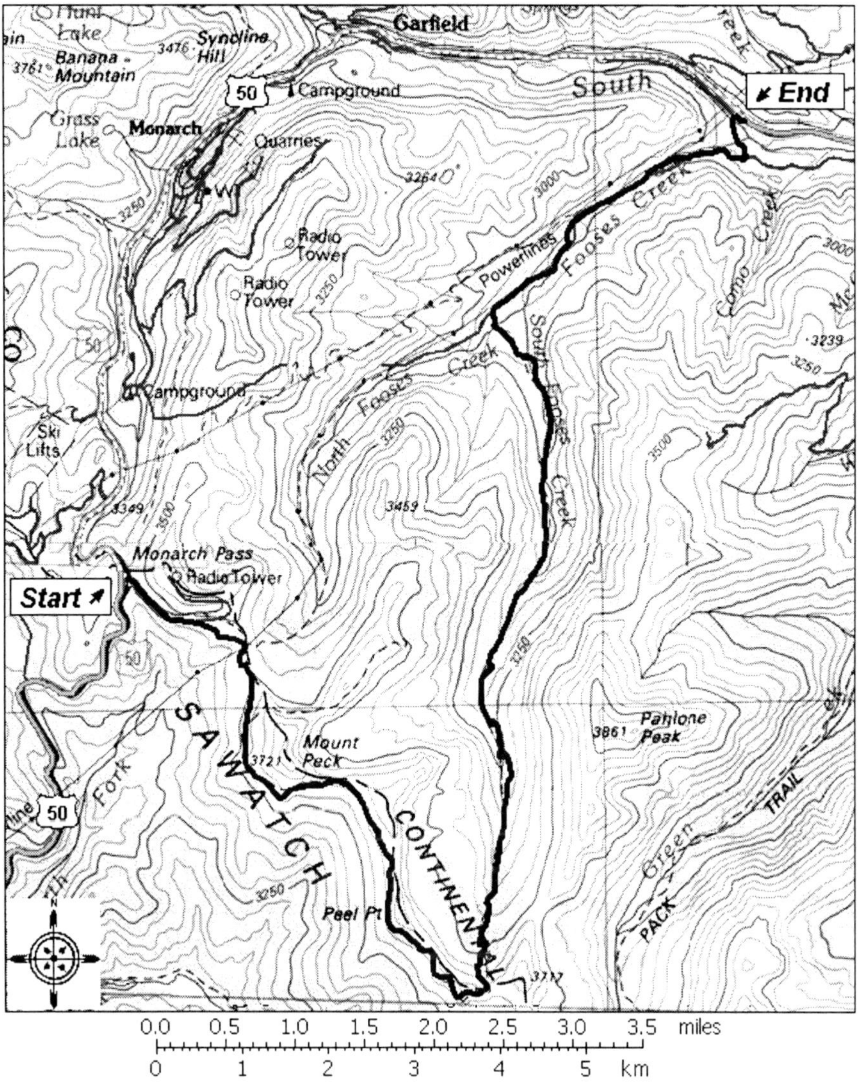

Map 39: Monarch Crest descending South Fooses Creek (copyright National Geographic)

This is an excellent ride combining tasty portions of two area classics: the Monarch Crest section of the Continental Divide Trail and the South Fooses section of the Colorado Trail.

The descent on the South Fooses Trail starts with a hairy, technical drop from the Divide. You'll want to break out the camera and capture it forever. Clean that section and you'll have something to brag about when you get home. The rest of the ride is a classic romp over some amazing single-track. As miles fly under your wheels, you will remember why you started mountain biking all those years ago.

Elevation profile:

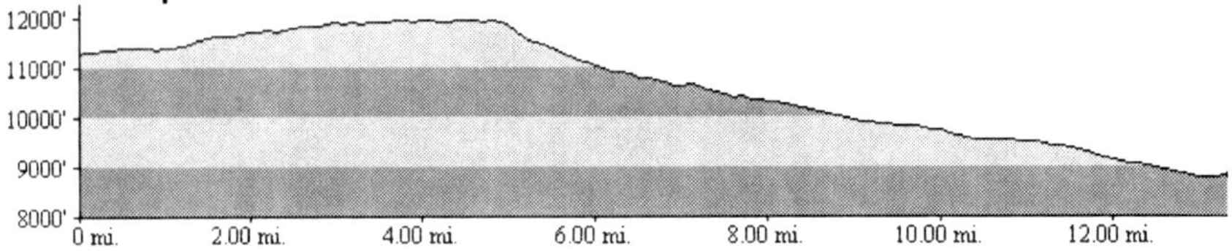

Ride length: 13.3 miles
Ride type: one-way with shuttle
Riding time: 2 hours
Surface: jeep road (4.0 miles); single-track (9.3 miles)
Elevations: start 11,300'; end 8,870'; max 11,960'; min 8,800'
Total climbing: gain 715' – loss 3,180' = total -2,465'

Aerobic level: moderate (easy climbing, but altitude might make it feel tough)
Technical level: 4 (one hairy steep, some rocks/roots)
Season: July through October
USGS Quadrangles: Pahlone Peak, Garfield, Maysville

Trailhead GPS coordinates: 38° 29.784' N; 106° 19.541' W

Getting there: from the intersection of US 50 and US 285 (from US 50), drive approximately 9.7 miles west on US 50 to the intersection with CR 225. There is a large pullout on the left (south) side of the highway at the intersection. Leave the drop vehicle here.

Take riders and bikes to Monarch Pass. Continue west on US 50 for about 8.4 miles to the summit. The ride starts from the large parking lot between the store and tram ride.

The ride:

0.0 From your car, ride up the paved drive leading to the tram.
0.3 Bear right onto the Continental Divide Trail. The single-track looks awesome but don't forget to sign the trail register!
1.0 Pass under some power lines then bear right onto the jeep track leading uphill.
1.5 Bear right and leave the jeep track for another helping of single-track. Trail markers a map board lead the way.
2.7 Amazing views! Can it get any better?
2.8 Pass the sign for Middle Fooses Creek on your left.
4.7 Round a big bend and Mount Ouray comes into prominent view.
5.0 Turn left and ride over the grassy knoll at the intersection with the Colorado Trail/South Fooses Creek. Whether the initial descent looks awesome or terrifying is a matter of perspective. The surface is rocky and loose, and excessive braking is the best way to eat dirt. If you aren't up to the challenge, walk to the bottom; the rest of the trail is nowhere near as steep or technical.
5.2 The steep is over.
5.8 Stream crossing.
6.1 Stream crossing.
7.2 Nice! Let it rip as the rocky section ends and the trail gets soft and loamy. Watch for roots!
8.2 Cross the bridge.
8.8 Cross another bridge.

9.8 Cross yet another bridge.

10.3 Guess what: another bridge. Continue 50 feet to the trailhead. Another 100 feet and you'll intersect a road. Turn right and ride the road downhill.

10.6 Turn right at the intersection with FSR 225. From this point, you'll intersect US 50 in approximately 3 miles. Stay on the main road throughout the descent as spurs cut in-and-out under the power lines.

12.5 Continue straight on the main road. You'll pass a pit toilet on your right in another 50 yards and Fooses Lake on the left.

13.2 Turn right at the "T" intersection. Look for a blue diamond trail marker on the tree to your right for reassurance. Make the short climb to the highway.

13.3 Arrive at the intersection with US 50. Some rides end too soon...

Options: if shuttles aren't your thing, start the ride at the intersection of US 50 and CR 225. It's an easy 8.4 miles to the summit of Monarch Pass, but use extreme caution when riding along the highway. Expect to spin some of those miles on a sandy, soft shoulder and be prepared to dodge wide load trucks and RVs.

Monarch Crest at the intersection with South Fooses Creek (copyright Tim Goodacre)

Salida

There's a reason Salida made *Outside* magazine's 2004 list of best towns in the United States. The town's proximity to so many world class recreational areas combined with its laidback vibe and unpretentious attitude make it an outdoor paradise. Unlike so many other mountain towns with similar claims, Salida is a place of genuine soul. You won't have to sidestep a parade of Hummers and Porsches when you cross the street, and nobody will look twice if you enter a store with dirt under your fingernails.

Originally founded as a rail center, Salida is now the largest town in Chaffee County and serves as its county seat. In addition to a wide variety of retail stores and other amenities, three great bicycle shops in town can meet your every need; check them out for up-to-date trail conditions and information.

A group of committed, hardcore local riders are working hard to establish Salida as Colorado's next big mountain biking destination. The superb new single-track around Tenderfoot Mountain is one example of their work. These locals are some of the friendliest I've encountered anywhere and most are more than happy to share their knowledge and offer direction.

Extending about 100 miles from the Continental Divide to Music Pass south of Westcliffe, the Rainbow Trail is a true Colorado epic. Initially built as a lumber and mountain access route for Arkansas Valley and Wet Valley settlers, construction of the trail began in 1912. Over the years, the various sections were connected until the final route skirted the eastern slope of the Sangre de Cristo Mountains like a giant rainbow. The segments south of Salida offer some of the best single-track in the southern end of the Arkansas Valley and the stretch between Bear Creek and Methodist Mountain is first rate.

Rainbow Trail local

***Note-** to make your visit easy, there are several free parking areas in town: the cul-de-sac at the north end of F Street, just past the F Street Bridge, adjacent to the Safeway at the intersection of Third and H Sts, and next to the skateboard park at First and G Sts.*

Ride 40: Bear Creek to Methodist Mountain Loop

38°29.106' N, 105°58.537' W WGS84

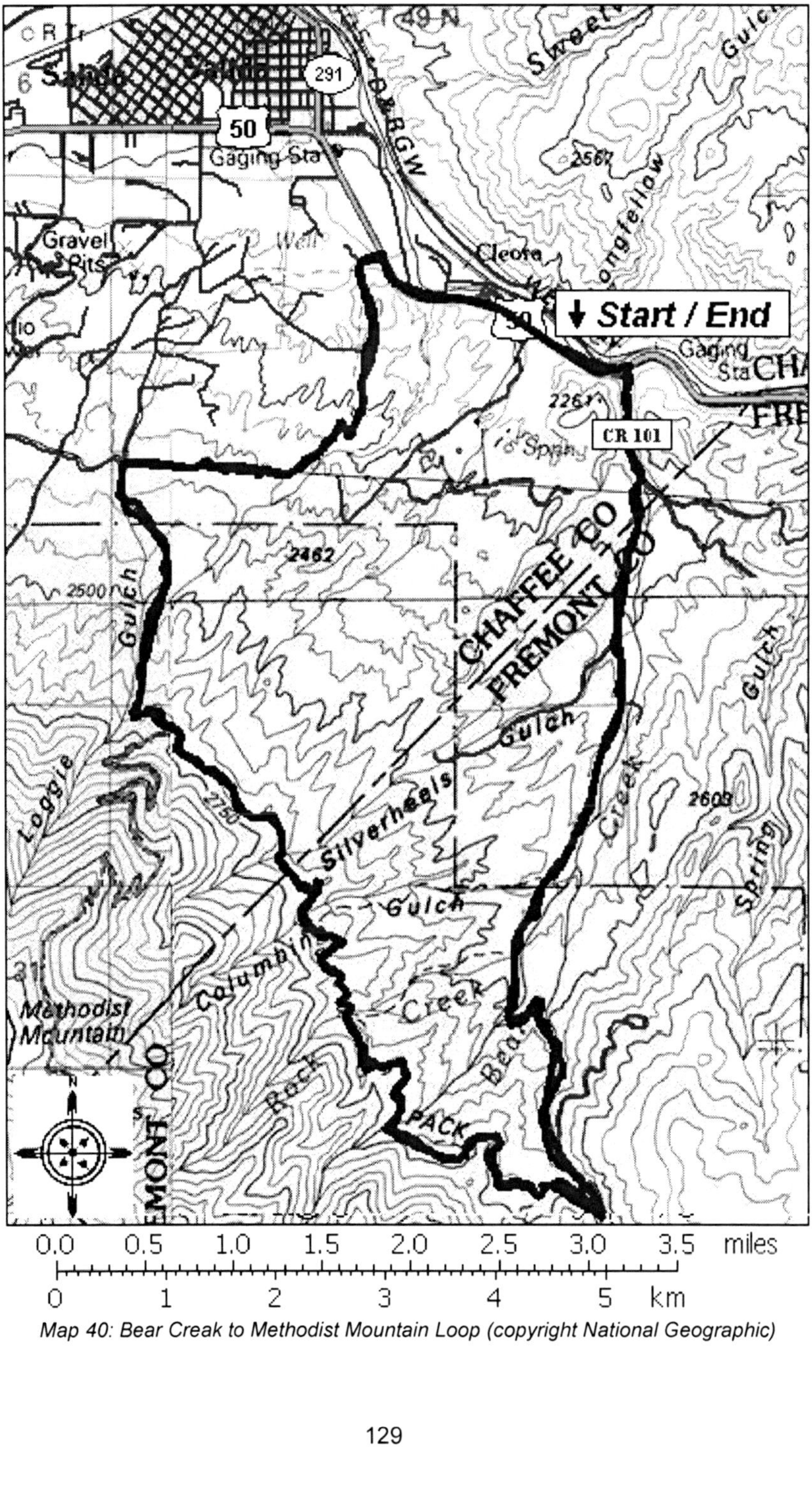

Map 40: Bear Creak to Methodist Mountain Loop (copyright National Geographic)

Do you want to know why local riders regard Salida as one of Colorado's best mountain biking towns? Do this ride.

This section of the Rainbow Trail is a local single-track staple and there are many well-documented variations of the route. This version, a clockwise loop incorporating fun sections of the BLM area east of CR 108, serves as a sampler for two popular riding areas.

The first area, the Rainbow Trail single-track between Bear Creek and Methodist Mountain, is first rate. The trail is fast with excellent transitions and flow. The terrain and scenery, if you slow down long enough to look around, are spectacular. It's a cross-country rider's dream.

The second area, the power line road, is a popular early and late season playground, and a fine alternate when snow covers higher trails. Single-track and jeep spurs abound in this rugged terrain just south of town. Find a local to take you out and show you some of the prime circuits.

Elevation profile:

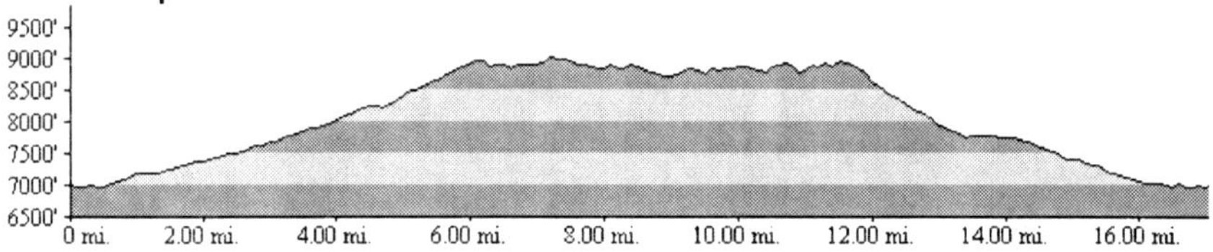

Ride length: 17.2 miles
Ride type: loop (clockwise)
Riding time: 2-3 hours
Surface: paved roads (1.8 miles); dirt road/jeep track (9.9 miles); single-track (5.5 miles)
Elevations: start/end 6,995'; max 9,020'; min 6,995'
Total climbing: gain/loss 3,015'

Aerobic level: strenuous (climbing-more than 3,000' of it)
Technical level: 3 (some tricky rocks and loose sections; some laterally eroded side-cuts)
Season: May through October
USGS Quadrangles: Salida East, Wellsville, Poncha Pass

Trailhead GPS coordinates: 38° 30.422' N; 105° 57.646' W

Getting there: from the intersection of 1st St. (CO 291) and F St. in downtown Salida, drive 1.0 miles east on 1st St. to the intersection with US 50. Turn left on US 50 and drive 1.9 miles east to the Salida East river access area on the left. Turn into the area and drive about 0.2 miles west to the day use/boat launch parking area. Ride bikes back out to the highway where the ride starts.

The ride:

0.0 From the entrance of the Salida East area, cross US 50 and ride east (left). The shoulder is wide and comfortable.

0.5 Turn right at the intersection with CR 101. Be aware that this public road crosses private land; stay on the road!

1.4 Cross into Fremont County. The road you are on is now CR 49. Continue climbing.

3.6 Pass a parking area on the right and cross a cattle guard at the National Forest boundary. The road, now FSR 101, is considerably rougher and steeper, but you can do it. No problem.

3.8 Pass an unmarked spur on your left.

4.1 Pass an unmarked spur on the right.

5.7 Continue straight up FSR 101 as you pass the intersection with FSR 101A on your left.

6.0 Stream crossing. Continue uphill. After 100 yards, you'll intersect the Rainbow Trail (TR 1336). Turn right to ride toward Methodist Mountain (6 miles). At the trail entrance, sign the trail register. The next 6 miles are fantastic.

7.0 Stunning views here. *Now, this is Colorado!*

10.3 Another beautiful meadow.

11.5 Arrive at the Methodist Mountain trailhead. Turn right and brace for a rigorous downhill.

11.7 Pass the Rainbow Trail entrance on the left. Continue downhill on the main road. ***Note-*** *from this junction it's about 9 (not 6) stiff, single-track miles to US 285.*

13.0 Pass a gated road on your left at the forest boundary. Continue straight downhill.

13.2 Pavement. Continue downhill.

13.4 Turn right (east) and ride the undulating, rugged dirt road under the power lines.

14.3 The road splits. Bear left and ride downhill away from the power lines.

14.8 After a small rise, continue straight downhill on the main road. Ride down another 100 yards, then turn right at the fork. ***Note-*** *there are so many spurs and trails intersecting the road in this area that it is nearly impossible to cleanly document the route. Don't worry about missing or making a wrong turn; most routes will eventually intersect US 50. When in doubt, ride downhill.*

14.9 Continue straight on the main road. (*A spur descends left into a gully.*)

15.1 Stay right on the main road, passing some single-track on the right. The road will become double-track in about 100 yards.

15.4 After a steep and rough descent, turn right on the unmarked road.

15.8 Pass through the signed exit from the BLM area. Ride downhill and turn right on the well-graded dirt road. Continue to the highway.

15.9 Turn right on US 50.

17.2 Arrive back at the entrance to the parking/camping area. Cross US 50 and find your vehicle. Had enough?

Options: there are many ways to ride this trail. Some people prefer riding just the single-track as an out-and-back. Drive CR/FSR 101 to the parking area at the trailhead; you'll want a high-clearance 4WD vehicle if this is your plan. As an alternate, you can drive CR 101/49 to the parking area at the San Isabel National Forest boundary (*approximately 3.1 miles from the highway*).

You can also do this as a one-way with a shuttle. Leave a drop car at the top of the paved section of CR 108 and start wherever you like. If you fancy something epic, leave the drop car at the intersection of US 285 and The Rainbow Trail (5.2 miles south of the intersection of US 285 and US 50). See *Ride 41* for more info. ***Note-*** *the Rainbow Trail is considerably rougher and tougher west of CR/FSR 108.*

Ride 41: Methodist Mountain to US 285 Loop

38°29.583' N, 106°02.973' W WGS84

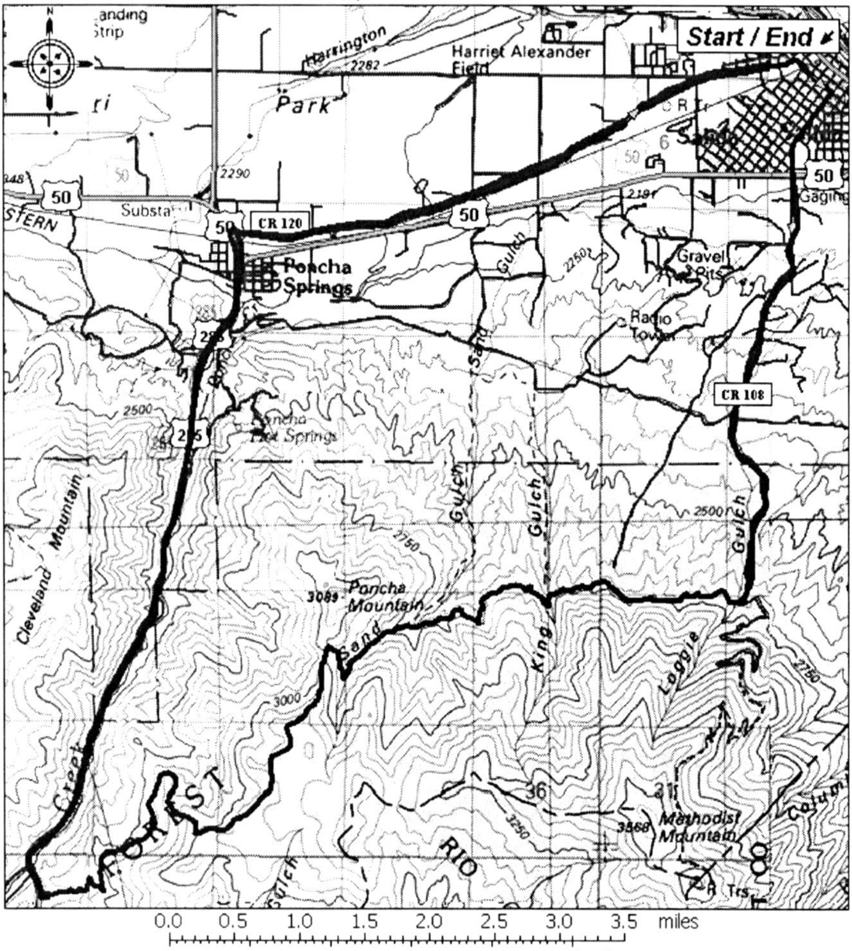

Map 41: Methodist Mountain to US 285 Loop (copyright National Geographic)

No doubt about it, this is a very difficult ride. First, the climb out of town is unrelenting and only gets tougher as CR 108 changes from pavement to well-graded dirt to sloppy rocks. Things level off a bit once the single-track starts, but short technical steeps abound. The crux climb, nearly 1,500 grunting feet up a soupy mix of dirt and rocks, will be a very long hike-a-bike for all but the strongest riders.

If you find yourself struggling between miles 8 and 10, rest assured, the downhill is a sweet reward that more than justifies the effort it takes to get there. Think fast, technical, and exhilarating. When you finally drop onto the highway, you'll wish the descent continued for another dozen miles.

Elevation profile:

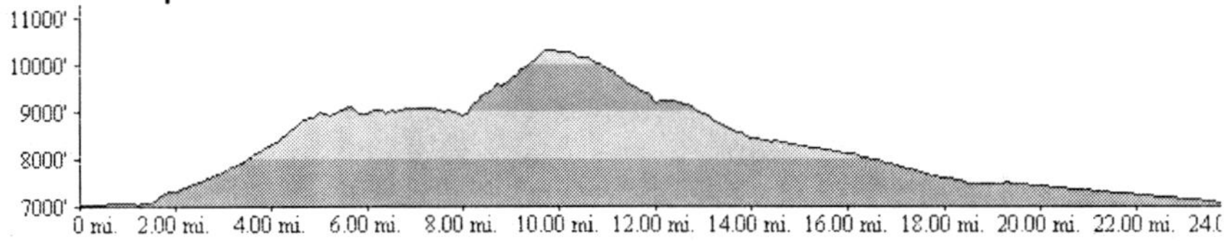

Ride length: 23.4 miles
Ride type: loop (clockwise)
Riding time: 3-4 hours
Surface: paved roads (12.9 miles); dirt road/jeep track (1.5 miles); single-track (9.0 miles)
Elevations: start/end 7,055'; max 10,320'; min 7,055'
Total climbing: gain/loss 3,900'

Aerobic level: strenuous (lots of climbing on steep, loose terrain)
Technical level: 5 (steep and loose descents; much of the climbing demands good line selection)
Season: May through October
USGS Quadrangles: Salida East, Poncha Pass, Salida West

Trailhead GPS coordinates: 38° 32.168' N; 105° 59.731' W

Getting there: this ride starts from the public parking lot adjacent to the Safeway at 3rd and H Sts. in downtown Salida. From the traffic light at 1st (CO 291) and F Sts. in the heart of Salida's historic district, travel 2 blocks southwest on F St. to 3rd St. Turn right at 3rd St. and travel 2 blocks northwest to the public parking lot.

***Note-** it's possible to start this ride from any number of places in Salida, but parking south of US 50 is somewhat limited due to narrow county roads and private property. Wherever you end up parking, be sure that it is okay to leave your vehicle for at least three or four hours.*

The ride:

0.0 From thc public parking lot adjacent to the Safeway supermarket at 3rd and H Sts., turn left and ride southeast on 3rd St.

0.3 Turn right (southwest) on D St. Look for the post office on the corner of 3rd and D St. as a visual marker.

0.8 Turn left on New St. This intersection may not be signed, but look for Salida High School. After turning left, ride along the athletic fields as you head toward the traffic light at the intersection of New St. and US 50.

1.0 Cross US 50 at the stoplight. CR 107 starts at the south side of this intersection.

1.6 Bear left at the fork and ride up the hill toward Methodist Mountain in the distance. Once again, this intersection may not have any signs, but you are now ascending on CR 108. (*CR 107 forks right and heads toward the gravel pits.*) You will continue climbing on CR/FSR 108 until you intersect the Rainbow Trail (#1336) in approximately 3.0 miles from this point.

1.7 Look down at Woodlawn Cemetery on the right as you pedal uphill. This final destination was established in 1889.

3.1 Continue straight on CR 108 as you intersect the power line road. (*This is a popular off-season riding area.*)

3.2 Bear left as the pavement ends at a fork. (*Right is CR 108A while the middle fork is a private drive.*)

3.4 CR 108 bends left (east) as you pass a driveway on the right.
3.5 Continue straight as you enter the San Isabel National Forest. The road (now FSR 108) gets considerably rougher beyond this point.
3.6 Stay left at the clearing. Continue climbing on FSR 108.
4.7 Turn right on the Rainbow Trail (#1336) single-track. ***Note-*** *according to the sign, it is 6 miles to US 285, but the actual distance is approximately 9.0 miles. How did that happen?*
6.5 Cross a small stream and stay left at the fork. (*The single-track spur on the right heads into private property.*)
7.9 Turn left as you intersect a rough ATV trail. The crux climb of the ride starts here. Not many cyclists can ride this line, so be prepared for some possible hiking. If you can clean it, then go-kat-go!
8.7 Turn right at the switchback and continue ascending.
9.8 The grade eases as you approach the top. Finally. Get ready for your reward.
12.0 A tiny, technical uphill puts a break in the action.
13.6 Stop and sign the trail register on your left.
13.7 Turn right (north) on US 285 and sail down the wide shoulder.
19.0 Pass through the heart of Poncha Springs and continue straight on US 50/285 past the intersection with US 50.
19.3 Turn right (east) on CR 120. This is a nice, relatively traffic-free alternative to US 50. Stay on CR 120 through all intersections. CR 120 becomes Poncha Blvd. once you enter Salida city limits.
23.1 Pass the Chaffee County Courthouse. Poncha Blvd. will dump you onto 3rd St.
23.4 Turn into the public parking lot and find your vehicle. Whew.

Options: if any ride is a solid candidate for a one-way shuttle, this may be it. Eliminate up to 12.9 miles of pavement spinning by driving as high as you want on CR 108 and leaving the other vehicle at the parking area at the intersection of the Rainbow Trail and US 285 (0.2 miles south of the intersection of CR 200 and US 285).

And, if you're going to shuttle, why not start at the Rainbow Trail's Bear Creek Trailhead? This adds more than 6 miles of moderate single-track to the ride. Drive about 2.2 miles east of Salida on US 50. Turn right (south) on CR 101 and drive about 5.4 miles up CR 101 to the trailhead (you'll want a high-clearance vehicle). See *Ride 40* for more info.

Ride 42: Spiral Drive/Tenderfoot Mountain

38°32.141' N, 105°59.793' W WGS84

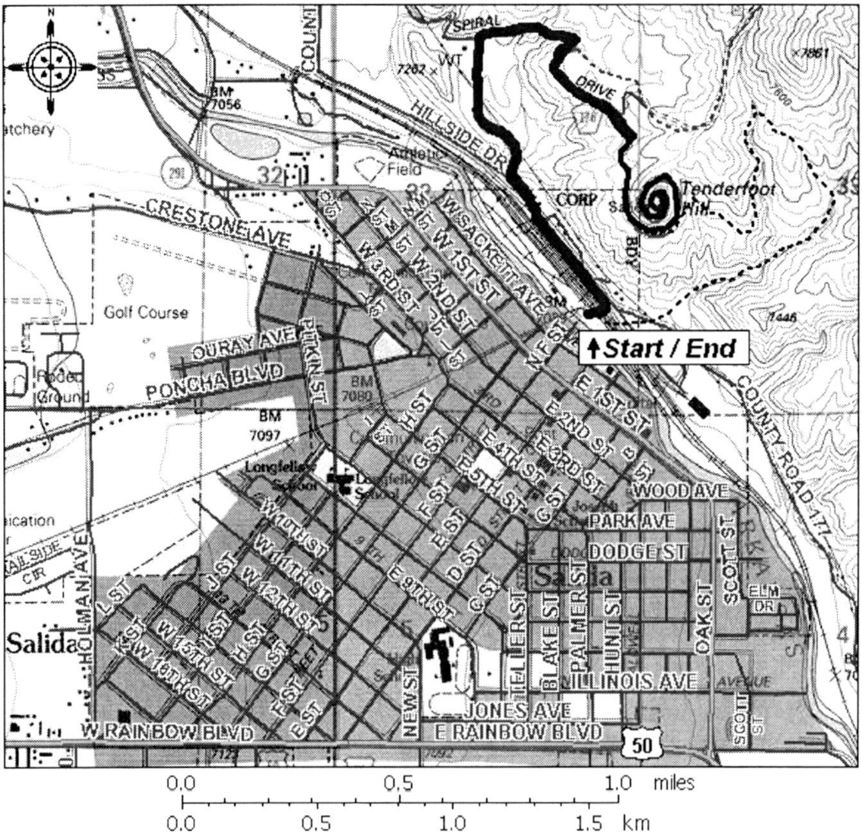

Map 42: Spiral Drive/Tenderfoot Mountain (copyright National Geographic)

This easy outing takes you from historic downtown Salida to the top of Tenderfoot Mountain. Sometimes called "S" Mountain, Tenderfoot is the hill adorned with the giant "S" just north of town. The ride up is easy and suitable for families and riders of all abilities. At the top is a sheltered observation deck with unsurpassed views of the Sawatch Range to the west, the Sangre de Cristo Range to the south, and the bottom half of the Arkansas Valley to the northwest.

The ascent is an easy, steady effort on a well-graded dirt road. The descent is equally gentle, but you'll want to control your speed and watch for hikers. You may also encounter some light auto traffic, so keep your eyes open.

Once at the top, you may want to sample the single-track built by volunteers from Salida Mountain Trails in 2006. While a fun challenge for intermediate riders, the route gets a little steep and offers some technical obstacles not suitable for novice bikers.

Elevation profile:

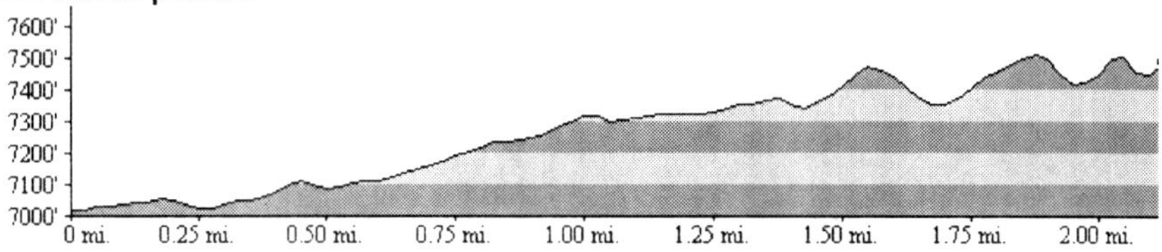

Ride length: 4.2 miles
Ride type: out-and-back (or loop on optional single-track)
Riding time: 1 hour
Surface: dirt road (4.2 miles); single-track (1.4 miles)
Elevations: start/end 7,020'; max 7,510'; min 7,020'

Total climbing: gain/loss 1,010'
Aerobic level: easy
Technical level: 2 (the single-track descent option is 3+)
Season: all year (if snow-free)
USGS Quadrangle: Salida East

Trailhead GPS coordinates: 38° 32.28' N; 105° 59.39' W

Getting there: from the intersection of 1st St. (CO 291) and F St. in downtown Salida (the only traffic light downtown), drive northeast on F St. until you reach the parking area past the bridge at the end of the road. The ride starts at your vehicle.

Additional parking is available in several other downtown locations.

The ride:

0.0 Ride through the gate at the northeast corner of the parking lot. Cross the railroad tracks and turn left when you reach the road (CR 177).
0.3 Turn right on CR 177 (unmarked) and start to climb.
0.5 Continue straight on the main road as you pass a gated spur on the right.
0.8 Pass the colorful water tank on your left then turn right on CR 176 (Spiral Drive).
0.9 Continue straight on the main road.
1.4 Ride through the gate or around it if it's closed.
1.7 Pass under the "S," then pass the entrance to the optional single-track descent route on your right.
2.1 Pick a side, any side: both forks lead to the top. Continue for another 100 yards to reach the highpoint of the road. Ditch the bikes and climb the stairs to the covered observation deck. After you finish observing, descend along the same route you took to the top.

Optional descent route (mileage continues from the top):

2.5 Turn left at the entrance to the single-track. ***Note-*** *this descent option may not be suitable for novice riders.*
2.7 Turn hard right at the intersection with an unmarked trail.
3.5 Drop into a sandy drainage ditch.
3.8 Stay left at the fork. Ride 100 feet then stay right at another fork. You will arrive at a junkyard in another 100 feet or so.
4.0 Descend to CR 177. Cross the tracks to return to the parking area.
4.2 The end.

Ride 43: Ute Trail Loop

38°33.785' N, 105°58.831' W WGS84

Map 43: Ute Trail Loop (copyright National Geographic)

This ride packs a lot of punch and offers great views of the southern Arkansas Valley. The big, technical descent on CR/FSR 273 is one of the best in the Arkansas Valley; it's not single-track, but line selection is so critical that it may as well be.

Start with a climb that, if you push hard enough, is guaranteed to purge your body of nasty toxins and negative thoughts. The mellow climbing/traverse across CR 181 is just long enough to allow the sweat to dry from your jersey. A few quick climbs will protect you from dangerous pleasure overloads on the technical descent.

Elevation profile:

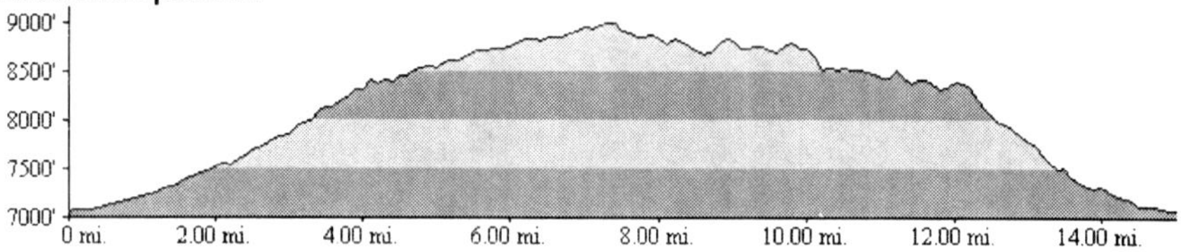

Ride length: 15.4 miles
Ride type: lollipop-loop (clockwise)
Riding time: 2 hours
Surface: paved road (2.5 miles) dirt road (6.4 miles); jeep trail (6.5 miles)
Elevations: start/end 7,060'; max 8.990'; min 7,060'
Total climbing: gain/loss 2,410'

Aerobic level: moderate (for the most part, the climb is a long middle-ring grind)
Technical level: 4 (steep, loose, and rocky descent)
Season: April into November (snow may linger into April on CR 273)
USGS Quadrangles: Salida West, Salida East

Trailhead GPS coordinates: 38° 32.65' N; 106° 0.377' W

Getting there: from the intersection of 1st St. (CO 291) and F St. in downtown Salida, drive approximately 1.0 miles west on 1st St. to the intersection with CR 175 (*look for the big Spiral Drive sign on the right just past the 2-mile marker*). Turn right onto CR 175 and immediately turn right again, toward the entrance for Sands Lake State Wildlife Area. Before entering the wildlife area, turn left and park in the parking area next to the river. The ride starts on the bridge over the river on CR 175.

The ride:

0.0 Starting from the bridge over the Arkansas River on CR 175, ride north 150 yards and turn right on CR 175. Pass intersections with CR 150 and CR 153 on the way.
0.3 Cross the railroad tracks then turn left, staying on CR 175.
0.5 Continue straight on CR 175 past CR 176 (Spiral Drive) on the right.
0.7 Continue straight on CR 175 as you pass CR 178 on the right.
1.2 Continue straight on CR 175 as you pass another intersection with CR 178 on your right.
1.9 Continue on CR 175 as it turns to dirt. Pass CR 156 on your left.
2.3 Continue straight on CR 175.
4.3 Pass the US Forest Service signs. The road is now FSR 175.
5.7 Continue straight on FSR 175, passing an unmarked road on the left.
6.4 Turn right onto FSR 181. An ATV sign marks the entrance.
6.7 Cross a small stream.
7.3 Follow the main road left, passing an unmarked spur on the right.
7.4 Turn right onto FSR 173.
8.3 Stay right on the main trail, passing a double-track spur on the left.
8.7 Bear left to stay on FSR 173, passing a spur on the right.
9.1 Stay on the main road.
12.4 Continue straight, passing an unmarked spur on the left.
13.6 Stay on the main road as you work your way down to the backside of Tenderfoot Mountain and Spiral Drive (CR 176). ***Note-*** *you'll pass a couple single-track spurs on your left. Explore them if you like. Most*

lead to CR 177 along the river. From there, ride west on CR 177 and Hillside Dr. back to CR 175 and your car.

13.7 Pass a few uphill spurs as you blast downhill. Many jeep spurs intersect the route as you approach Spiral Drive (CR 176). Your ultimate destination for this section is the graffiti-covered water tank on Spiral Drive. See it to your right in the distance? Just take the most obvious descent line and don't worry about making a "wrong" turn. Most of these tracks eventually intersect Spiral Drive.

13.8 Follow the main track down to the left.

13.9 Intersect CR 176 (Spiral Drive), a well maintained, gently descending dirt road. Turn right and ride downhill toward the water tank.

14.4 Stay on CR 176 past the water tank and CR 177 on the left.

14.8 Turn left at the intersection with CR 175 (paved). This closes the loop.

15.2 Turn left at the stop sign. Cross the bridge over the river.

15.4 The parking area is on your left. Another ride under your belt.

Options: if you want to extend the ride, climb another 1.5 miles to the top of Tenderfoot Mountain. Turn left on CR 176 at mile 13.9 and wind your way to the top. Explore the single-track descent routes from the top. See *Ride 42* for optional routes to the F St. Bridge in downtown Salida.

Or, start the route from downtown Salida and ride out to CR 175 on CO 291.

Ride 44: Upper Bighorn Sheep Canyon

Gather the family for a ride on the "Pathway Through History." This route, an easy outing through the magnificent Upper Bighorn Sheep Canyon of the Arkansas River, has twelve interpretive signs that provide an historical perspective to your journey. In addition, you might see some of Colorado's official state animal, the bighorn sheep, grazing in the canyon.

This is an easy ride, so take it at a relaxed pace and read the interpretive signs along the way. As the first sign suggests, try to let your imagination carry you back to the time when this road was a simple dirt path.

Note- *Badger Creek may be impassible when water levels are high and attempting to cross it in winter is hazardous. In addition, some parts of the road may flood during times of high water.* ***DO NOT ATTEMPT TO CROSS ANY FLOWING, FLOODED AREAS OF THE ROAD.***

Elevation profile:

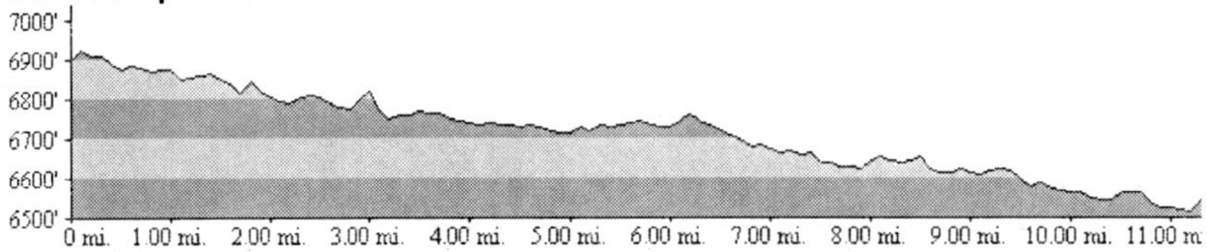

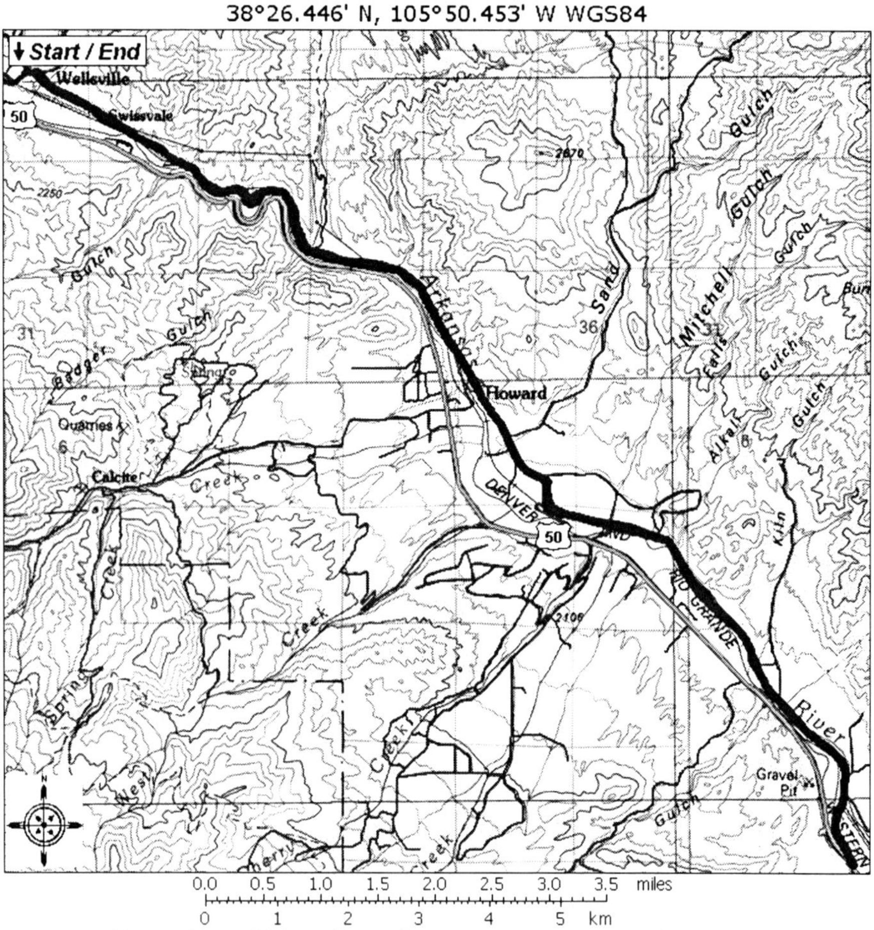

Map 44: Upper Bighorn Sheep Canyon (copyright National Geographic)

Ride length: 22.4 miles (or any length you choose by turning back before Vallie Bridge)
Ride type: Out-and-back
Riding time: 3-4 hours
Surface: dirt road
Elevations: start/end 6,900'; max 6,925'; min 6,515'
Total climbing: gain/loss 560'

Aerobic level: easy
Technical level: 2- (some beginners may struggle through the mile of rocky and sandy road adjacent to Badger Creek)
Season: April through November
USGS Quadrangles: Wellsville, Howard

Trailhead GPS coordinates: 38° 29.216' N; 105° 54.554' W

Getting there: from the intersection of 1st St. (CO 291) and F St. in downtown Salida, drive approximately 1.0 miles east on 1st St. to the intersection with US 50. Turn left on US 50 and drive 4.9 miles east to the intersection with CR 7/45. Turn left onto CR 7/45. Drive over the bridge and continue for approximately 0.6 miles. Cross the railroad tracks and a cattle guard then park in the clearing on the right.

Additional parking is available at the pullout on the north side US 50 just east of CR 7/45 (this adds 1.2 miles to the ride).

The ride:

0.0 From the parking area, turn right (north) onto CR 45. The entire ride is on CR 45.

0.2 Pass a spur on the left. The first set of interpretive signs is on your right.

1.8 Pass under the railroad bridge and turn left.

2.0 Bear right at the fork and take the double-track to the next sign.

2.5 Turn right for the next sign and a toilet.

2.6 The next sign is on the right.

3.4 See the sign on the right?

3.5 Cross Badger Creek. If water levels are high, you may need to turn around here. Use good judgment and be cautious: water currents may be stronger than they appear. Turn left and ride toward the trestle; the trail continues right just before you cross under the tracks. ***Note-*** *for an interesting diversion, continue straight under the tracks and ride toward the gate. A single-track spur leads to a green BLM gate. Pass through the green gate and follow an old jeep trail that parallels Badger Creek for approximately 4 miles. The route is technical, aerobically demanding, and route finding is extremely difficult. If you go, be sure to stay within your limits and don't get lost!*

3.6 Another sign for you.

5.2 Look for the sign on your left.

5.5 Pass Howard Hall on your right. Look for the sign on the right, at the intersection with CR 56.

7.5 Stop at the stop sign then continue straight on CR 45.

8.6 Look for the sign on the left.

9.9 Another sign on the right.

11.2 Vallie Bridge recreation area is on the right. This concludes the ride and the interpretive sign tour. Turn around and return along the same route. ***Note-*** *if you use the picnic facilities at Vallie Bridge, please pay the daily use fee ($3.00/person, April 2007).*

Options: ride out and turn back at anytime along the route. CR 45 crosses US 50 at mile 11.4; ambitious riders may want to continue for another 1.9 miles to Coaldale.

Or, elect to do this as a one-way ride with shuttles. Leave your drop vehicle at the Vallie Bridge Recreation area. From 1st and F Sts. in downtown Salida, drive 1.0 miles east on 1st St. to the intersection with US 50. Drive about 16 miles east on US 50 to the Vallie Bridge recreation area entrance. There is a self-service fee station; auto parking is $5.00 (April-2007).

Other interesting rides

These routes don't fit easily into the geographic groupings of the others in this guide, but are too good to not include.

Ride 45: River Park to River Park- Buena Vista to Salida

Ever wondered about an all-dirt route between Buena Vista and Salida? Wonder no more. This long ride takes you from Buena Vista's River Park to the F Street Bridge in Salida's historic downtown.

As epics go, this one is fairly easy. I say "fairly" because the spaghetti single-track climbing from Buena Vista gets slightly challenging and the descent to Salida along CR 173 is downright tough. In between, however, are many miles of pleasant rolling on dirt roads.

If you enjoy traveling the back roads of Colorado, you will love this ride.

Elevation profile:

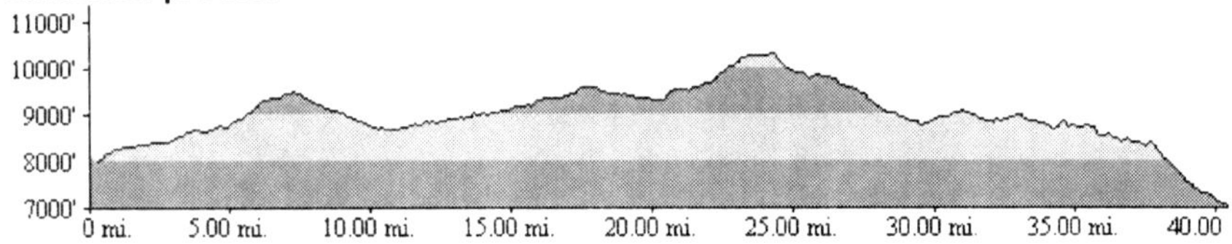

Ride length: 40.1 miles
Ride type: one-way with shuttle
Riding time: 4-5 hours
Surface: single-track (0.9 miles); dirt road (32.8 miles); jeep trail (6.4 miles)
Elevations: start 7,960'; end 7,020'; max 10,300'; min 7,020'
Total climbing: gain 4,950' – loss 5,880' = total -930'

Aerobic level: strenuous (this is a very long ride with lots of climbing)
Technical level: 4 (the final descent on FSR/CR173 is steep and technical)
Season: May into November
USGS Quadrangles: Buena Vista West, Castle Rock Gulch, Cameron Mountain, Salida East

Trailhead GPS coordinates: 38° 50.822' N; 106° 7.328' W

Getting there: leave your drop car at the parking area just north of the F St. Bridge in Salida. From the intersection of 1st St. (CO 291) and F St. in downtown Salida (the only traffic light downtown), drive northeast on F St. until you reach the parking area past the bridge at the end of the road.

The ride starts at the Buena Vista River Park. From the intersection of US 24 and Main St. in Buena Vista (the only stoplight in town), drive east approximately 0.5 miles to the end of Main St. Bear left into the Buena Vista River Park parking lot.

38°46.761' N, 106°02.505' W WGS84

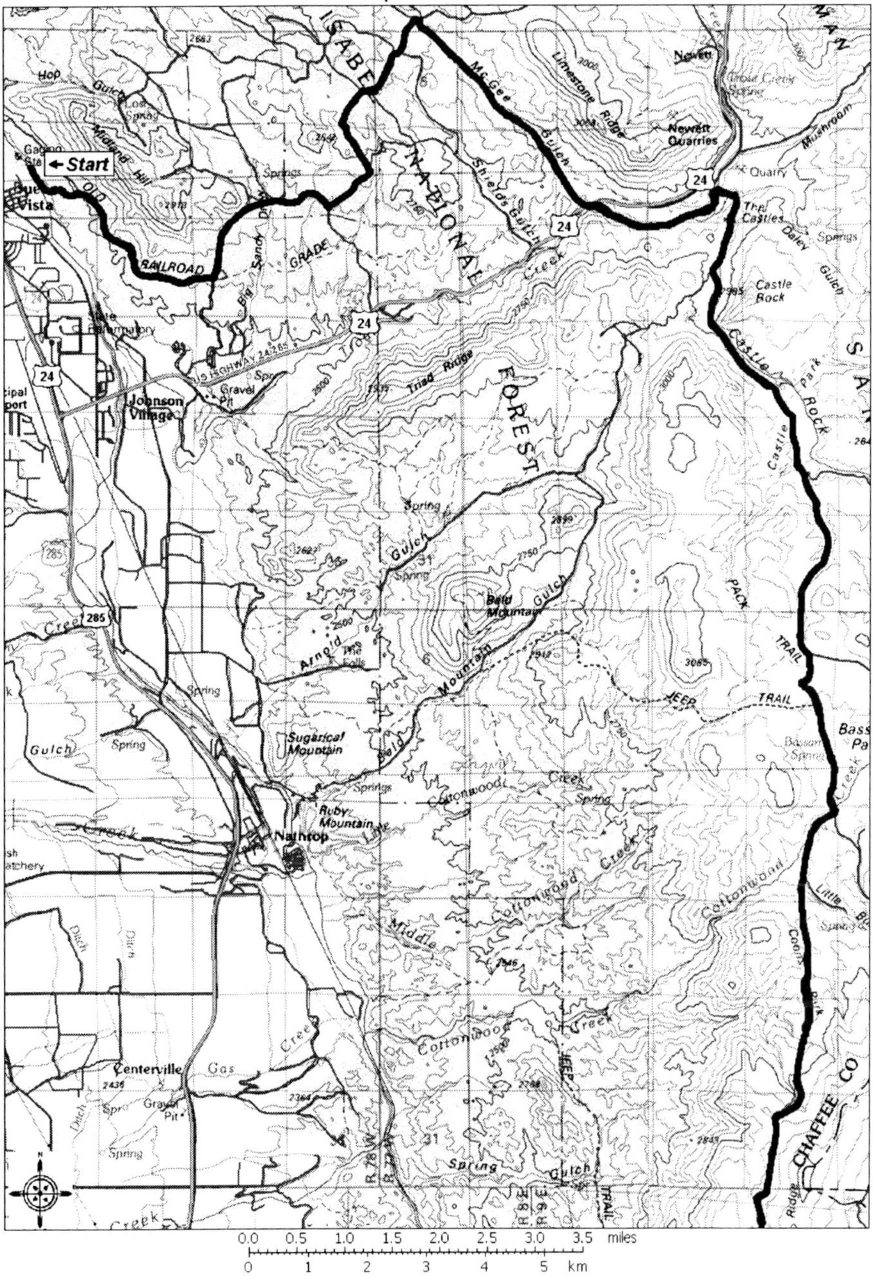

Map 45a: River Park to River Park - map 1 (copyright National Geographic)

38°36.573' N, 106°00.709' W WGS84

Map 45b: River Park to River Park - map 2 (copyright National Geographic)

The ride:

0.0 From the west side of the river, cross the footbridge over the river to start the ride.

0.1 Stay right at the split.

0.2 Pass the shaded bench area with 4 interpretive signs.

0.3 Stay right at the fork.

0.9 Go right at the intersection with CR 304. Stay on this road, passing all spurs and driveways for the next 2 miles.

2.9 Go left at the three-way intersection. This sandy spur is a shortcut that feeds into FSR 376A. (*The middle fork is the Midland Bike Trail and right is CR 304.*)

3.0 Merge with FSR 376A and continue left, riding uphill.

3.3 Stay right on the main road, passing a spur on your left.

3.4 Stay right on the main road, passing a spur on your right.

3.9 Turn right, passing a large, gated drive on the left.

4.3 Bear right, staying on the main road as you pass a double-track on your left. Keep climbing.

5.0 Continue climbing on the main road as you pass TR 1450A on the right. FSR 376A is now rutted and moderately technical.

5.3 Continue climbing on the main road as you pass a campsite on the right.

5.6 Continue climbing, passing the double-track spur on your right.

6.0 Continue climbing on the main road as you pass a spur leading to an awesome campsite.

6.3 Stay left on the main road, passing a spur on your right.

6.5 Turn right as FSR 376A ends at a "T" intersection with FSR 376 (*the Lenhardy Cutoff*). Continue straight (east) as a spur heads left (north). Continue straight on FSR 376 as numerous campsite spurs intersect the main road for the next 0.2 miles.

6.7 Continue straight on FSR 376 as you pass the intersection with CR/FSR 315 (*Shields Gulch*) on the right. (*The route now overlaps both the Lenhardy Cutoff and the Midland Bike Trail.*)

7.0 Continue straight on the main road, passing a spur on the left.

7.6 Continue downhill on FSR 376 as you pass the intersection with FSR 376B on the left.

7.7 Turn right on CR/FSR 305 to descend McGee Gulch. (*The Lenhardy Cutoff and the Midland Bike Trail continue straight on FSR 376.*)

10.5 Cross US 24/285 as CR/FSR 305 ends at the highway. Head left 50 yards then turn right onto CR 307, following the sign to Castle Rock Gulch.

12.1 Turn right onto CR 187. (*CR 307 continues toward Trout Creek Pass.*)

13.2 Stay on the main road as you pass the intersection with FSR 300 on the right.

15.9 Continue straight on CR 187 as you pass the intersection with FSR 188 on the left.

16.7 Stay on the main road as you pass a trail area on the right.

17.9 Turn right on FSR185, following the sign to Aspen Ridge (*5 miles*).

18.0 Continue on the main road as you pass a spur on the right.

18.5 Continue descending straight on the main road.

19.6 Stay right on FSR185 as FSR185C spurs to the left.

20.4 Bear right on FSR185 as the main road becomes FSR 185B and leads to Elk Mountain Ranch. Continue climbing and look right for some nice views of Sawatch 14ers (Antero, Shavano, and Tabeguache). The road

gets rougher for about the next 9 miles.
21.0 Continue straight on the main road as you pass a spur on the right.
21.6 Stay on the main road as you pass a double-track on the right.
22.1 Cross a cattle guard and pass through the seasonal closure gate as you enter the Aspen Ridge State/Trust Wildlife Management Area. Stay on the main road.
22.7 Continue straight on the main road, passing 2 double-track spurs on the right. Continue climbing.
23.3 Stay left in a clearing as an unmarked spur heads right. Check out the big view on the right.
23.7 Stay on the main road as you pass spurs, first on the left then on the right.
24.5 Cross through a fence and over a cattle guard. From this point, you will see the northern peaks of the Sangre de Cristo Range to the south.
26.1 Stay right as you pass through a seasonal closure gate. You are now leaving the Aspen Ridge State/Trust Wildlife Management Area.
26.2 Stay right as a double-track splits left.
26.8 Turn left at the unmarked intersection and continue riding downhill.
27.1 Keep right on the main road and continue descending. (*An unmarked road heads uphill on your left.*)
29.4 Pass the intersection with FSR 184A on your right and continue descending on FSR 185. ***Note-*** *FSR 184A leads to the ghost town of Turret.*
29.8 Continue on the main road to begin a short climb as you pass a road on the right.
31.2 Intersect and merge right onto FSR 175. The road surface improves here.
31.8 Continue descending on the main road, passing an unmarked road on your left.
32.2 Take a sharp left onto FSR 181. The route now overlaps the Ute Trail Loop and leads to a very technical descent. ***Note-*** *for a less technically demanding descent, continue riding down FSR/CR 175 until it intersects CO 291. Turn left on CO 291 and ride approximately 1 mile to the intersection of 1st St. (CO 291) and F St. in downtown Salida. Turn left at the traffic light and ride 2 blocks north to the F St. Bridge and the parking area.*
32.8 Stay left on the main road, passing a spur on the right.
33.2 Stay left on the main road as you pass a double-track on the right.
33.3 Turn right onto FSR 173.
34.1 Stay on the main road as it wraps around an exaggerated switchback. You'll pass an unmarked spur at the start of the big bend.
34.5 Stay left on CR/FSR 173 as an unmarked spur heads right.
36.0 The downhill begins to get serious.
38.1 Although you have great views of Salida here, you are not down yet! This may be the most technically formidable portion of the descent. You've already ridden many miles, so dismount and walk if you are tired or not comfortable on the terrain.
39.4 Stay on the main road as you work your way down to the backside of Tenderfoot Mountain and Spiral Drive. ***Note-*** *you'll pass a couple single-track spurs on your left. Explore them if you like; most lead to CR 177 along the river.*
39.5 Pass a few uphill spurs as you descend like a rock in water. Many jeep spurs intersect the route as you approach CR 176 (Spiral Drive). Your

ultimate destination for this section is the graffiti-covered water tank on Spiral Drive. See it to your right in the distance? Just take the most obvious descent line and don't worry about making a "wrong" turn. Most of these tracks eventually intersect Spiral Drive.

39.7 Intersect CR 176 (Spiral Drive), a well maintained, gently descending dirt road. Turn right and ride downhill toward the water tank. ***Note-*** *turning left will take you to the top of Tenderfoot Mountain. Check it out if you still have something left in your ride-weary legs.*

40.2 Turn left at the intersection with CR 177 to descend past the colorful, graffiti-covered tank on the right.

40.7 Turn left on the paved road.

41.0 Look right for the path over the tracks and the opening in the fence at the parking lot. Ride that way, but you'll probably have to carry your bike over at least two sets of the tracks.

41.1 Arrive at the F St. Bridge and the Salida whitewater park. Did you leave your kayak back in Buena Vista?

Ride 46: Salt Creek-McQuaid Loop

38°58.792' N, 106°02.218' W WGS84

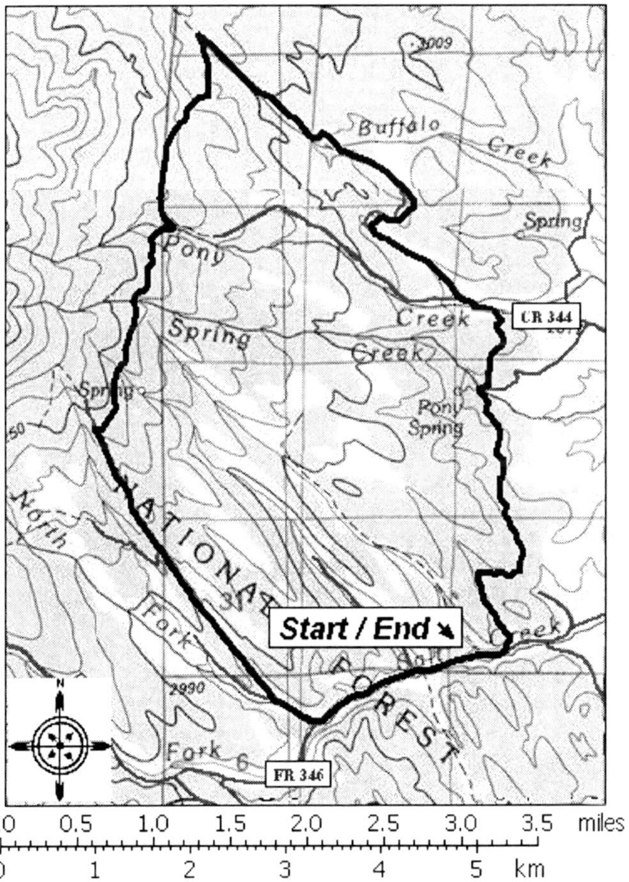

Map 46: Salt Creek-McQuaid Loop (copyright National Geographic)

What could be better than finishing the weekend with one more outing on pristine single-track? Because this route provides easy access to both US 24 (*to Colorado Springs*) and US 285 (*to Denver*), it's an excellent one to hit on the way home.

Start with a three-mile, gentle climb up FSR 435. Hit the single-track for about another 0.5 miles of climbing to the highpoint of the route. Next, the trail roller coasters until the final drop to FSR 434. Sail down FSR 434 until you intersect the McQuaid Trail single-track. The remainder is an easy glide on more pristine, skinny single-track.

Riding the loop clockwise puts the majority of the climbing on a gently graded road, saving extremely fun single-track and rutted jeep trail for the descents. The route traverses some dense stands of aspen and mid-September is an especially nice time to ride it. The trail passes through several open range areas, so please close and chain all gates after passing through them.

Elevation profile:

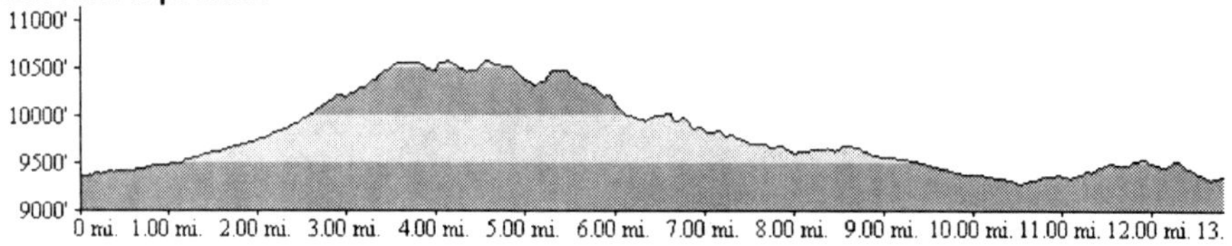

Ride length: 12.8 miles
Ride type: loop (clockwise)
Riding time: 2 hours
Surface: dirt road (3.0 miles); single-track (6.4 miles); jeep track (3.4 miles)
Elevations: start/end 9,370'; max 10,570'; min 9,290'
Total climbing: gain/loss 1,950'

Aerobic level: moderate (some climbing and a few short steeps)
Technical level: 3+ (one steep littered with loose rocks; a long descent on tricky, rutted jeep trail)
Season: May through October
USGS Quadrangles: Marmot Peak, Jones Hill

Trailhead GPS coordinates: 38° 57.381' N; 106° 1.051' W

Getting there: from the intersection of US 24/285, (2.4 miles south of Buena Vista), drive approximately 15.7 miles north on US 285 to the intersection with FSR 345. This intersection is difficult to anticipate, but it's approximately 1.7 miles north of the split between US 285/24 at Antero Junction. Look left for an opening in the fence and a stop sign. Turn left on FSR 435 and drive approximately 3.5 miles west to a parking area at a campsite adjacent to some beaver ponds on Salt Creek. *FSR 435 is an open range area so drive with caution.*

Note- *look right for the McQuaid trailhead after driving 3.3 miles on FSR 345. The trailhead is very difficult to see as you drive west, but two fiberglass posts and a sign mark it. The ride starts at the parking area 0.2 miles west of that trailhead.*

The ride:

0.0 From the campsite, turn left (west) on FSR 435.

1.2 Bear right at the fork to continue on FSR 435. Follow the sign to the Salt Creek Trail (2 miles). (*FSR 436 leads left to Trout Creek Pass in 6 miles.*)

1.5 Continue straight on FSR 435 as FSR 435.2C forks to the left.

2.3 Cross a cattle guard as the grade increases.

2.7 Continue on FSR 435 as you pass the entrance to FSR 435B on your left.

2.9 Continue straight on the main road.

3.0 FSR 435 ends at the intersection with the Salt Creek Trail. Take the right, single-track entrance to Trail #618. This entrance may not be properly signed because somebody uses it for target practice. The trail continues climbing for approximately 0.5 miles to the highpoint of the ride. ***Note-*** *the left entrance climbs for 0.1 miles before descending into a valley along broad switchbacks.*

3.5 Turn right at the intersection, continuing up into a stand of pine. (*Left leads into a stand of aspen.*)

3.7 Crest the highpoint of the trail and enjoy a break in the climbing.

4.7 Get ready for a steep and moderately technical downhill.

4.8 Stream crossing. Look left for the footbridge.

4.9 Bear left, staying on the Salt Creek Trail as it leads to Buffalo Peaks Road.

5.1 Pass an old well on the right. Use caution if you choose to explore the area around it.

5.6 Pass through a gate.

6.4 Cross a small creek then turn right on FSR 433. (*The Salt Creek Trail continues left and uphill.*)

7.1 Cross through a gate.

9.6 Cross a cattle guard and turn left, continuing downhill on FSR 433. (*The road on the right is FSR 433.2B.*)

9.8 Turn right on the McQuaid Trail single-track. The entrance is faint, but there's a sign to help you find it.

10.4 Intersect FSR 434. Ride left about 20 yards and look for the entrance to the single-track. Once again, this intersection is faint, but there is a sign about 50 yards from the road to help you find it.

10.6 Cross a small footbridge. Ride 20 yards, then stay right past a very faint spur heading left.

10.9 Cross through another gate and continue straight as cattle trails intersect from the right and left.

11.6 Pass through another gate.

12.6 After a nice and easy downhill, turn right at the intersection with FSR 435.

12.8 Arrive back at your vehicle. Watch the cow patties as you pack up the bikes for the drive home. See you next weekend.

Options: Take some time to explore the Salt Creek Trail and the myriad of jeep trails in the area.

More rides!

This guide is a companion to the free, on-line e-Guide: ***www.arkvalleymtb.com***.

On this site, not only will you find rides that didn't make the editorial cut for this printed edition, but more area rides set to appear in the next printed edition. Rides are posted weekly throughout the summer and the content is constantly growing. You'll want to check back often.

In addition, .gpx files (GPS routes) for every route in this guide are available as free downloads from the site. These files can be imported into most recreational mapping software packages, such as ***National Geographic's TOPO!***, or load them directly into your GPS unit.

You will also find useful area information and other things to help you get the most from your visit to the Arkansas Valley.

Check it out and tell your friends!

End of the road

Local resources

Bike Shops

Cycles of Life
504 Harrison Ave.
Leadville, CO 80461
(719)486-5583
pbbicycles.com

The Trailhead
707 N. Hwy 24
Buena Vista, CO 81211
(719)395-8001
www.thetrailheadco.com

Absolute Bikes
330 W. Sackett Ave.
Salida, CO 81202
(719)539-9295
www.absolutebikes.com

Otero Cyclery
248 W. Hwy 50
Salida, CO 81201
(719) 539-6704
www.oterocyclery.com

Subculture Cyclery
246 1/2 East 1st St.
Salida, CO 81202
(719)539-5329
www.subculturecyclery.com

High Valley Bike Shuttle
6250 Hwy 285
Poncha Springs, CO 81242
(800)871-5145
(719)539-6089
www.monarchcrest.com

Colorado Division of Wildlife

6060 Broadway
Denver, Colorado 80216
(303)297-1192
wildlife.state.co.us

Arkansas Headwaters Recreation Area

307 W. Sackett Ave.
Salida, CO 81201
(719)539-7289
parks.state.co.us/Parks/ArkansasHeadwaters

US Forest Service

Salida Ranger District
325 West Rainbow Blvd.
Salida, CO 81201
(719) 539-3591
www.fs.fed.us/r2/psicc/sal

Leadville Ranger District
810 Front St.
Leadville, CO 80461
(719)486-0749
www.fs.fed.us/r2/psicc/leadvile

Campground reservations:
www.recreation.gov

Hospitals

Heart of the Rockies Medical Center
448 East 1st St.
Salida, Colorado 81201
(719) 539-6661

St. Vincent's Hospital
822 West 4th St.
Leadville, CO 80461
(719)486-0230

Lodging and area information

www.leadvilleusa.com
www.coloradoheadwaters.com

Printed in the United States
115307LV00001B/9-10/P

9 780615 194134